David Shipman was born in Norwich in 1932 and has lived in London, Singapore and Paris: for many years he travelled extensively throughout Western Europe as publishers' representative. After a brief period back again in a London publisher's office he became a writer, with immediate success with the two best-selling books, *The Great Movie Stars* (on the stars of 'the golden years' and the post-war era). His subsequent books have included his monumental two-volume *The Story of Cinema* and for the Consumers' Association *The Good Film and Video Guide*. His most recent work is a compilation of real-life quotes, *Movie Talk: Who Said What About Whom in the Movies*. He was Associate Editor for a time of *Films and Filming*, and has frequently broadcast and contributed to major publications. He is also an occasional programme planner for the National Film Theatre and has just mounted a season on Marlon Brando to coincide with the publication of this book.

MARLON BRANDO

David Shipman

SPHERE BOOKS LIMITED

SPHERE BOOKS LTD

Published by the Penguin Group
27 Wrights Lane, London w8 5tz, England
Viking Penguin Inc., 40 West 23rd Street, New York, New York 10010, USA
Penguin Books Australia Ltd, Ringwood, Victoria, Australia
Penguin Books Canada Ltd, 2801 John Street, Markham, Ontario, Canada 13r 1b4
Penguin Books (NZ) Ltd, 182-190 Wairau Road, Auckland 10, New Zealand

Penguin Books Ltd, Registered Offices: Harmondsworth, Middlesex, England

First published as The Movie Makers: Brando, in 1974 by Macmillan London Limited.
This revised and extended edition published
by Sphere Books Ltd, 1989.

Copyright © by David Shipman 1974, 1989.
1 3 5 7 9 10 8 6 4 2

Printed and bound in Great Britain by
Richard Clay Ltd, Bungay, Suffolk

Contents

I

Beginnings

Marlon Brando is his real name, and the mysteries – typically – begin right there: the name is either an Anglicization of the French 'Brandeau' or the Dutch-Alsatian 'Brandau'. His father was also a Marlon Brando; he married Dorothy Pennebaker; Marlon Jr was born on 3 April 1924, the youngest of three children and the only boy. They were living then in Omaha, Nebraska, where Mrs Brando was a director of the local Community Playhouse. She was an enthusiastic amateur actress, and had acted with Henry Fonda – then living in Omaha – before he turned professional.

When Marlon Jr (nicknamed 'Bud') was six, the family moved to Evanstown, Illinois; they moved again, to California, and then returned to Illinois, to a town called Libertyville – a name which is appropriate in view of the fierce independence Brando has carried with him through life.

He was rebellious from the outset, insecure and arrogant at the same time; and so hypersensitive that he was literally unable to respond to anyone he considered a phoney or dishonest – *could* not rather than *would* not. Already there was that element of conflict within him, for he lived in a world of fantasy, of play-acting. Most children do, but this one more than most wanted to impress other children. He himself loved to show off, to be the centre of attraction, to dare – to see how much he could get away with, particularly in front of his father's friends. That did not help a marriage already under strain.

They were comfortably off. Again, accounts vary as to what Marlon Brando Sr did for a living. He was 'involved in' agricultural products, or a 'salesman for' or 'manufacturer of' same. Since the family kept servants, what seems most likely is that he was an executive for a company or companies which sold farming goods – but that did entail frequent absences from home. It was presumably during these times that he indulged in womanizing – for on his home ground he was a respected member of the community and a pillar of the Episcopalian Church. He was also a martinet and the sort of 'man's man' who regarded his wife's acting ambitions with tolerance rather than enthusiasm. He also had scant sympathy with her view that the boy be restrained as little as possible. Doubtless she hoped that young Marlon's posturings and play-acting might lead to something theatrical – or at least artistic – but that was the last ambition Brando Sr had for the boy. Later in life Brando was to claim that his mother meant everything to him, but that his father was either not satisfied with or not interested in anything he did.

According to one report he 'drove everybody nuts' – though this would not seem to include his mother. His sisters, Jocelyn (called 'Jody', three years his senior) and Frances ('Fran', eighteen months older), learned to cope with his precociousness and constant competitiveness; they may have been drawn together by learning in their teens – initially, it would seem via a telephone call from a barman, requesting that someone get her out of here – that Mrs Brando had a drink problem. Bud's school record could have been of no consolation to her.

He was twelve when he enrolled as a pupil at Libertyville Township High School, whose principal was to recall that 'he wasn't a mean boy. Just irresponsible.' His acting ability was recognized, but he seldom participated because the drama classes coincided with the punishment period. He began to take an interest in athletics and weight-lifting, activities over which his parents disagreed, since his father approved and his mother did not. Studying and scholarship held little appeal; at the age of sixteen he left – he says he was expelled – for smoking in the gymnasium. It would seem rather, that his father felt that he needed the discipline for which America's military academies are renowned.

So, in September 1941, over Mrs Brando's objections, he was packed off to his father's old training ground, the Shattuck Military Academy at Faribault, Minnesota. Curiously, he enjoyed close order drill on the parade ground, but otherwise, in his own words, he 'hated it every day I was there'. He was to claim that the school bell (chiming every quarter-hour) so irritated him that he climbed to the top of the belfry and prized off the clapper. He spent much time feigning illness and for a long time affected a limp. One teacher remembered: 'Anything to duck out of assignments, classes, duties.' He developed a taste for reading Shakespeare and joined the school drama group – whose taste in plays did not lie in that direction. Brando's first thespian appearance was in 'A Message From Khufu', a melodrama inspired by the discovery of Tutankhamun's tomb; he played the hero, an explorer on the trail of an Egyptian mummy, but although the school magazine reported 'a new boy who shows great talent' he seems to have had smaller roles in two subsequent productions – perhaps because he randomly changed the dialogue. These were the old farce, 'Is Zat So?' and 'Four on a Heath', during the course of which he was hanged for highway robbery. The school tolerated him till May 1943, when he was expelled – for smoking, done less from enjoyment or conviction but simply because it was forbidden. Once again his own version differed from that of the authorities: he said he had

3

constructed a bomb from firecrackers to be positioned against the door of a teacher he particularly disliked, but that the trail of hair-tonic – lit as a fuse – led straight to his room instead of disappearing as it burnt.

Had he graduated he would not have joined millions of fellow-Americans now fighting for Uncle Sam in Africa and the Pacific: he had been graded 4-F because of a trick knee. His choice was then that not so distant one between religion and show business. He expressed an interest in becoming a minister and that recommended itself as he had long shown sympathy for any underdogs encountered; but the family thought him too introverted for public speaking – and not exactly rich in tact when it came to handling people. He started a five-piece combo, 'Brando and his Kegliners', but bookings proved elusive. He then tried the traditional job for black sheep, troublesome sons and free spirits: ditch-digging. But after six weeks with the Tile Drainage and Construction Company he quit. By this time his father did have his own company, and a life in insecticides seemed to loom ahead – but that was not a prospect Brando Sr viewed with unmitigated pleasure. Accordingly he offered to finance Bud for training in whatever trade or profession he cared to follow – for a trial period of six months. He chose acting, which was not what his father considered a manly profession. He was nineteen.

He had liked an audience as long as anyone could remember. In this respect school plays had been less rewarding than in the parlour at home or with his contemporaries. He had, while on vacation from Shattuck – in March 1942 – acted alongside his mother with the Libertyville Village Players, when the advertised play was suddenly cancelled and replaced by an impromptu effort, 'Curse You, Jack Dalton'! His mother's influence had already pointed Jocelyn towards the theatre, and the fact that she had already appeared in one mainstream Broadway play, albeit a short-lived one, may well have been instrumental in Brando

4

Sr's allowing the boy to try the same. And Bud was already in New York, living with Fran, who was studying art. It was unlikely that he was paying her rent, since he existed on a series of elementary, almost-bumming jobs which seemed to confirm his penchant for failure. Jocelyn was now understudying, but that was not such a come-down since the lady concerned was Broadway's newest sensation, Dorothy McGuire, in the season's most sought-after (non-musical) ticket, 'Claudia'. Brando's later claim that he drifted into acting, 'My sister Jocelyn was already acting and I thought I'd give it a whirl too' may have been one of his more honest public statements. It paid better than washing-up in a greasy spoon.

At Jocelyn's suggestion he enrolled in Erwin Piscator's Dramatic Workshop of the New School for Social Research, where she was studying under Stella Adler. She found the course stimulating and believed that its radical atmosphere would be absolutely suited to her brother's temperament. Miss Adler, then in her early forties, had had a sound training in theatre and a long record of success, both with the Yiddish Theatre and on Broadway. Her entry in 'Who's Who in the Theatre' notes that her parents were distinguished actors and producing managers, that she studied under her father, under Maria Ouspenskaya, Richard Boleslavsky and Constantin Stanislavsky. She taught acting to the principles laid down by Stanislavsky. These, briefly stated, include complete realism, ensemble acting, and an absolute identification with the character – which can lead to complexities whereby the actor might delve into the character's subconscious, or move in his time-and-space process. The layman knows this as Method acting, or as 'the Method', and it has been much dissected and analysed since Brando became famous (and the two matters are not coincidental). The discussions, I suspect, were of little interest to audiences, who had already discerned the fact that all good actors have a method.

5

Laurence Olivier has said so; so has Bette Davis – and in passing we might note her comment (in her memoir) on the Method and Brando: 'They have simply learned to express themselves; and I'm terribly happy for them. When they learn to express the character, I shall applaud them ... Then there's the question of style. Without it, there is no art. As personal as these troubled actors are, there is – aside from much of a muchness – the same of a sameness. They are all so busy revealing their own insides that, like all X-ray plates, one looks pretty much like the other. Their godhead, the remarkably gifted Marlon Brando, may bring (as all true stars do) his own personal magnetism to every part, but his scope and projection are unarguable. He has always transcended the techniques he was taught. His consequent glamour and style have nothing to do with self-involvement but rather radiation.'

The Method – the one with the capital M – may be said to refer to the practitioners of the Stanislavsky rules, as adopted by some earnest theatre people in New York whose thoughts and theories on the subject were coming to fruition at the time Brando took up acting. The names of the teachers and trainers are as well known outside the profession as their features are cloudy: Miss Adler, Robert Lewis, Lee Strasberg, Herbert Berghof and Elia Kazan, among others. With these people and the Actors' Studio would be associated almost every major American acting talent to emerge over the next generation. Discontented or ambitious Hollywood stars – like Marilyn Monroe and Shelley Winters – went to the Studio classes as 'observers'; Anne Bancroft studied there after her Broadway success in 'Two for the Seesaw'.

The renown and fame of the Studio – the fact that the general public heard of it – is directly attributable to Brando, often in connection with the 'mumbling' and 'scratching and itching' which are supposed to have characterized his work – and I am quoting from 'Actors Talk About Acting' by Lewis Funke and John E. Booth, in questions about Brando put to Morris Carnovsky and Maureen Stapleton. Both performers refuted the suggestion that such gestures were typical of Method acting; and on another occasion Miss Stapleton observed that 'someone like Marlon Brando is so complete a talent that he can draw on things inside himself for what he needs. He has more equipment for doing this than most people.'

It took Brando a long time to live down such accusations (those interviews were published in 1961), and they were directed at him because he was the most famous of the alumni – though, of course, his first famous role was not exactly brother to John (or is it Ernest?) Worthing. Kim Hunter, who played with him then, later noted one of his major qualities: 'an uncanny sense of truth. It seems absolutely impossible for him to be false. It makes him easier to act with than anybody else ever. Anything you do that may not be true shows up immediately as false with him.' One of the things he was doing was pushing realism to the extreme.

The new realism could be said to have been demanded by wartime and postwar audiences, no longer content to be lied to; but realism had been with theatre audiences, long before it was ever chanted by Stanislavsky. Nineteenth-century audiences had wanted to see realistic flames when the barn burned down in the last act; old playbills boast of waterfalls and avalanches. Popular successes like 'The Scarlet Pimpernel' and 'The Only Way' realistically re-created the Terror when their actors donned the clothes of that era; it was the view of the Universe which was romantic till the first chill notes were struck by Ibsen. Later, a Galsworthy or so, offered a 'social conscience' play but amidst so many melodramas and farces realism lay like a slumbering dog. Its eventual awakening was inevitable once the cinema took over the mass-marketing of fairy-tales – for the cinema was obviously a realistic medium, proffering not only Mary Pickford's curls and Chaplin's jaunty walk but the revolutionaries of Pudovkin's *Mother* and the peasants of Dovzhenko's *Earth* – and I cite Russian examples because the new realism of the American theatre in the thirties was distinctly left-wing, though the reason (if directly attributable at all) has probably less to do with the experiments in Soviet Russia than the Depression. The most influential theatre organization of the time, the Group Theatre, was founded in 1931 by a group of breakaways from the Theatre Guild, the most prestigious and successful New York producer – to wit, Cheryl Crawford, Lee Strasberg and Harold Clurman (who was married to Stella Adler at the time Brando was her pupil). Luther Adler, Stella's brother, acted for the Group; so did Carnovsky, Franchot Tone, Lee J. Cobb and John Garfield, all in their tyro days. Robert Lewis and Kazan were trained with the Group. They put on 'realistic' plays by Irwin Shaw, Robert Ardrey, Sidney Kingsley and William Saroyan – and Clifford Odets, whose 'Waiting for Lefty' and 'Golden Boy' were the Group's biggest successes.

With time and fame, the Group broke up and dispersed: the reforming zeal of Odets evaporated, and without it his plays were mediocre – unless, as some sceptics claim, the mediocrity of the earlier ones had gone unnoticed in the general zeal and dedication, being only 'real' when set against the frivolities of Broadway, where 'serious' meant The Classics or adaptations from literature and Eugene O'Neill. Broadway's biggest success at this time was a sentimental family drama, 'Life With Father'. It did have its lighter moments, but that was in the American theatrical (and movie) tradition. Only The Classics and O'Neill were allowed to be gloomy for an entire evening.

'Life With Father' and 'Oklahoma!' were Brando's sole experience of professional theatre when he began at the New School. Within a week's experience of her tuition Miss Adler pronounced that a year from hence 'he will be the best young actor in the American theatre'. Many years later she would say: 'He lives the life of an actor twenty-four hours a day. If he is talking to you he will absorb everything about you – your smile, the way your teeth grow. His style is the perfect marriage of intuition and intelligence. If he must learn to ride a horse for a movie, he will watch that horse like no one else has watched a horse and when he does the scene he will be both horse and rider.' She also observed that she taught him nothing, 'I opened up possibilities of thinking, feeling, experiencing, and as I opened up those doors, he walked right through . . .'

Some sources state that Brando studied under Piscator before moving on to Miss Adler, but she was teacher for the Dramatic Workshop and Piscator rather its impresario – a hand-me-down version of his own mentor, Max Reinhardt. Piscator directed the student productions – and conceived a play that they put on for an outfit called The Children's Theatre at the Adelphi Theatre in New York, 'Bobino', written for the occasion by Stanley Kauffman. Brando had two roles in what is regarded as his professional debut: a giraffe and a guard. He had another dual role in a once-famous German play by Gerhart Hauptmann, 'Hannele's Way to Heaven' (known simply as 'Hannele' in Britain). In Act One it is he as her lover and teacher who carries the dying waif onto the stage; hallucinating for the rest of the play, the angel she sees has, unsurprisingly, the same face. The production illustrated Piscator's lectures, 'The March of Drama', concentrating on plays which the students performed. This one caught the attention of George Freedley, the critic of *The Morning Telegraph*, who thought 'Easily the best acting of the evening was contributed by Marlon Brando' – which may be why, two months later, in July 1944, Piscator invited Brando to join him for a stock season at the Sayville Summer Theatre on Long Island, where he repeated his teacher-angel and played Sebastian in 'Twelfth Night'.

He did not, however, find Piscator any more worthy of respect than the regimented instructors at Shattuck; he considered him a petty tyrant – as he said, 'His Prussian nature just couldn't understand how to deal with Americans.' Translated, this meant that Brando couldn't resist needling him – preferably unseen, and a golden opportunity was provided because Piscator insisted that the larder should be under padlock: it did not keep Brando out. He was officially sacked for fraternizing with the females in the cast, strictly forbidden by Piscator.

Hollywood, however, beckoned. With many of their male contract players in the Armed Services, the studios were avid for new talent. Among the New York agents searching for it in the stock theatres that summer was Maynard Morris, a nervy bachelor with a stammer. He arranged for Brando to be looked over by the studios' executives in New York, one of whom – at 20th Century-Fox – arranged for a screen test. Brando arrived for it looking sullen and indifferent; his look turned to boredom halfway through and he took out a yo-yo to divert himself. 20th Century-Fox showed no further interest – which may be why for so long, after achieving Broadway success, he insisted that movies didn't interest him. Another contradiction of this time is the impression he later gave of indifference towards his career, while Morris's colleagues recall him hanging around the office as often as not.

Morris did arrange for him to see Rodgers and Hammerstein, who were producing 'I Remember Mama', John Van Druten's dramatization of a memoir by Kathryn Forbes, concerned with a Norwegian-American family in San Francisco. Brando was asked to audition, a new ordeal for him, and one which he confronted by mumbling, not seeming to be able to read the script either with feeling or indeed, literally. Van Druten found in him, over the objections of the producers, a quality likely to serve in the role of Nels, the 15-year-old son of the Mama being played by

Mady Christians. The play opened at the Music Box Theatre in October 1944 to a good press, but only Robert Garland of the New York Journal-American singled out our hero: 'The Nels of Marlon Brando is, if he doesn't mind me saying so, charming.' Just conceivably a few other critics were unimpressed by the pompous biography published in the programme: 'At present is delving into philosophy, "getting a smattering of Schopenhauer and Spinoza", he says. Likes music, particularly primitive African music ...' The piece located his birthplace in Calcutta, but it was to move over half the Orient in subsequent theatre programmes. His stated view was that it was unimportant, 'What difference does it make where you're born? It's such a curious thing to talk about.' Few would disagree; but since it is unimportant why lie about it? This issue would seem to establish Brando as a man questioning or poopoohing accepted convention or received opinion while also behaving in a mysterious, enigmatic way, a blending of opposites which would become second nature. Such behaviour would always draw attention to him. In an odd honest moment he admitted that to get that he would walk across Times Square on a tightrope. In the event, he never needed to: his talent did it for him.

Attracted to that then was Edith Van Cleve, a former actress now working for MCA, the country's leading talent agency. Her view of his performance in 'I Remember Mama' was of concentration, because or although he had little dialogue, but 'when he did say something, he seemed to come from another country compared to the rest of the cast. He was so *natural*.' Backstage, she learned that he had no agent (he had not signed with Morris) – nor did he want one. If he changed his mind, she said, he could contact her, and one day during the run, on a winter's day horrible even by New York standards, he turned up at her office, still undecided. She sensed, she said, 'that there could be no big agent double-talk, no lying ... It all had to be straight-shooting or I'd lose him.'

Her faith in him was not shared by all her colleagues at MCA, for it became clear that he was hopeless at auditions. As the run of 'I Remember Mama' drew to a respectable close – 713 performances, but a long way after 'Life With Father', the first and longest-running of a slew of dramatized reminiscences – she sent him to see the pre-eminent acting partnership of Broadway, Alfred Lunt and Lynn Fontanne, who were casting for 'O Mistress Mine', the Terence Rattigan play which they had done in London (under the title 'Love in Idleness'). They apparently thought him too old for the role and that was that; but years later Lunt heard that Brando claimed to have walked on the stage, growled 'Hickory-dickory-dock, the mouse ran up the clock', and sauntered off. Lunt commented, 'I imagine that when he became famous, Brando decided to make a character for himself, and rudeness was part of this character.' More likely it was Brando's belated reaction to the inflated reputation of the Lunts, who as performers were gracious, mechanical and almost totally without real feeling – the antithesis of his own approach to acting. He may not have seen them on stage, for they had been acting in London since 1943, but he knew what they represented – they were the darlings of Manhattan's theatregoers; but by inventing the lie he was thumbing his nose at a fake bogey. The incident may indeed have happened – auditioning for someone else; but it sounded better if the insult was aimed at one of the leading members of the theatre establishment. It obviously represented a way of revenging himself for the humiliation of having to audition – to be judged by those in authority, like his father and his instructors at military school. It also betokens insolence and a certain self-confidence, whereas it is more likely that his lack of confidence was the reason he always failed to give a halfway decent reading.

If Brando 'read' for 'Truckline Cafe', he did so with the support of Stella Adler – whose husband, Clurman, was directing. It was the first venture of a production company which he had formed with Elia Kazan, another alumnus of the Group Theatre, working in conjunction with The Playwrights Company. Kazan had been offered a partnership by another prominent producer – Kermit Bloomgarden – but he preferred an alliance with Clurman, because he was one of the few figures he thought challenging; but neither had expected some immediate dissension about the quality of the play and the cast. The author was Maxwell Anderson, whose previous work included a verse-drama on Elizabeth I and the Earl of Essex (for the Lunts) and 'Winterset', a dour piece about criminals and New York's deprived people, the first recipient of the New York Critics Drama award. 'Truckline Cafe' was of the same genre as 'The Time of Your Life' and Tennessee Williams's 'Small Craft Warnings' – all of life there is, as seen over a glass of beer. Mr Anderson tended to regard life and its ills from 'a lofty artistic plane' (as Brooks Atkinson once put it), but that did not on this occasion include the rewriting promised when Kazan thought it unsatisfactory. The setting was a West Coast diner whose patrons were contemplating the postwar world; its patrons included a young ex-soldier, Sarge McRae, who goes outside and kills his wife after learning of her infidelity during his absence. Kevin McCarthy, who auditioned for the role, learnt that 'Gadge [Kazan] got some young guy who is a student of Stella's'. McCarthy was given another role, supporting Virginia Gilmore and David Manners (the best known names in the cast). Kazan said later, 'Although two small parts were brilliantly played by two unknown actors (Karl Malden and Marlon Brando), the central roles were limp, in both the writing and performance.' The critics agreed: 'Except for a brief bit by Marlon Brando as the former soldier who blew his top,' said Burton Rascoe in the *New York World-Telegram*, 'the acting was indifferently bad', while Vernon Rice in the *New York Post* observed that 'the poignant playing of Ann Shepherd and Marlon Brando as the ill-fated husband and wife' would be remembered long after the play and the other characters had been forgotten. It turned out that there would be only another twelve opportunities to sample them, despite the advertisements castigating the critics placed in *The New York Times* by Clurman, Kazan and Anderson. Because of Miss Adler's casting coup Brando's fellow-players showed some initial resentment, but soon admired the sustained emotional pitch he brought to the role; years later the director Jules Dassin recalled his own reaction: 'And this kid walked on and I said, "Oh shit, this kid is great."'

Wanting to sample this greatness were Katherine Cornell and Guthrie McClintic, for one of their periodic revivals of 'Candida'. She of course would be Candida; the husband (McClintic) would direct; and Wesley Addy and Cedric Hardwicke had been cast as Morell and Burgess respectively. Brando would play Marchbanks, the young poet who worships the older Candida (Shaw specifies thirty-three; Miss Cornell was forty-eight at this time) and is confident that he can woo her from her parson husband. The role was played in an earlier Cornell production by the previous *wunderkind* of American show business, also then in his pre-fame days, Orson Welles. The play opened in April, and Brando's performance was, on the whole, well received; but I have spoken to several people who saw it, and they shudder at the memory: 'unfortunate' is one summing-up of the interpretation. Marchbanks is not easy to play, despite Shaw's clinical description: 'a strange, shy youth of eighteen, slight, effeminate, with a delicate childish voice, and a hunted tormented expression and shrinking manner that show the painful sensitiveness of very swift and acute apprehensiveness in youth . . . Miserably irresolute, he does not know where to stand or what to do.'

'Young Mr Brando stepped right out of the stage directions,' said Robert Garland in the *New York Journal-American*. 'It is he and his performance that the enthusiasts at the Cort [Theatre] may still be cheering for all I know to the contrary.' Other critics – as others have done down the years – commented that the role is unplayable. Mr Rascoe in the *New York World-Telegram* thought 'Mr Brando did as well as he could', while Mr Rice in the *New York Post* thought it 'certainly to Marlon Brando's credit . . . that a wave of nausea' did not pass through the audience. According to John Chapman in the *New York Daily News* he 'achieved a believable lovesick introvert by playing very quietly', but Lewis Nichols for *The New York Times* did not agree: Brando, he said 'emphasises the weakness and banks the fire, the result being a somewhat monotonously intoning poet. His version is not believable . . .' Had Miss Cornell been active fifty years later we should probably have a videocassette record of her celebrated Candida. My friend Felix Brenner says she was a warm Candida – just as she had been a majestic Cleopatra, that she had grace and a mellifluous voice, qualities which put her ahead of the other ladies who fancied themselves in classical roles. I never saw her (she never made a film), but I did see Helen Hayes and Miss Fontanne on the stage, and he shares my inconsiderable opinion of them.

Obviously, we have a record of Brando the screen actor, but what was it like, this 'theatre' he joined and left so precipitously and permanently? He was to revolutionize American acting, but would the stage have found the roles for him? Most Americans who have seen British casts in Shakespeare, Shaw or Chekov might hesitate before seeing these dramatists done by their countryman. And I must say that *easily* the worst production and performances that I've ever seen were contained in Lee Strasberg's Actors Studio presentation of 'Three Sisters', which went to London in 1965 with Kim Stanley, Nan Martin, Sandy Dennis, George C. Scott and Luther Adler. The reviews were appalling, but then hadn't we just seen Olivier's production of 'Uncle Vanya', with himself, Michael Redgrave, Rosemary Harris, Joan Plowright and Sybil Thorndike? That much-esteemed production was recorded on film, yet viewed twenty-five years later it's no great shakes. The acting is very good, and in the case of Olivier and Redgrave brilliant: but everyone, including them, is performing in a different style. The conclusion to be drawn is that in the intervening years a gigantic advance has been made in ensemble acting, which brings me to my point: that despite McClintic, recognized at the time as a tyrant and perfectionist, and whatever was thought at the time, Cornell and Brando were working in totally different styles.

Once he became a star he had an added magnetism: judging him from his film performances I think he would have required a great deal of self-discipline to be a stage star, playing alongside other people. But once he became a star what discipline he had was simply tossed away.

Certainly by the time Brando was done with Marchbanks, he was going lightly on neither 'the hunted tormented expression' nor the irresolution. Jim Henaghan, later the Hollywood columnist, knew Brando at this time and says that except in one respect, Marchbanks was the reverse of Brando as he then was. He was remarkably self-assured, Henaghan says, but he was certainly effeminate; the mannerisms thus implied disappeared when he went on stage in 'A Streetcar Named Desire' and, Henaghan adds, in life as well around the same time. He was always polite and friendly towards Henaghan; to other columnists he was rude, but he wasn't entirely unjustified. Whichever reaction he took it is doubtful whether he knew who Sheilah Grahame was when he interrupted Jessica Tandy, introducing them, with 'Your mother?' (Sheilah was the same age as Miss Tandy, and very pretty). Sheilah did not then know that Tandy disliked him – 'an impossible, psychopathic bastard' she once called him, partly because he was unreliable on stage. There was also the matter of his playing bongo drums distractingly backstage and such wheezes as poking a cigarette up his nostril when she was downfront in one of her big scenes. 'Marlon's humour,' wrote Miss Grahame, 'is mostly of the little-boy kind. He will stick a piece of paper into the side of his shoe, raise one leg over the other so that you see it, and when you bend down to read what is written on the paper, you will find "What the fuck are you looking at?"' Elaine Stritch (who had been with Brando at the New School and in the Sayville Company) told one biographer of fleeing Brando's apartment when he appeared in pyjamas (whilst admitting her own 'innocence' in going there in the first place); wanting revenge – she thought – Brando appeared in her convent dormitory with a prop gun. He stepped on her stomach with his bare feet, drank a pint of milk, stepped on her again, and still 'grim and unsmiling', left. Once during the run of 'I Remember Mama' he substituted salt for the caster sugar used by Oscar Homolka to sweeten his tea – and it was a little whim of the play that he liked it very sweet. Brando's joke was the sort actors have perpetrated on each other since time immemorial: what makes this unpalatable, however, is that he was the most junior member of the company and Homolka an ageing star actor with a distinguished career behind him.

Later, in Hollywood, he telephoned Miss Grahame with the information that he was getting married that evening, hanging up before she could respond. She supposed that he had somehow learnt that she was a dining *à deux* with a very rich man who she hoped would propose to her, but who was wavering because he feared that her career as a columnist was of overwhelming importance. She spent most of that evening on the telephone trying to contact friends of Brando without success; the engagement ring was not forthcoming. That was among the last occasions Brando spoke to her. Like Henaghan she was and is completely honest and dispassionate about the 'monsters' amongst whom they moved and from whom they made their living – so that writing about him in 1969 she admitted that since he did not (then) make himself available to the press, 'I have done the next best thing, talked with his friends and associates to understand what goes on behind the mumble and the sullen exterior. Everyone with whom I spent long hours agreed that Brando is self-destructive.'

Except in that respect he is as much an enigma to colleagues and casual aquaintances as to journalists. I was with Kazan once when someone mentioned a rumour that Brando had been found dead; and Kazan said, 'I'll say this much: the going of him will not be ordinary. Marlon is the most perfectly mysterious man I have ever met.' His friends would have agreed. He might appear unexpectedly, and disappear as quietly as he came; sometimes it seemed he materialized in order to eat all the food in the house or change his clothes (for those of the host; socks, mainly).

This last was not a complicated operation. He favoured dungarees or jeans with a T-shirt, at a time when other budding actors wore ties and jackets – at a time when *Esquire Magazine* ran colour pages of colour coordination from fedoras to garters. Men who had recently been in uniform preferred to remain in conformity. 'Marlon was the original hippie' observed Sheilah, 'He was twenty years before his time with his torn shirts, leather jacket, dirty sneakers' – but she does not go on to reflect how much he influenced the apparel worn by the youth of the 50s and 60s. She surely is quite correct, however, when she goes on to refer to '. . . his hatred of authority and affluence' and pointedly, 'His father looked like a conservative banker when I met him one lunch-time at Paramount.'

That he had, beneath the rebellious outfit and the bonhomie and the practical jokes, problems, was evident to Kazan, who sent him to his own analyst. Two words sum up Brando's private life: ambiguous and ambivalent. You might add, devious. The total sum of his interviews, his public statements and reported remarks are consistent only in being inconsistent; some people have found him blindingly intelligent, and others stupid; with some he has been co-operative, with others not. He has frequently said that he despises acting, but before returning to his career we might pause at a statement he made in 1960: 'An actor must interpret life, and in order to do so he must be willing to accept all experiences that life can offer. In fact, he must seek out more of life than life puts at his feet. In the short span of his life, an actor must learn all there is to know; experience all there is to experience; or approach that shape as closely as possible. He must be superhuman in his endless struggle to inform himself. He must be relentless in his efforts to store away in the warehouse of his subconscious everything he might be called upon to know and use in the expression of his art. Nothing should be more important to the artist than life and the living of it, not even the ego. To grasp the full significance of life is the actor's duty, to interpret it his problem, and to express it his dedication.'

2

Broadway Fame

'One young actor to benefit from Katharine Cornell's far-sightedness was an appallingly rude young man,' wrote Cedric Hardwicke in his autobiography. 'The young man, in my judgment and others', was useless in the role [of Marchbanks], but I for one detected talent in him. My friend George Jean Nathan, on the contrary, did not ... and bet me an even ten dollars that the surly youngster would come to nothing at an early date.' 'Candida', in fact, had been staged for matinees only when the McClintic presentation of Anouilh's 'Antigone' failed to draw audiences. At some time during the brief runs of both – 'Candida' lasted only twenty-four performances – Brando took over the role of the Messenger in the latter play. It was an effective role, rushing on in the final moments with the bad news – and Laurence Olivier (who later starred in and presented the London premiere) caught him one evening whilst in New York: 'Marlon had a very small part – no more than one speech, really, but he was electrifying. It was obvious that he was a star in the marking.'

Brando agreed to tour in both plays. Miss Cornell kindly recalled 'his portrayal as Marchbanks was erratic from performance to performance, but at the top of his form he was the finest Marchbanks I ever had' (and she also observed that 'as a human being I found him warm and friendly and interesting'). He apparently over-acted wildly when the play opened in Chicago, but on other occasions went to the extreme: 'Marlon often let his performance go,' said Mildred Natwick, who played Prossie, 'He would forget lines. Guthrie lost his temper with him.'

In September, Brando opened at the Alvin in a play sponsored by the American League for a Free Palestine, 'A Flag is Born', a pageant by Ben Hecht with music by Kurt Weill. The cast was headed by Paul Muni and Celia Adler; Brando had the third most important role, as David, an embittered boy who rings down the curtain – after Muni's death on stage – exhorting audiences to defy Britain and show their solidarity with those about to build a Jewish state in Palestine. Partly because of his involvement with the Adler family, Brando did the play – against the advice of MCA; his belief in the rights of minorities continued to grow and he thus gave his ardent support to a piece which was more propaganda than drama (around the same time he returned the playscript of Terence Rattigan's frivolous comedy to the impresario John C. Wilson with the words, 'Don't you know there are thousands of people starving in Europe?'). He did not, however, show much fervour in rehearsals and Stella Adler had constantly to reassure brother Luther, who directed, that he would 'give' on the night. He did, not entirely to the delight of Muni, who had to lie onstage each night and know that it was Brando's performance the spectators would discuss as they filed out. 'Marlon Brando, the young actor who was so generally acclaimed last season, is a bitter and impassioned David . . .' said Ward Morehouse in the *New York Sun*; '[his] accusations sear when his bitterness bursts out' wrote William Hawkins in the *New York World-Telegram*, while 'Marlon Brando was called upon again to provide some dramatic fireworks' commented Vernon Rice in the *New York Post*. Brando 'is the bright particular star of the Ben Hecht pageant' said Robert Garland in the *New York Journal-American*, 'His David is enduring in the memory.'

'Pageant' was also a word used by Brooks Atkinson in *The New York Times*, going on to observe that 'the mixed values of Mr Hecht's script leave this reviewer ungratefully reluctant' – to support its cause, despite the recent suffering of the Jews and Muni's performance. Adler directed, and took on Muni's role when the play moved to the Music Box the following month. It did not run: like most good causes allied to art, neither was well-served, and ethnic interest was little stirred.

Brando had already left the cast, after being presented to John C. Wilson as the ideal lover – on the strength of 'Candida' – for Tallulah Bankhead in 'The Eagle Has Two Heads', Jean Cocteau's wish-fulfilment fantasy, written to please his lover Jean Marais, who had given instructions that he do nothing in the first act, everything in the second, and die dramatically in the third. Thus, a peasant assassin comes to kill a Queen but stays to fall at her feet – till, like Stanley Baldwin in 1936, her advisers decide that the liaison must end: but in this play the lovers choose death rather than abdication. Postwar Paris audiences found escapism in this odd Hapsburg revival (and curiously, some depth); they cheered Edwige Feuillère as the Queen – a performance about to be committed to celluloid for posterity, along with that of M. Marais. In London, in the translation by Ronald Duncan to be used for Miss Bankhead, it had made a star of Eileen Herlie. The dialogue did not work for American audiences, and Wilson was apparently unable to make any valid artistic combination out of the opposing acting styles of Brando and Bankhead. According to Noël Coward's diaries, Wilson (who had been his lover) was a weak personality and a devious colleague – hardly the man to handle an actress famous for her temperament, her on-stage extravagance, her hedonism and a distrust of anyone who did not grovel at her feet (not to mention her rampant bisexuality). This latter characteristic she interpreted with a certain elasticity, especially after she had been drinking, and it did not include Brando, who was wary of her at first and then increasingly disrespectful. He was neither the first nor the last man to find her hostility miraculously gone – Kazan was another, when he directed her in 'The Skin of Our Teeth' – as she stumbled into his hotel room after the first night fiasco when the play tried out in Newhaven (he fled from her, screaming 'I'm a virgin').

The play is at best a folderol, even with Mme Feuillère, and by all accounts it was not Miss Bankhead's most shining hour: but that does not explain why, during her 20-minute First Act speech (one reason the piece attracted her in the first place), Brando should have scratched, picked his nose, examined his fly, etc. One night when Wilson caught his performance he was also, after killing the Queen, an unconscionably long time a-dying, threshing about the stage till he found a suitable resting-place. He was replaced by Helmut Dantine, an Austrian-born Warner Bros second lead of the war years. Neither he nor the play were well-received when it arrived on Broadway; it lasted only twenty-nine performances.

Several versions exist of the reasons for Brando's dismissal; the most favourable to all concerned has Bankhead incensed at Brando refusing to socialize with her, preferring instead the company of the black actor playing her major-domo, Cherokee Thornton – a friendship wrought from a shared passion for bongo drums. 'He's terribly talented, but rather strange,' she said of Brando, as he began to exercise his 'strangeness' both back- and onstage; for his part, he seems to have realized that he was part of a debacle – from which being fired was the desired objective. He was reportedly devastated when it actually happened – and unhappy to realize that he had now acquired his own reputation for temperament. For the first time in two years there were no immediate offers. He was free to attend classes at Kazan's newly-formed Actors' Studio.

The project was born from Kazan's dissatisfaction with

most of the cast of 'Truckline Cafe': 'One thing was clear to me . . . We needed our kind of actors to play the leading roles in our productions.' He mentioned the idea to Clurman, whose response was to say that he would speak to his wife. Kazan had once had a run-in with Miss Adler, after she had been brought in to coach a young actress performing under his direction. With the financial and practical assistance of the impressario Cheryl Crawford he set up shop instead with an old colleague from the Group Theatre as his partner – Robert Lewis, who coincidentally had been the diplomatic adviser when Brando and Bankhead had first discussed working together. He stayed only a year and was replaced by Lee Strasberg, who had been his teacher. 'Over the years, respect became hero worship and hero worship idolatry' said Kazan, himself tactfully refraining from comment on the position Strasberg holds in Brando's career. Strasberg was always happy to take credit for that, despite the fact that he was not there when Brando became a Broadway success; he was also, ungratefully, to point to Brando as an actor who 'sold out' to Hollywood.

At this point Brando advised MCA that he would be willing to make a film – but Edith Van Cleve reported back to him that the studios were only prepared to gamble with an actor of his (slight) reputation if he would sign the standard seven-year contract. The only one prepared to take him for one film was 20th Century-Fox, and that was due to the clout held by Kazan, about to direct *Gentlemen's Agreement*. John Garfield – an old associate, now a second-rank star – was hesitating over the role of the Jew, which was easily secondary to that of Gregory Peck, playing the gentile journalist who passed as a Jew. When he accepted it, Kazan abandoned the idea of using Brando instead.

It was Kazan who suggested Brando for the role of Kowalski in 'A Streetcar Named Desire'. Tennessee Williams's writing, after a flop play ('Battle of Angels' in 1940) and a spell as an MGM scriptwriter, had found eloquent expression in a memory piece, 'The Glass Menagerie'. Returning to New Orleans, he resurrected from earlier one-act plays (many of his later three-act plays are reworkings of his early plays and stories) the character of a faded Southern belle on the edge of self-destruction, Blanche du Bois, who arrives in New Orleans to stay with her sister Stella and her husband, Stanley. Stanley Kowalski is, as the play says, a Polack, and even without Blanche's pretensions it is clear that Stella has married beneath her, probably for what a later generation would call 'a good screw'. Kowalski is elemental; as Williams describes him: 'Animal joy in his being is implicit in all his movements and attitudes. Since early manhood the centre of his life has been pleasure with women . . . with the power and pride of a richly feathered male bird among hens. Branching out from this complete and satisfying centre are all the auxiliary channels of his life, such as his heartiness with men, his appreciation of rough humour, his love of good drink and food and games, his car, his radio, everything that is his, that bears his emblem of the gaudy seed-bearer. He sizes women up at a glance, with sexual classifications, crude images flashing into his mind and determining the way he smiles at them.'

In 1947 on Broadway there were serious plays about British justice ('The Winslow Boy'), a Henry James spinster ('The Heiress') and USAF executives ('Command Decision'). It was unthinkable that anyone would want to write or present a play in which a man sizes up his sister-in-law sexually. At a cursory glance, 'Streetcar' is a study of sexual antagonism. The 'plain man', Stanley, rebels at Blanche's dreams and fantasies – of the now-gone family mansion – because they remind him too forcibly of his own inferiority ('I'm afraid I'll strike you as the unrefined type'); he resents her airs, so he's jubilant when he can expose her: 'That's why she's here this summer, visiting royalty, putting on all this act – because she's practically told by the mayor to get out of town! Yes, did you know there was an army camp near Laurel and your sister's was one of the places "Out-of-Bounds"?' He's actually intrigued: the cuckoo in the nest is a whore. In turn, Blanche criticizes him to Stella: 'He acts like an animal, has an animal's habits! Eats like one, moves like one, talks like one! . . . Thousands and thousands of years have passed him right by, and there he is – Stanley Kowalski – survivor of the Stone age.' His discovery of her past, and her acknowledgement of his animalism lead to sexual congress: with Stella in hospital, he rapes Blanche, saying, 'We've had this date with each other from the beginning.'

The line is, fortunately, not typical of the play, but it is impossible to under-estimate its effect on audiences at the time. Our drama does not lack for 'fallen' or 'kept' women, but they are either trying to live down the past and find true love (like Anna Christie) or turning down true love from the noblest motivations (like Marguerite Gautier); and it is certainly mealy-mouthed on what they actually did to please their men. Williams does not say that Blanche turned to prostitution from poverty, another theme of modern drama, especially during the Depression: worse, he infers that after discovering that her husband was a homosexual (a word which then seldom appeared in print) and a suicide she became so deranged that she frequented, for the love of it, the sort of places where men went looking for sex. Many reviewers referred to her as a nymphomaniac (another rare word), but the text does not entirely support this. (Kazan thought the play autobiographical, inasmuch as Williams was a homosexual compulsively seeking partners, with a knowledge that what the play calls 'the kindness of strangers' was often brutally unlikely: but when taxed on this, Williams would neither deny nor confirm.) Together with the implication that Stanley's chief attraction for Stella was that he was 'good in bed', the subject-matter was heady stuff for the time. Many people, not necessarily moralists, in New York and later London, were genuinely shocked or scandalized. Critics recognized that the play ranked with Arthur Miller's 'Death of a Salesman' as the two landmarks of the postwar theatre; and it was immediately realized that Williams had written a compassionate, poetic piece, rough-romantic, tough-tawdry, silken-sophisticated; and he had created two remarkable leading characters. Blanche and Kowalski offered one of the classic confrontations of twentieth-century drama: she is a lady, a butterfly, a hypocrite, 'a cultivated woman', as she puts it, 'a woman of intelligence and breeding'; he is a rough diamond, a slob, an honest Joe, the guy in the street. He will crush her – though this was not (see below) Williams's own view.

This time Garfield's vacillation was Brando's gain. He feared that the role of Blanche overshadowed that of Stanley – which was untrue, and Williams was then and thereafter happy to rewrite to accommodate colleagues. Both Irene Mayer Selznick, producing, and Kazan, directing, felt that a Hollywood name, returning to the stage after a long absence, was to be preferred commercially if the compromise was not too great: but as negotiations dragged on it became clear that Garfield's movie career was again in the ascendant; and it was suspected that Mrs Garfield did not want to uproot the family for a long run. 'Garfield' said Kazan, 'was as good-hearted a kid as you'll find in the annals of show business; he half meant what he said.' What he – or his agent – now said was that he would play the role for four months, and then only if guaranteed it in any film version, but Selznick and Kazan refused to meet these terms.

Robert Mitchum has said that he was offered Stanley, but was advised to turn it down as being harmful to his movie career. None of the participants concerned has mentioned Mitchum, which may mean that it was his agent who suggested it; or Mitchum might have been up to replace Brando later. Burt Lancaster claims that both Kazan and Williams wanted him, 'but I had to go back to Hollywood for a film'. Mrs Selznick remembered differently: she asked to see Lancaster on the strength of his work in *The Killers*, but sensed – rightly, as it turned out – that his agent, Harold Hill, was really only interested in a film career for his client; and she was mildly incensed when Hill lectured her – the daughter of Louis B. Mayer and the wife of David O. Selznick – on the making of movies.

The casting of Blanche was equally difficult. Mrs Selznick wanted Margaret Sullavan, the choice of Joshua Logan, whom she had invited to direct – till Williams sent the play to Kazan, and she deferred to his judgement in that matter. Williams himself wanted Pamela Brown, but Kazan couldn't see a British actress in the role (the final choice was British, and he would direct a British actress in the film version), while Kazan himself thought that Mary Martin, the musical comedy star, was most suitable (partly because she was Southern).

It was Kazan's friend Hume Cronyn, the actor, who supplied him with the first Blanche. With the Actors' Lab, a haven for those alumni of the Group Theatre working in Los Angeles, he mounted a production of 'Portrait of a Madonna', the one-act play Williams reworked (as he did on other occasions) into a full-length one, i.e., 'A Streetcar Named Desire'; in the leading role was Jessica Tandy, Mrs Cronyn, and she solved, said Williams, 'our most difficult problem in a flash'. Brando was one of Kazan's 'beginners' in the class at the Actors' Studio which Kazan started on returning from working on *Gentleman's Agreement*. He chose him, he said later, because of a letter from Williams which explained, among other things, that 'Blanche must finally have the understanding and compassion of the audience. This without creating a black-dyed villain in Stanley.

It is a thing (Misunderstanding) not a person (Stanley) that destroys her in the end.'

He sent Brando to see Williams, and in an interview in *Esquire* Williams spoke of their first meeting: 'He arrived at dusk, wearing Levi's, took one look at the confusion around him, and set to work. First he stuck his hand into the overflowing toilet and unclogged the drain, then he tackled the fuses. Within an hour, everything worked . . . Then he read the script aloud, just as he played it. It was the most magnificent reading I ever heard and he had the part immediately. He stayed the night, curled up with a quilt on the floor.'

Kazan chose Karl Malden to play Mitch, the card-playing crony of Stanley's whom Blanche almost manages to marry; and Mrs Selznick found the Stella in Kim Hunter, an actress 'who hadn't quite made it in Hollywood'. Mrs Selznick remembered her first meeting with Brando: 'He didn't behave like someone to whom something wonderful had just happened, nor did he try to make an impression; he was too busy assessing me . . . He was wayward one moment, playful the next, volunteering that he had been expelled from school, then grinning provocatively at me. I didn't take the bait. It was easy going after that. He sat up in his chair and turned forthright, earnest, even polite. One thing he wanted me to know was that he'd never make a movie.' She interpreted this remark as his assurance that he would fulfil his contractual obligation to stay with the play for twenty months – but given his reputation ('moody, restless, unpredictable') she thought she would be lucky if she kept him.

According to her, Brando had a terrible struggle with the role; she watched Kazan, with infinite patience and tenderness, coax the actor to the extent that it was hard on the others: 'Gadge in his infinite wisdom let Marlon get away with just muttered snatches of his speeches. His performance was becoming so powerful that Tennessee remained unruffled' – a rather ambiguous statement, but understandable when coupled with Kazan's own comment on the possibility of Brando overwhelming Tandy: 'I looked toward my authority, Tennessee. He was no help; he seemed enraptured by the boy. "The son of a bitch is riding a crush," I said to myself.' Tandy's performance grew stronger throughout the try-out tour, and the occasion was a triumph for all concerned when the play opened at the Ethel Barrymore in New York on 3 December 1947. Her notices were perhaps the best, but as Brooks Atkinson said in *The New York Times*, 'The rest of the acting is also of very high quality.' Brando was 'brilliant' (Louis Kronenberger in *P M*), 'brutally convincing' (Howard Barnes in the *New York Herald Tribune*) 'magnificent' (John Chapman in the *New York Daily News*), playing 'with an astonishing authenticity' (William Hawkins); Richard Watts in the *New York Post* was converted ('I have hitherto not shared the enthusiasm of most reviewers for Marlon Brando, but his portrayal of the heroine's sullen, violent nemesis is an excellent piece of work') and Robert Garland in the *New York Journal-American* was confirmed in his opinion ('our theatre's most memorable young actor at his most memorable'). The play was judged the best of the year by the Drama Critics Circle and it was awarded the Pulitzer Prize; it was easily the hottest ticket in town, and went on to play 855 performances.

During the run Miss Tandy was succeeded by Uta Hagen, with the curious result – rare in the theatre and a tribute to both performances – that the leading role was thereafter identified with two actresses. Queried about the best of the Blanches in 1973 (when the play was revived on Broadway with Rosemary Harris and James Darren), Williams agreed that possibly Miss Hagen was the one, but he'd always felt 'closest' to Miss Tandy; he volunteered the information that no one had equalled Brando as Kowalski, and added that no one should try to imitate his performance.

In his 'Memoirs' (1975) Williams wrote, 'I think he is probably the greatest living actor; I think he is greater than Olivier.' The same source reveals that he has only ever written roles with three actors in mind – the others were Donald Madden and Michael York, and the plays written for them were among his minor work, done in his later years. Brando, he says, 'was just about the best-looking young man I've ever seen, with one or two exceptions; but I have never played around with actors, it's a point of morality with me and anyhow Brando was not the type to get a part that way.'

As far as Williams is concerned, this would seem to contradict something I learnt in researching this book, that one young actor, widely known as heterosexual, had 'serviced' both 'Tom Williams and Bill Inge' while appearing in a movie based on Williams' material – and I take the source as impeccable, since only Williams' closest friends called him Tom. Most biographers of Brando refer to rumours of homosexuality and I heard these myself when researching the original version of this book in the early 70s. Since the text then dealt almost exclusively with his career I was not inclined to mention the rumours. I believe that a public figure has a right to a private life and that the tabloids have done untold damage by not sharing this view. However . . .

Stuart Little (former drama critic of the Herald Tribune) and Arthur Cantor (a producer active in both Broadway and London) have penned a study of sexuality backstage and they say: 'Some variation from the norm seems present in most actor's sex lives. While other people hold back from sexual experimentation because of fear, actors often behave in a counterphobic fashion, which is to say they are challenged to plunge in and do the very things they're afraid of. Athletes and dare-devils share this characteristic. To them the challenge is physical, while to the actor it's psychological.' They conclude that the emotional barriers through which an actor must hurdle on stage may tempt him to try 'any number of sexual variations'.

It is as well to bear this comment in mind when reading Shelley Winters's autobiography – the passages, anyway, which deal with her dalliance with Brando. This actress had made some progress as a Hollywood starlet and had taken over as Ado Annie in 'Oklahoma!'; she met Brando by dropping in on the Actors Studio as an observer and was acting in the same capacity – with Brando's connivance – at the rehearsals of 'Streetcar' (because she wanted to watch Kazan direct). Brando invited her to the cold-water flat – 'there was ice on the *inside* of the windows' – that he shared with Wally Cox. Apart from a minute bathroom, it consisted of a kitchen and a living-room, both of which contained a double-bed. (There was also Brando's pet raccoon.) The place was lit by candles in beer-bottles, a set-up which terrified Miss Winters, in view of the paint-cans lying around. Dinner consisted of canned tomato soup, cold cauliflower in sour cream, brown rice with nuts, kasha with raisins and green peppers, followed by grapefruit with brown sugar, and washed down with a gallon of wine laced with gin. Coffee was made by plugging the pot into the overhead light fixture. After Winters had shared the washing-up with Cox's girlfriend, that lady and he closed the door on their bed; Brando did some weight-lifting while discoursing on Kazan's methods of directing, before offering his own version of come-hither, 'My body generates a great deal of heat.'

This does not suggest much in the way of sexual variation, but equally obviously it hardly seems a romantic prelude – despite the candles – to the act of love. Double-dating in this case is suspect, though it was common enough in the 40s: but Brando evidently found it especially soothing, or so implies Carlo Fiore in his book, 'Bud: the Brando I Knew'. Fiore's account of their friendship, which began when they were acting together at Sayville, is both touching and revealing – as, for instance, when first bunking down in Sayville, Brando invited him to join him 'in the upper berth'. When Brando's mother visited them, Fiore confessed that he was sexually attracted to her; and after watching them dancing together much of one evening Brando said, 'I can see you want mother. Why don't you go to bed with her?' They also tended to share girlfriends, Fiore taking over when Brando tired of the lady. It was a friendship which endured, and when Fiore's acting aspirations came to little Brando found him employment – as his stand-in on *On the Waterfront*, for instance, and as one of the screenwriters on *One-Eyed Jacks*; Brando remained exasperated by Fiore's drug addiction – heroin and cocaine – but when he first started making good money on Broadway he would often pay for his fix.

Brando's other life-long companion-in-arms was in contrast to the snappy-suited Sicilian. Wally Cox was a childhood chum, encountered again by chance in a New York supermarket. Brando introduced him to Dick Loving, who was courting (and would marry) his sister Fran; the two men went into partnership as silversmiths, making cuff-links and other accessories for men. However, he also harboured show business ambitions – or, at least, was prompted to do so after Brando had watched him perform a monologue at a party. With several of these he began a professional career at the Village Vanguard, a Greenwich Village nightclub – a career which reached its highest peak only four years later, in 1952, in the role of an NBC series, 'Mr Peepers', in which he played an ineffectual science teacher. They were an odd couple, the skinny, wiry, introverted Cox and Brando, who had 'the face of a poet and the body of an animal'.

This description was given to one biographer by one of Brando's girlfriends – for a book which exhaustively lists, it would seem, every one of her species. The number of his 'chicks' (the word is Williams', in his autobiography, used of Brando's companion when they first met; but, as we have seen, she was omitted from his earlier account of this) is well-attested to: so the reader may well resent my innuendo. But while the writer concerned has an index entry, 'Brando and homosexuals' he does not seem to know that in 1975 Brando gave an interview in which he discussed his homosexuality. I do not know why he did, unless in middle-age he could think of nothing else to continue his tradition of shocking the bourgeoisie; it would seem a strange confession – unprompted, it would seem, by those interviewing him – from a man who has had several wives and who has a grown-up family: but it is certainly manna to a biographer.

He said (and I translate from the French as it appeared in *Ciné-Revue*): 'Homosexuality is so fashionable these days that no one bothers to talk about it. The proof? – I've dabbled in it. Perhaps to counteract that image that seven out of ten women have considered me, probably wrongly, a sex-symbol. For me sex is something you can't describe. If you like, let's say that sex has no sex. Like the vast majority of men I've had several homosexual experiences and I'm not remotely ashamed of it.'

Earlier, while working with the actor Cameron Mitchell, Brando had blurted out, 'I'm trisexual', which suggests a less positive response to his sexual identity. It was not easy at this time to be a successful actor and a homosexual – at least in the United States and even more so in Hollywood. Montgomery Clift – whom Brando admired, and whom he considered his greatest challenge – did not marry, but his homosexuality was one of the factors which turned him into an alcoholic. If Brando's solution – marriage and a girl for every public occasion – seems preferable, it confirms the conflict and contradiction we have already noted. These qualities had already intruded upon his career: happily, they would not reappear – at least publicly – till he had enjoyed the sort of acclaim accorded no other actor.

3
Into Films

Brando fretted during the run of the play. Reputedly he refused to rehearse when Miss Hagen took over the role of Blanche – and Kazan, incidentally, had also backed away, unwilling to direct 'the strong-minded' Miss Hagen. Devilishly, he recommended Clurman as his successor, and he reckoned that he gave it a conventional reading. Both ladies toured with the play – opposite Anthony Quinn, who was playing Stanley; and with Ralph Meeker it played another six months on Broadway after Brando left in June 1949. Brando was not only bored with doing the same thing every evening, but was increasingly subject to lapses of memory. It amused him to find audiences panting for his next word when he hadn't the least idea what it should be. He consoled himself during this period by the reflection that he was now a stage star, which meant, in practical terms, that the next time round he could command a higher salary than at present ($550 weekly) and have greater freedom in his choice. Although the publicity line, later, was that he turned down scores of offers, Jim Henaghan says that Brando begged him to get him a film contract, but no producer was interested – which cannot be strictly true, since Brando was interviewed by two independents, Hal B. Wallis and David O. Selznick. Wallis had recently raided Broadway, coming away with Kirk Douglas and Burt Lancaster, but he did not find Brando equally impressive; Selznick had no active plans to re-enter production, though he kept a dwindling but profitable stable of stars to be loaned to other producers – but he did not foresee much income from Brando. A Warner Bros executive did discuss *Rebel Without a Cause* with the actor, but the film was not made (till six years later).

The fact is that Hollywood had at that time all the new faces it needed, for the public then was showing a marked preference for the old ones. The accredited male box-office stars in 1949 and 1950 were Bing Crosby, Bob Hope, Abbott and Costello, John Wayne, Gary Cooper, Cary Grant, Humphrey Bogart, Clark Gable, James Stewart, Spencer Tracy, Clifton Webb and Randolph Scott; hovering just below the top-listed ten in the *Motion Picture Herald*'s compilations were Tyrone Power, Errol Flynn, Alan Ladd, Robert Taylor and James Cagney. Leaving aside Abbott & Costello and Webb as special cases (they were 'funny-men'), Ladd was the only one who had been around less than ten years (i.e., as a star); most of the others, went back fifteen years or more. The studios were, as ever, industriously finding vehicles for them, and if they wanted new blood, there was some around: some independent, none tied exclusively to one studio – Gregory Peck, Kirk Douglas, Burt Lancaster, Montgomery Clift. And if they were being offered more work than they could handle, there were lesser contract stars to be kept busy, like Glenn Ford and William Holden at that time.

Even when these artists had favourable, non-exclusive agreements (Lancaster and Douglas, for instance, with Wallis) they had little artistic freedom. As a result, Brando felt, 'I do not think that anybody connected with the films in the United States has ever made a sincere effort to avail himself of their fullest potential the way they do, say, in France.' He expressed a wish to make films in France, concluding, 'I just feel dead inside, coming away from most Hollywood screenings.' Among the French movies

Brando most admired was *Les Enfants du Paradis*, which starred Arletty, 'I mean, I was really in *love* with her.' When he left 'Streetcar' he went to Paris, where she was starring in the French production of the play. He asked to meet his 'ideal woman' but 'Wow! Was that a mistake, was that a disillusionment. She was a tough article.' The disenchantment was mutual. Mlle Arletty had not expected one of Broadway's leading actors to turn up in jeans and a T-shirt.

On his vacation – travelling in France and Italy – Brando did not stay in the class of hostelries favoured by major stars; and he looked like a bum when Maynard Morris came across him in Paris. He wired MCA with Brando's address and MCA promptly mailed a script – to be produced by Stanley Kramer, who had in fact had Brando in mind for a movie since seeing him in 'Streetcar'. Brando had turned down the project, on the basis of a synopsis, before leaving for Europe; the veteran director, Lewis Milestone, encountered in Paris, advised him to accept on the basis of the talents involved. Kramer operated an independent company which couldn't afford – and for this venture certainly didn't want – a high-priced name. Pencilled-in for the role, till Brando accepted, was Richard Basehart, officially a 'star' at 20th Century-Fox, but despite his talent one who seldom looked like striking box-office gold. The film was *The Men*, and it was the effort of a group of men – a felicitous coming-together of talents – considered the industry's new white hopes. Critics and what can succinctly be described as serious film buffs looked to these men to provide relief from the fantasies of the dream factory – to face film life more realistically and with maturity. They were Kramer, Carl Foreman, author of the screenplay, and Fred Zinnemann, who was to direct. Their recent credits were clearly of the sort to appeal to an actor who thought that American films were 'removed from all reality whatsoever' – but they were, despite their 'promise', old Hollywood hands.

Kramer had begun in films in 1933 in the research department of MGM; he had been cutter and casting director, and in the early forties had assisted Albert Lewin on the production of *So Ends Our Night* and *The Moon and Sixpence*. Lewin was a producer who did not underestimate public taste (though the public often had little taste for the ambitious works he offered it); his philosophies seem to have rubbed off on Kramer, who, after a minor comedy in 1948, *So This is New York*, embarked on a series of resolutely non-escapist films. The first, *Champion*, was a fierce and unsentimental study of a prize-fighter (Kirk Douglas); made on a modest budget and liked by both press and public, it made a lot of money. *Home of the Brave*, the second venture, was a version of a Broadway play about racial intolerance in the army: there was prestige but little profit. United Artists distributed both, and they would handle *The Men*, but for that Kramer had had to find a new backer. UA had provided some finance in the past, and would do so again in the future – when the company became a producer as well as a distributor; but at this time, after years of squabbling between Mary Pickford and Charlie Chaplin (the survivors of its four founders) its financial state was so precarious that backing had to be found elsewhere. *Champion* had been an immense shot in the arm; Kramer's output comprised almost its sole link to quality at this point.

Foreman had co-scripted or adapted Kramer's productions up to now. He had been in Hollywood since at least 1941, when he received a credit as one of the writers of *Spooks Run Wild*; after working on such ignoble projects as *Bowery Blitzkrieg*, *Rhythm Parade* and *Dakota*, he finally managed, with Kramer, to make the sort of films he wanted to make.

The only one of the three of any real accomplishment was Zinnemann. Born in Vienna, he worked in Germany on *Menschen am Sonntag*, in 1930, before reaching Hollywood. In 1937 he started work at MGM on their 'Crime Does Not Pay' series; he had moved over to features – B pictures – in 1941. In 1944 he directed Spencer Tracy in *The Seventh Cross*, one of the best of all anti-Nazi pictures (it concerned an anti-fascist on the run in the prewar Reich), and made his reputation with *The Search*, in 1948, a film about displaced children in postwar Europe.

'There were various things that convinced me Fred would be a good addition to the team,' said Kramer. 'We were a small company with a modest budget and at that time Fred did not come too expensively.' Zinnemann himself anticipated working outside the constraints imposed by a big studio (he had been under contract to MGM). And there was the subject-matter. He had also made *Act of Violence*, a thriller about a guy whose wartime experiences have turned him into a psychopath. He seemed the right person to direct another (his third) movie concerning the aftermath of war – for *The Men* was a study of paraplegics. There were 2,500 of these in the US at the time, relics of the war, men permanently maimed – or in dictionary terms, with the lower half of their body paralysed on both sides. Foreman (who wrote both story and screenplay) and Kramer talked to many of them at the Birmingham Veterans Administration Hospital near Los Angeles, and it was there, later, that much of the piece was filmed – and it was because some of them were to have small roles that the leading role was played by someone unknown to the mass audience, therefore the more easily blending in with them. Brando insisted on living in the hospital before filming began. There was also considerable rehearsal before the cameras were set up, which was unusual at the time, and although Zinnemann described Brando's performance to me as 'astonishing' and 'all his own work. I can take no credit for it,' it did not seem that way at the time.

Kramer had wondered whether the quietly-spoken but

forceful Zinnemann could control an actor whose reputation for temperament had preceded him to the West Coast; so he watched with satisfaction as they learnt to trust each other, building the performance. Zinnemann says 'It was an interesting scene [at the beginning of the film] because the situation was that of the man telling the girl that he wanted nothing more to do with her, to get out, and Marlon played it that way quite ruthlessly, not involving Teresa Wright at all. She was wonderful in the first two takes, but was gradually affected by his lack of response, and I had somehow to control these contradictory things – a feeling that he was freezing out the other performer, but this self-absorption absolutely fitted the character he was playing.'

One reason for the rehearsals was that everyone involved felt that the subject would benefit from a greater knowledge of the interplay of characters – and the result was a taut, tight film, with, paradoxically, a documentary-like spontaneity. The film was edgy, rough, and, by implicaton, deeply pacifist. Under the credits, soldiers advanced to the martial cry of drums; with a burst of machine-gun fire, the screen dissolves to the men in hospital – and then to a doctor (Everett Sloane) explaining to a group of women the meaning of paraplegia. He speaks of the malfunctioning of bladder and bowels – and that had not been done in a Hollywood film before. It is soon obvious that the makers have achieved their aim, to make a movie worthy of men permanently wounded in the war: yet when the doctor asks for questions it is the woman in the mink-coat who refuses to believe that money cannot pay for a cure.

However, in most instances the film does break with convention. There had been few screen doctors – this one was based on a real person – like this one before. They were usually like Brian Aherne in *Vigil in the Night* or Gary Cooper in *The Story of Dr Wassall*, but Sloane is not romantic; he has a salty tongue, an impish sense of humour and he can be very tough to his charges. Chief among these is an ex-officer, Ken Wilozek (Brando), alternating between gloomy silences and outbursts of self-mockery. He refuses to see his fiancée, Ellen (Wright), anxious to help him, because he feels that she is acting from pity; he greets the doctors with sullen sarcasm and is as prickly as a hedgehog when confronted with the kindness of fellow patients. They, like he, resort to irony, and he gradually emerges from isolation to mingle his bitterness with theirs. He also succumbs to therapy and training, and is finally encouraged to see Ellen. Her optimism falters when faced with a lifetime of coping with an invalid. His doctor (Sloane) can offer no reassurances and her family opposes the marriage; and on the wedding night they quarrel.

The critic Richard Winnington wrote in *Sight & Sound*: 'The scene in which two persons who love each other deeply pour out the fruit of all their torment in irrational words of hate, is a hallmark of the truth of the film. It is one of the few love passages of the cinema to encompass the pitiful ache of human love.'

Today it is one of the least convincing sequences in the film, heavily obvious in dialogue and motivation – and the most notable instance (of many) of Miss Wright's inadequacy. It is followed shortly by a particularly good one, an effective vignette of American life, in which Ken and a buddy are accosted by an overfriendly, drunk veteran of World War I. The film ends, however, foolishly, but making a plot point – that if Ken can make his marriage work there is no greater therapy: an inconclusive, but hopeful note.

It is conventional to say that a film like this must be moving: it is about sad matters, therefore it must be sad. It is inconceivable that it isn't so, but it is inconceivable without the tact, the passion and the honesty of the handling here. Zinnemann's ability to get it down plain even papers over some of the faults, seemingly indigenous at the time, to the 'social problem' picture. A difficult subject requires an exceptional talent, and he had it. Stanley Kramer, later, when he turned director, would be inadequate to almost every subject he handled; he, Zinnemann and Foreman would work together on another highly-praised – and much more popular – film, *High Noon*, but there was, later, no love lost between them, Zinnemann, an exceptionally modest man, observed of *The Men* that Kramer, 'overdramatized and sentimentalized it by adding Dimitri Tiomkin music and making violent cuts'. However, there is no doubt that in 1950 the three of them made a film better (i.e., better-made, more involving, with more substance) than any other American film that year.

The reviews were entirely laudatory, and Brando's ability was at once acknowledged. Winnington said that 'his combination of style, depth and range comes like a blood transfusion into cinema acting' and Otis L. Guernsey, in the *New York Herald-Tribune*, noted that the performance 'depends not at all on personality but entirely on understanding of character and technical virtuosity'. We were not accustomed to this in Hollywood pictures. Spencer Tracy, regarded by many as the best living screen actor at that time, delved deeper into himself instead of casting wider (and when asked why he always played himself, growled, 'Who do you expect me to play – Humphrey Bogart?'). We enjoyed the virtuosity of Bogart and Cagney, without kidding ourselves that they played other than variations of themselves. Only occasionally did a star actor maintain his position by exploiting versatility: Charles Laughton was one, and he had to, because he was not by nature a leading man; Paul Muni was another, and it was only after a while that it was realized that under the various beards there was the same performance going on. Unless you're content to play yourself, the use of make-up is a legitimate device: Laughton and Muni tried never to look the same twice – a theory to which Laurence Olivier, on stage and screen, was the most notable adherent. Brando would follow them but would use less artificial aids.

His achievement at this stage, in *The Men*, was to offer a complete study instead of the bits of himself a movie-star offers to the saying of the dialogue. We sensed rather than knew that it was a character performance: men under stress and neurotics are not unusual in movies, but even with natural-sounding dialogue there was something we hadn't experienced before. Ken Wilozek was outwardly tortured and inwardly twisted – the sort of terms in which such heroes could be summarized – but there was an un-expected sense of ordinariness: this was a young man who had never expected to amount to very much, he'd never expected he'd have to think deeply or read the right books, much less question the fate which had dealt him this blow, setting him apart from his fellows. Brando plays against his disability; he asks to be neither liked nor pitied.

He is vibrant, unexpected and powerful. There is some-thing of Stanley Kowalski here – the unexpected shifts of mood, in this case to express his physical infirmity. Obvi-ously there had been electric performers in film before – Cagney, evidently, but he worked chiefly in comedy and melodrama, where his ebullience would serve the material rather than disturb it. When I think of some of the greatest screen performances to this time – Walter Huston in *Dods-worth*, Bette Davis in *The Letter*, Barbara Stanwyck in *Double Indemnity*, Louis Jouvet, Harry Baur, Bogart and Tracy in practically anything, Olivier in *Carrie* (admit-tedly, made a year later) – I can see big emotions being reined in, talent working in subservience to the flow of the drama. Brando does not do this; he dares to go for the outsize emotions, relying mostly on his eyes and his hands. At the same time his Wilozek has the gentleness which for some of his friends was the keynote of his personality. As Zinnemann put it, 'He had an extraordinary instinct, a sensitivity that enabled him to understand the men in that hospital. He was also quick to understand how sometimes the least gesture could be the most effective in acting for the movies. And he was soft-spoken, which can be ideal in movies.' It is an absolutely truthful performance, as well as being wholly original, which is one reason why he and Miss Wright are so singularly ill-matched: there is nothing in hers that we hadn't seen a thousand times before in Hollywood's 'concerned' heroines. His performance was not nominated for an Oscar. These were: Jose Ferrer (who won) for *Cyrano de Bergerac*, Louis Calhern for *The Magnificent Yankee*, William Holden for *Sunset Boulevard*, James Stewart for *Harvey* and Spencer Tracy for *Father of the Bride*. Brando was not interested in the Oscar circus, but since he had broken most of the rules governing the behaviour of stars he had to be judged as an actor – and by the (uneven and unreliable) standards of the Academy he was found wanting. Those five performances nominated are in most cases to be noted for their professionalism – and Tracy's, certainly, is much more than that. But even that pales beside Brando. Watching *The Men* today is to be forcibly reminded how he changed the course of American acting.

4

Two by Kazan

The Men opened in New York at Radio City Music Hall, but its reception by the public reflected only the optimism of its backers. Kramer's avowed policy was to offer the best possible films on limited budgets, using inexpensive but appropriate talents. Brando's fee had been $40,000, while Miss Wright had agreed to do it for only $25,000 because she was persuaded that it would be an important picture. She says her usual fee at this time was $200,000 – which seems exaggerated when the certified box-office stars (which she was not) were getting on average $150,000; but in her honesty she tells us that the film's failure was so great that she found herself 'a $25,000 actress' working in Westerns. It did appear on several lists of the year's best films, but to the New York critics that year the best possible film was *All About Eve*. The public liked *Samson and Delilah*, Disney's *Cinderella*, *King Solomon's Mines*, *Battleground* and *Annie Get Your Gun*. The time had not yet come when queues formed at the instigation of critics.

But if Brando was praised in the reviews, the feature pages presented him as a surly young man who went about in T-shirts and blue jeans and was rude to Louella Parsons. Co-operative and conscientious on set, he was equally painstaking in showing contempt for Hollywood people. Sifting through all the stuff written about the young Brando, the 'rebel', I think it is clear that he set out to outrage or antagonize the self-important denizens of tinsel-town, but, like his rejection of the Oscar twenty-three years later, he seems to have taken them at their own importance. His antics read foolishly because you wish he'd been big enough to ignore the Heddas and Louellas and the cigar-chomping tin gods. The press has always trivialized colourful or independent minds working in show business: it's a shame, it is inconvenient, like a hangover. Brando never seems to have adjusted.

There had been, before, other actors – usually from Broadway – who refused to play the Hollywood game. Katharine Hepburn was one, and George Cukor later observed that it wasn't she who had grown up to Hollywood but vice versa. It is, Brando observed, 'a frontier town ruled by fear and love of money, but it can't rule me because I'm not afraid of anything and I don't love money'. 'They dress you up in a tuxedo,' he told the columnist Bob Thomas, explaining why he refused to sign a long-term contract, 'and tell you to go to this party and that. I would end up like Lewis Stone, waiting by the phone until the studio calls up and says I get a part playing a cannibal in a Johnny Weissmuller picture.' Hollywood would learn to love Brando, as it always loves success, but whenever it folded him to its bosom over the years, he struck back like a spoilt child. He chose that pool to paddle in: but whoever thought that actors should lay claim to diplomacy?

More than that was required by the feudal-minded studios, in which stars were treated as serfs. *Of course* the executives resented Brando's rebellion, springing as it did from his honesty and desire for independence. These were not qualities highly prized in Hollywood, but among those who did were George Glass, a partner in the Kramer organisation and its director of publicity, and Jack Cooper, the company's press agent. Cooper thought of him as 'very open, a little bashful and very, very sensitive', though professionally he was hardly delighted when he heard Brando describe his background as 'horrible' and his mother as 'a drunk'. Another lasting colleague whom Brando acquired at this time was Jay Kanter, MCA's West Coast correspondent, appointed to look after Brando by its president, Lew Wasserman. Except for his looks, Kanter was the antithesis of his new client – precise, aggressive but straightforward and excessively well-turned-out; he was also younger than Brando, not hide-bound in industry ways – and very much aware of the ways in which the imminent break-up of the studio system could benefit MCA and its clients.

However, it was by no means certain whether he could command for Brando a real star's fee, though a first film that is a critical success but a box-office failure is clearly better than one that is neither. Because movies so seldom accommodated an actor of this sort, it was widely thought that he would return to the stage – to eventually tackle the classics. He did a television play in 1950 – 'Come Out Fighting' for NBC, in which he played a prize-fighter – but has evinced little subsequent interest in that medium (he has been interviewed on TV, but less than ten times in forty years – less than some promoters do in a week). After *The Men*, he didn't lack film offers. At RKO, Wald and Krasna announced *The Harder They Fall*, saying that they had in mind Brando, Kirk Douglas or John Garfield as the pugilist (it wasn't made till six years later). Brando was often bracketed with Douglas as the new 'strong' actor.

His next film role was the expected one – in the film of 'A Streetcar Named Desire'. Despite the acclaim that had greeted it, no studio thought that it would pass the restrictions imposed by the Breen Office – Hollywood's own censorship set-up – without emasculation. The rights were eventually purchased by an agent, Charles K. Feldman, who had motion picture aspirations. In 1944, for Universal, he had produced *Follow the Boys*, an all-star jollity containing many of his clients. He returned to films in 1950, co-producing with Warner Bros the film of Tennessee Williams's 'The Glass Menagerie'; he arranged another deal with Warners for *Streetcar*, signing Kazan to direct and Williams to write the screenplay. Warners agreed to take Brando, Karl Malden and Kim Hunter from the New York production, but insisted on a name actress for Blanche. Kazan believes – because by this time he had a string of successful movies behind him – that he could have held out for Miss Tandy (who had only done supporting roles in films), but that he had already achieved from this play and these players as much as he could; he had only taken on the job because Williams had urged him to, and he felt the need of stimulation from a new Blanche. The role was offered to Vivien Leigh, who had played it in the London production: because of *Gone With the Wind* a decade earlier (it had not long been reissued) she remained a potent name in the States though her last two (British) films had not been successful. She declined to leave London and her husband, Laurence Olivier, and the role was offered to Olivia de Haviland, on the strength of her performances in *The Heiress* (for which she won an Oscar) and *The Snake Pit*. Feldman seriously considered casting her sister Joan Fontaine as Stella, but that idea came to nothing when de Havilland's husband, the novelist Marcus Goodrich, decreed that his wife could not sink so low as to play a loose lady.

Miss Leigh, meanwhile, changed her mind about doing the film, because Olivier had received a movie offer from Paramount – to star opposite Jennifer Jones in William Wyler's *Carrie*. Tennessee Williams now wanted Miss Leigh to play Blanche and no other. When he had first seen the London production, directed by Olivier, he had been so digusted by it – and the cuts made by Olivier – that he had refused to go backstage to meet the star. This mutual disappointment was banished when Williams and Leigh eventually met; he was enchanted with her. So that was that. She was paid $100,000 as opposed to Brando's $75,000.

The film was not a cast-iron proposition. Whatever the Broadway public had liked, movie audiences were accustomed to light relief in the heaviest of drama – they hadn't wanted to know about the film of O'Neill's *Mourning Becomes Electra* at all – and it was doubtful whether they would support a film which ends with its protagonist being led off to a mental institution. The ad-copy could emphasize the 'sizzling! scorching!' aspects, but though the Breen Office had passed the screenplay (with the insistence that Stella reject Stanley at the end, and with the exception of a tacit reference by Blanche to her husband's homosexuality) there was always the possibility of interference by local authorities, preventing cinemas from showing the film.*

Together Kazan and Williams had worked out a screenplay, opening it out, but at the last minute went back to the original play and filmed that. It remains the most persuasive of photographed plays. 'I think it's an awfully good film of a play,' Kazan told me. 'One reason it is so good is because of Brando. He's brilliant.' He went on to say that he had difficulties at first with Miss Leigh, who wished to keep the conception her husband had given her of the role, 'and I would say, "You're not doing it with Larry now, you're doing it with me."' She learnt to trust Kazan after a couple of weeks, and he grew to like and admire her 'enormously'; he also observed that she had little actual talent, but that he had never known anyone work so hard to use what she had.

She had this to say of Brando: 'I thought he was terribly affected. He used to say to me, "Why do you have to say

* The reason for the setting-up of the Breen Office – then the Hays Office – in 1921.

good morning to everyone?" and I'd say, "Because it is a good morning and anyway it's a nice thing to say, so why not?" I got to understand him much better as he went on with the filming. He is such a good actor and when he wants to he can speak English without a mumble. He is the only man I know who can imitate Larry accurately. Larry is awfully difficult to imitate. Brando used to do speeches from *Henry V* and I closed my eyes and it could have been Larry. Brando also had a nice singing voice; he sang folk songs to us beautifully.'

Karl Malden also had pleasant memories of working on the film. He thought the poker game sequence one of his best scenes, but at first Brando was 'horsing around' and treading on his lines. Since he was the star, he could get away with it, 'but he was also a nice guy and probably not thinking what he was doing to my part. So I put it to him straight' – and Brando was consideration itself.

Kazan starts the film with a cliché – an effect, anyway, which he admits he borrowed from the Garbo *Anna Karenina*: Blanche appears out of a puff of smoke. With that exception and the scene in which Mitch almost proposes to Blanche, relocated to the verandah of a riverside cafe, the entire action takes place either within or just without the Kowalski apartment. The effect is so dynamic that it's hard to realize that Kazan deliberately meant that apartment to be claustrophobic; he has gone for the 'meanings in the text' – the expression as used by Sidney Lumet of his version of *Long Day's Journey Into Night*, made ten years later – adding that its only connection with theatre is that it takes place within four walls. There is a fake poetry in the early reaches of the film, a combination of peeling stucco, Ufa lighting, Alex North's heartbreak-jazz score (the first time jazz had been used as background music in a movie); but it is entirely suitable to what Blanche is saying or dreaming. She is a larger-than-life figure confronted by another – Stanley – in a New Orleans of recognizably proletarian taste, but not of much realism. The effect is, intentionally or not, extraordinarily like the stylized Berlin of *The Last Laugh*, in which, in a different way, Jannings was as bizarre as Blanche; his dismissal is as effective as her expulsion from grace, in that with the shock they are both in an unreal, alien world. Kazan, in fact, found a texture to accommodate the text – and into it Brando slotted with ease.

Kowalski is perhaps one of Blanche's fantasies – the most substantial of them. Against her extravagances his excesses, even his bellowing and grunting, pale. Despite the title (Desire is a district of New Orleans), their mutual appraisal is dependent on selfishness rather than lust. Her posturing is somewhat antiseptic – at least the way Vivien Leigh plays her; it has rather to do with the hope that Stanley, or *someone*, will recognize her gentility. She has been a coquette too long to be very sanguine, however, that she can go on holding off advances – and of course she doesn't want to: nymphomania is primarily selfish. He is more obviously motivated by sexual gratification, but he's concerned with the quality of his orgasm, not with hers – and she's fully aware of that. Another set of actors, another director might not find these inferences in the text: because of their contributions, this is the definitive *Streetcar*. Miss Leigh is over-theatrical, and since the camera cuts away from her so insistently (in the middle of a sentence, even a word) it looks as though Kazan could not control her and left the editors to 'create' her performance. She is never still, hogging the screen as if afraid that the Americans would take the film from her, causing her to hang on to what she thought was her one advantage, the directions Olivier had given her. Even so, vain and vulnerable, a beautiful woman trying to look ravaged, she is fascinating. No other Blanche is conceivable to me. My memories of her performance on the stage are now cloudy, but I have watched this one on film so often, with such admiration, that I've never had the least wish to see another Blanche – till 1984, when I found myself curious about a version filmed for television (which used, incidentally, this screenplay but restoring, from the play, the changes demanded by the Breen Office). Ann-Margret (Blanche), Treat Williams (Stanley), Beverly d'Angelo (Stella) and Randy Quaid (Mitch) gave well-integrated performances, and the whole thing is so well-done that it was nominated for no less than eleven Emmy Awards: but two days later you have forgotten it while Kazan's version sears the memory. Miss d'Angelo is better-casting than Kim Hunter, because she is more earthy: but her scenes with the also excellent Williams do not carry the impact of those between Hunter and Brando, who are superlative. They *enjoy* each other – the way each other looks and talks; they long to be together after a quarrel (those caused by Blanche); there is sex and sanity in their interaction, in complete contrast to Blanche's sleazy past. Brando's Stanley, a creature of fire and air, encompasses everything that Williams had imagined into the character and set down in the text; and his presence made both silences and shouting awesome. One recognized, more than in *The Men*, that he generated the same electricity as Cagney: you felt that nothing either of them did was without danger, without tension. Brando was less volatile, and probably a better actor. As Kowalski, it was as if a spring uncoiled, and he became the most discussed actor in the world.

He was later to say that *Streetcar* was the only one of his films he liked. He must have liked the reviews. In the *New York Herald-Tribune*, Otis L. Guernsey Jr found him giving 'a remarkably truthful performance of a heavy-muscled, practical animal, secure in the normalcy of marriage and friendship, cunning but insensitive, aware of Blanche's deceits but not of her suffering. This performance is as close to perfect as one could wish.' Bosley Crowther in *The New York Times* thought him no less brilliant than

Miss Leigh, carrying over 'all the energy and the steel-spring characteristics that made him vivid on the stage. But here, where we're closer to him, he seems that much more highly charged, his despairs seem that much more pathetic and his comic moments that much more slyly enjoyed.' The British critics, who had not had an opportunity to experience Brando's stage Stanley, were no less enthusiastic. He represents, said Milton Shulman in the (London) *Evening Standard*, 'probably the lowest human denominator yet to be presented seriously in motion pictures. His uncouth, physical crudity is fascinatingly repulsive. It is a shocking, but memorable, characterization.' C. A. Lejeune in *The Observer*: 'Marlon Brando's performance as the monstrous, mumbling, almost subhuman brother-in-law is acting of a different sort. No sheath of gold for Brando, only the cave-man's skins and the naked man beneath them. But his brute exacts the same sort of pity as Caliban, and is one of the strongest and most selfless performances I remember seeing in the cinema.' Richard Winnington in the *News Chronicle*: 'the performance of Marlon Brando is terrific. As the primitive, defiant, repellent Kowalski, "the Polack" who resents and rapes his sister-in-law, Brando burns with a sullen glow that one will not easily forget.' The film was cheered at the Venice Film Festival and the New York Critics Circle chose it the best of the year. Kazan was the Critics' best director and Miss Leigh their best actress – but as far as they were concerned the best actor was Arthur Kennedy in *Bright Victory*, the study of a blinded ex-soldier undergoing rehabilitation. It is a capable performance, but not – since the comparison presents itself – in the same class as Brando's in *The Men*.

At the Academy Award ceremony, Oscars went to Miss Leigh, Miss Hunter and Mr Malden. Kazan lost to George Stevens, who had directed *A Place in the Sun*. It had been predicted that that film and *Streetcar*, Hollywood's two coming-of-age productions, would sweep the Oscars, but

the members of the Academy, impressed by the 'arty' clim-
actic ballet of the musical *An American in Paris*, voted
that the Best Picture. *Streetcar* did win Best (black and
white) Art Direction for the veteran designer Richard Day
– though Kazan's contribution to that should not be ignored
(his insistence, for instance, that the Kowalski apartment
should look increasingly cramped, its walls dripping with
water). Irene Sharaff was nominated for her costume designs, but lost to *A Place in the Sun*. We should note,
however, her influence in creating the Brando image –
blue jeans and torn, sweaty T-shirts.

He may have worn these in real life, though almost all
the portraits taken of him till this period show him correctly attired in collar and tie; but a comparison of the
stills of the stage* and screen versions of Williams's play
demonstrate the extent to which Miss Sharaff redefined
the 'slob' image, rendering it more powerful, individual,
sexy. This was the way the world got to know Brando,
and though the film industry might have pretended disdain
it was something it understood – in the way it had always
liked a handle (Mary Pickford's curls, Chaplin's bowler-
hat, Garbo's desire for solitude, Gable's large ears).

Brando, of course nominated for an Oscar, lost to
Humphrey Bogart in *The African Queen*, which could
mean that the Academy wanted to slap him down or even
that its members loathed Kowalski as much as Brando
said that he himself did. It is much more likely that Bogart
won from a combination of sentiment and merit: not then
recognized as the ikon he is today, he was a box-office star
and considered a darn-good actor. *The African Queen* was
his first real 'character' role, and though there was some
surprise that Brando was overlooked in favour of it, it
stands today as one of the less idiosyncratic of best acting
awards. Also, Hollywood people are sometimes realists (in
things which concern Hollywood), and it was clear that

* For which Lucinda Ballard designed the costumes.

Brando would be heard from much in the future. His third picture had been shown before the Academy ballots went out, and if things went on this way, the three feathers in his cap would be an Indian head-dress.

The film was *Viva Zapata!*, and Brando played the Mexican revolutionary leader, at the insistence of Kazan, again directing. Kazan had been considering a movie on this subject since 1944, and he had engaged the novelist John Steinbeck to write the screenplay (though Howard Hawks once told *Cahiers du Cinéma* that he had turned down the project). Steinbeck's source, uncredited on the screen, was a novel by Edgcumb Pinchon, 'Zapata the Unconquerable,' which MGM had bought in 1940 as a vehicle for Robert Taylor (MGM had some years earlier had a big success with *Viva Villa!*). In 1949, it was sold to 20th Century-Fox, who already owned a property about Zapata called 'The Beloved Rogue'. It was perhaps because of this that Kazan and Steinbeck went to Darryl F. Zanuck at Fox. Zanuck had earlier produced the movie of Steinbeck's 'The Grapes of Wrath', at the time, and since, regarded as one of the proudest moments in the history of the studio. Nevertheless, Zanuck was not enthusiastic, and Kazan believes that he only agreed to make the film because of Kazan's excellent commercial record. Until the actual shooting started the project often looked doubtful.

The great Mexican cinematographer Gabriel Figueroa read the screenplay and demanded changes in the name of historical accuracy; without these, he decreed, there was no possibility of shooting on location, since the cooperation of the Mexican film industry would be withheld. Steinbeck, however, had had experience of shooting in the country when his novella *The Pearl* was filmed there in 1946; he believed that there was no 'official' in the country immune to a little payback and he contacted Oscar Dancigars, his producer on that occasion (and who was now beginning his association with Luis Buñuel). Dancigars's offer to cooperate was vetoed by Zanuck, who produced an affadavit proving that he was a Communist – and, as we shall see, it was dangerous to be a Communist in the US at this time. (Zanuck at one point suspected the script of being Communist.) It was eventually decided to film on location in Texas, as close to the Mexican border as possible.

Brando was not Zanuck's choice for Zapata: Tyrone Power was – or, failing him, Anthony Quinn, who was eventually cast as Zapata's brother. Zanuck had disliked Brando's performance in *The Men* because of his 'mumbling'; but he was assured that the film of *Streetcar*, then in post-production, was going to be a commercial success – and Kazan was adamant that he didn't wish to make the film without Brando – whose agent asked, and got, the fancy sum of $100,000. The gifted stage actress Julie Harris was tested for the role of Zapata's wife on the strength of her performance on Broadway in *The Member of the Wedding*, but the role went to a studio contract player, Jean Peters (who not long thereafter retired when she married Howard Hughes).

'Marlon delighted me,' Kazan wrote in his memoir. 'In *Streetcar* he'd been playing a version of himself, but in *Viva Zapata!* he had to create a characterization. He was playing a peasant, a man out of another world. I don't know how he did, but he did it; his gifts go beyond his knowledge.' Zapata's twenty-six bigamous marriages have in Steinbeck's script become one wooing and wedding to the miscast Miss Peters, and even that seems an afterthought – for Kazan and Brando were agreed that Zapata 'used' women and then passed on. Sex came a good last in a life where the peasants' rights were the prime concern. Brando, Kazan says, was also like that. He goes on: 'I've watched several white women (he preferred women of colour) make it known to him that they were interested and available. Perhaps this was discretion or shyness, but the warmest relations I've seen him involved in have been with men.' These would not include Anthony Quinn, who complained that Kazan was favouring Brando – despite the fact that the rapport between star and director was so well established that Kazan gave him increasingly fewer instructions, especially after discovering that Brando had found Zapata within himself. The two actors competed in being the most macho, which on one occasion resulted in a urinating contest in the Rio Grande. Quinn later said 'Marlon was a very peculiar young man. An original young man. He never seemed to want to talk to me, to have a normal conversation. It was always a pretend conversation.' He was not, of course, entirely pleased to be in a supporting role when he had been considered for the lead (and later interviews find him resentful that Brando's name was indelibly associated with 'Streetcar' when he had played it for much longer, 'two whole years'): but he had sweet satisfaction when his performance won the Best Supporting Oscar – and Brando did not win (on his second nomination).

That these were the film's sole nominations disappointed Zanuck, but he was not surprised. 'It's just a big Western,' he had said, '*The Scarlet Pimpernel* with a dignified motif.' He had put his name in the film all the same – a custom dating back to the 30s, when those films likely to be both prestigious and profitable were advertised as 'Darryl F. Zanuck presents', the name being almost as big as those of the stars.*

As the film has it, Zapata is a Mexican Indian, well-born but penniless. In 1909 he was one of a party from a remote

* On *All About Eve*, the stars' names are in uppercase, Zanuck's in upper and lower, so the D, F and Z are in the same size. His name as producer is in the same size as Joseph L. Mankiewicz, who wrote and directed – and who charged that Zanuck only decided to 'produce' after reading the script. Mankiewicz's dispute over Zanuck's billing on his films was one reason he left 20th Century-Fox.

province, Morelos, come to Mexico City to complain that their arable land has been enclosed, leaving them only the barren hills; his expressed dissatisfaction with the response of the president, Diaz, puts him in danger, and when he rashly rescues a prisoner from the local militia he becomes an outlaw. Urged on by a strolling intellectual, Fernando (Joseph Wiseman), he supports the exiled Madero against Diaz, and becomes the leader of his forces in the South as Pancho Villa is in the North. Diaz flees, and Madero takes his place; but he is a puppet president, in the hands of the leader of the army, Huerta, who has him assassinated when he tries to express solidarity for the men who fought for him. Zapata and Villa return to arms, and, successful in victory, seek to find a leader for the country. Unwillingly, Zapata takes the job, but, a while later, he responds to some petitioners from his own village with no more reassurance than had Diaz years before: realizing that with power his idealism had gone, he returns with them to Morelos – specifically to investigate their complaints against his brother (Quinn). New leaders take his place, and, egged on by the always surviving Fernando, they decide Zapata is a threat to their regime. He is trapped and shot.

The real Zapata remains an enigma. His creed was 'Tierra y Libertad', and his cause was land for the Indians; he remains a hero in Mexico because, unlike other dissidents, he took nothing for himself. His integrity was unquestioned although, in the accepted manner of brigands, he pillaged and murdered indiscriminately – matters on which the piece is mute. Steinbeck was aware of the damage to his reputation if he tampered with history to produce the usual Hollywood concoction but, with Kazan's co-operation, tamper he did. His most serious distortion concerns Zapata's relinquishment of the presidency, which was far more complex than a desire to return to decency (and, in fact, after Villa and Zapata had succeeded in overthrowing despotism, they maintained a joint – if uneasy – control for eight years, not the few months the film suggests for Zapata's presidency).

However, if the film takes liberties, chances and sometimes leave of its senses, it is still a challenging thesis on great matters, unequivocally the best movie – there are few competitors – on revolt between Eisenstein in the 20s and *La Battaglia di Algeria*. It also manages a vivid picture of a country at war with itself, of an uneducated and listless peasantry, of an opportunistic and vicious militia; it suggests both the highs and lows of a revolutionary's life – and it does it with incisiveness (Kazan says that he learnt from *Paisa* 'to jump from crag to crag, rather than going all along the valleys'). There are several things which no longer work (the parallels between the two petitions, the symbolic use of Zapata's horse in the final shot) and the pseudo-poetic dialogue was never admirable. Both the photography and the score help to patch together the disparate elements – palace intrigues, violent fighting and the placid, almost-asleep life of the villages.

Brando's intensity provides what is then needed. His make-up establishes the image of the photographs; for the rest, he is sunk in contemplation till conscience beckons him into obstinacy or fury. As with Kowalski – and some later performances – he makes much of the man's inability to communicate or think deeply (this Zapata is obsessed by the fact that he can't read, by his lack of education – and it might be worth noting that some of Brando's comments on his own success refer back to the fact that he was a school drop-out). He sometimes gives the impression of being a small, lost boy, but he's simply different from those actors (Cooper, Gable, Tracy) who normally play leaders; never one to play the accepted way, he doesn't so cheerfully accept the burden. He refuses the leadership at one point, claiming, 'I don't want to be the conscience of the world, I don't want to be the conscience of anybody,' and with any other actor it would have been self-assertion;

59

Brando is too honest to play it except with a lingering note of regret. It was the first time in films he played a man of destiny, a role to which he would return again and again; and, of course, the role comprehended the other side of his screen persona, the inarticulate, uneducated underdog. Whether he could have played the real Zapata remains unknown, but he could play Steinbeck–Kazan's Zapata; Zapata the idealist. The film was made because they wanted to express the ineffectiveness of idealistic revolutionaries.

Just before it opened Kazan publicly described it as 'an anti-Communist film'. Throughout its preparation and production he had had cause to consider his political affiliations, past and present. The witch-hunt – the quest to disgrace American Communists and deprive them of work, the purpose of the House Un-American Activities Committee as sanctioned by the US House of Representatives – had begun in 1947. Show business personalities, because of their high profile, were particularly vulnerable – and the Group Theatre had had avowed left-wing policies. Kazan had been a member of the Communist Party between 1934 and 1936, so he knew that he would have to testify – and he did so, naming names, a month before *Zapata* opened. In my opinion, it is neither anti- nor pro-Communist, but it does reflect the deliberations of a man knowing that he has to disavow his former political beliefs. He has said: 'I believe in democracy. I believe that democracy progresses through internecine war, through constant tension – we grow only through conflict. And that's what a democracy is. In that sense, people have to be vigilant, and the vigilance is effective. I truly believe that all power corrupts . . .' Kazan's explanation of the reasons behind *Zapata*'s philosophy can, in fact, be applied to virtually every 'political' film made in Hollywood, so we need not suppose that he discussed them with Brando. The same beliefs can certainly be found in virtually every film, later, over which

Brando had power (as well, of course, in the next, a version of Shakespeare's 'Julius Caesar'); and if you look at most of them carefully, you might well suspect a hankering to play Zapata again and again. (And in real life, he would take up the cause of land for the Indians.)

5
Screen Stardom and Screen Shakespeare

The excellent reviews for *Zapata* and its star (and he was judged the best actor for it at the Cannes Film Festival that year) cemented his position as the most solicited actor in town, or, in industry terms, the hottest property. After *The Men*, interest had been considerable; now, it was engulfing. Brando hesistated. *The Men* had opened in July 1950, *Streetcar* in September 1951, *Zapata* in February 1952; supremely confident of his ability to floor Hollywood, he turned down long-term contracts with all the major studios, and wasn't concerned whether he went another year between films. His discernment (and he made six films before he blundered) only increased the admiration radiated in his direction.

He cast his eyes towards Europe, and flirted with a Zavattini script, *Stazione Termini*, with Autant-Lara directing, and which at one time Gérard Philipe had actually started. Ingrid Bergman was supposed to be the co-star of either actor, but then Selznick bought the property for Jennifer Jones (who made it with Montgomery Clift). Fred Zinnemann offered Brando a life of Van Gogh, and something called *The Red and the Blue*; Warner Bros hopefully announced *Black Ivory*, a pirate story which would reunite him with Vivien Leigh. Hardly less likely was an immersion in screen Shakespeare.

After three disastrous expeditions into Shakespeare in the early Talkie period, Hollywood had left the Bard well alone and/or to Laurence Olivier in Britain. However, at MGM, John Houseman, a more enterprising and more cultured producer than customary (he had been Orson Welles's partner at the Mercury Theater), had persuaded the Front Office that he could do a *Julius Caesar* for little cost (there were lots of togas left over from *Quo Vadis?** and they had only to be shipped from Rome) and much expectation of prestige. There would be several weeks' rehearsal, and the director would be an adroit handler of dialogue – Joseph L. Mankiewicz, returning to MGM for the first time since his days there as a producer. The cast would be paid, for the privilege of being part of the venture, less than they could normally command.

MGM's choice for Mark Antony originally lay between Charlton Heston (who had played the role in a 16mm version, before his Hollywood career) and Leo Genn (who had impressed them in *Quo Vadis?*). Mankiewicz plumped for Richard Burton, but he was under contract to 20th Century-Fox, who had him lined up for *The Robe*, which they believed would be the most important film in the company's history. Burton had not at that point made his debut as a Shakespearean actor, but Mankiewicz had heard of another young British actor, Paul Scofield, who on the strength of his performances at Stratford-upon-Avon was being hailed as the heir to Olivier. The film debut of that sort of talent would create press interest and help the box-office. In London Mankiewicz saw Scofield playing Don Pedro in John Gielgud's production of 'Much Ado About Nothing', in which Gielgud played Benedick – and as a result signed Gielgud to play Cassius (the actor's first American film and his first in more than a decade). Scofield was apparently in the process of being tested when

* *Quo Vadis?* cost $5 million and *Julius Caesar* only $500,000. The average budget for a movie at this period would be around $1,200,000.

Houseman thought of Brando – and Brando in Shakespeare, 'Old Mumbles' himself as Mankiewicz called him, would provide even bigger opportunities for publicity.

Brando refused to test 'but agreed to record a tape', wrote Houseman in his memoirs, 'for which he chose Mark Antony's dramatic entrance into the Senate after the assassination. It was a powerful recording that convinced Joe and myself.' Mankiewicz told me, 'I myself was terrified – a Yankee swine taking on what was left of the British Empire. Really, Shakespeare and how dare I? . . . Marlon called me; he had a terrible pad on 57th Street – oh, it was filthy – and there were tape recordings all over the place. He locked the door and started playing these tapes. What he'd done, he'd gone out and bought discs of Olivier, Gielgud . . . I mean, he went back to Gerald du Maurier. So he imitated them, and I said, "Marlon, you sound like June Allyson."' Mankiewicz also recalled that the casting of Brando gave stand-up comics a field-day (understandably, in as much as comic imitations of Brando in *Streetcar* were as common as those of Charles Laughton as Captain Bligh). The actor and director 'worked hard and long together, just the two of us; he worked his ass off, preparing by himself'. Houseman gave his reason for casting Brando in *Theatre Arts Monthly*: '. . . there is no question in my mind that in natural equipment, temperament and application, he is one of the very great actors of our time.'

James Mason (whom Mankiewicz had directed in *Five Fingers*) was cast as Brutus; Louis Calhern was to play Caesar and Edmond O'Brien Casca (both had worked with Houseman at the Mercury Theatre; Houseman had directed Calhern as Lear). MGM contributed Greer Garson and Deborah Kerr from their contract list, for box-office ballast, though their roles – Calpurnia and Portia respectively – hardly gave them twenty lines in total. Budget restrictions notwithstanding, MGM offered Technicolor, but Houseman felt that 'the familiar and concentrated tones of black and white' were less likely to 'swamp' the production.

MGM happily used a still of one of the very great actors of our time stripped to the waist, to advertise the film, plus a simple but not-telling slogan, 'Greater than *Ivanhoe*!' In fact, the reviews sold it. It was an austere but straighforward account of the play, strong where it is strong, and faltering where the play is weak. The original has an unsatisfactory construction: it builds to the assassination of Caesar and Mark Antony's subsequent oration, then wanders into the matters of the rival factions which resulted, and their battles. In the film, the battle scenes were scrappily done, and it further suffers because it's a toss-up as to which actor will predominate; the later reaches of the play always seem to be searching for a tragic hero. It should be Brutus – but James Mason doesn't make it. He is up to the role, and his reading of it is intelligent, but his nobility is self-conscious, as if assumed for the film. By sheer skill, John Gielgud should make it; his Cassius is perfectly judged, and he wields the verse as a champion swordsman his weapon – but not even a study of this quality can hold Cassius to an audience. In his company, Brando is an amateur, and that is why, for all its qualities, his Mark Antony doesn't make it.

It is an astonishing performance (and it was more so then, when we didn't know his range), wrought with authority and a fierce controlled passion. It is by all means a success; the verse is well-spoken and without doubt to its meaning. But a vowel does get swallowed now and then, and Brando is neither suave enough nor elegant – a Roman general, perhaps, but a Roman statesman never. He is not dwarfed, and the film has almost the unity of Olivier's Shakespeare films. The play is very much the thing: you're never less than aware of Shakespeare's musing on the dangers of dictatorships, and of the mechanics to bring about their end, but in the end, the film is less a film than a record of some performances.*

It was premiered in New York in June 1953, to prove that Shakespeare on the screen was not Olivier's sole prerogative. Despite the praise of American critics Mankiewicz was so afraid of their British counterparts that he fled from London (where he was preparing *The Barefoot Contessa*) to Paris. But, he notes, reading the British notices is one of the most treasured memories of his life. There was universal praise for Gielgud and qualified approval of Mason's portrayal; it was Brando, however, who drew most attention. In *Sight & Sound*, for instance, Gavin Lambert devoted a very long paragraph to it, noting that it wasn't an orthodox Shakespearean performance, that his verse-speaking 'has its limitations and rough edges' and that he could be 'academically faulted': but for each of these reservations there was a compensation – the performance 'assimilates itself into the drama and the text by sheer emotional grasp and passion', that it is 'electric' and 'as a piece of dramatic interpretation it shows a rare, exciting talent'. Physically he had 'the glamour, desirable but seldom found for the part, and his "shrewd contriver's" speech on the Senate steps after Caesar's murder is rendered with extraordinary power'.

Mankiewicz offered an insight into Brando's methods: 'Marlon plunges into acting the way a deep-sea diver goes overboard. He keeps his eyes shut for hours to see what it's like to be without sight – in case he ever had to play a blind man. He practises using only his left hand for days so he'll know what it's like to play the part of a character who's lost his right hand.' Houseman in his memoirs notes that Brando abandoned the Actors' Studio method of exploring the 'sub-text': 'Now, suddenly, he had discovered

---

* In his autobiography, discussing the control of directors, James Mason writes 'And Mankiewicz, though far from average, did not quite impose an individual style upon his *Julius Caesar*.'

that, with a dramatist of Shakespeare's genius and in a speech as brilliantly and elaborately written as Antony's oration, it was not necessary nor even possible to play *between* the lines.' He goes on to say that Brando was 'helped in this by Mankiewicz's faith and patience. Also by the help he received from John Gielgud who, throughout rehearsals, showed a generosity that is rare among actors.' Gielgud himself found Brando 'very self-conscious and modest ... enormously responsive'; when he asked for advice, 'I found that he had taken note of everything I said and spoke the lines exactly as I had suggested.' (He recalls Brando's rehearsal tapes as being of Maurice Evans and John Barrymore.)

Gielgud also recalled an enthusiastic Mankiewicz inviting him to watch the rushes of Mark Antony's great speech, but he did not like them very much: 'I thought he was giving a bad imitation of Olivier, but it was hardly my place to say so.' That actor was also unflattering. 'I thought, God, that's me, it's so awful, is that all I've given to the world?' Olivier's other comments on Brando, delivered on NBC's 'Today Show' in the early 70s, are revealing. Asked which actors he admired, he said 'Well, there's the obvious one: I adore Marlon Brando.' Pressed, he said they had something in common: 'Something, I can't describe it ... the same channel of message, somehow, I think. He is a marvellous actor. I wouldn't compare myself to him.' Asked about Brando and the Actors' Studio technique – to 'get themselves into the part and it's inside out', he replied, 'Don't believe Marlon. Don't tell me he searches inside himself for everything. He looks out, too. He's peripheral, just as any other character actor is peripheral.'

Julius Caesar did respectable business. The reviews and curiosity about Brando's participation resulted in its 'first national weekend box-office take' – records Houseman – 'being 5 per cent higher than the corresponding gross of *Quo Vadis?*', but the boondocks were less responsive. By this time Brando had been to France and back. A French producer, Paul Graetz, had offered him the role of Sorel in a film version of Stendhal's 'Le Rouge et le Noir', and he had accepted. A few days before the agreed start, Brando changed his mind because, it was understood, he couldn't agree with the director, Claude Autant-Lara. Graetz sued for $150,000 – presumably the salary paid to Brando – and a few months later began the film with Gérard Philipe.

He turned down the remake of a French film, *Human Desire* (it had been *La Bête Humaine*), which Fritz Lang directed with Glenn Ford; he was one of several actors unwilling to be overshadowed by Judy Garland* in *A Star is Born* which James Mason eventually did. He was offered an independent *Sodom and Gomorrah*, and he may have turned down *Prince of Players*, a life of Edwin Booth which 20th Century-Fox announced as a vehicle for either him or Olivier (Richard Burton later played it). Because of the success of *Julius Caesar* there was a move at MGM to do either an *Antony and Cleopatra* with Brando and Ava Gardner, or a *Romeo and Juliet* with him and Pier Angeli: the later, more probable project was abandoned when the Rank Organisation announced a British version to be directed by Renato Castellani. He was committed to *Pal Joey* at Columbia, with Billy Wilder directing him and Mae West, but the negotiations were tricky and the project abandoned (some years later, Frank Sinatra played it).

In the summer of 1953 he did a summer stock tour in the Northeastern States – to the consternation of MCA, who did not care for their stars, when they were as big as Brando, playing the straw hat circuit. In the company would be his friends Carlo Fiore and William Redfield. And the play would be Shaw's 'Arms and the Man'. When Fiore asked him why he didn't choose a contemporary play he replied 'I told you. I don't want to

* Though according to his friend Richard Erdman, who had a collection of her records, he loved her 'passion, vibrancy, attack'.

work. I want to fuck around. And I want to try comedy for a change. A farce. I want to leer, wear a moustache, make asides to the audience like Groucho Marx.' He played Sergius, the cynical, vain and rather ridiculous officer who loses the heroine to Bluntschi, the plain man, 'the chocolate soldier'. Bluntschi was played by Redfield, who noted later – in 'Letters from an Actor' – that Brando's performance varied from day to day, from town to town. Sometimes he walked through the role; on other occasions he imitated other, famous, actors. When Redfield reproached him, after being confronted at the stage door by disappointed spectators, Brando replied, 'Man, you don't understand. This is summer stock.' Despite this attitude and what Fiore calls a 'slipshod production' it played to packed houses.

It was the last time he acted on the stage. Gielgud had begged him to play Hamlet, offering 'to direct him if he did, but he said he never wanted to go back to the theatre'. Years later Mankiewicz encountered him on the street, 'and he was getting chubby. I said "Champ, have you one more good fight left in you?" and he said, "What are you talking about?" I replied that if we could work as we'd worked on *Caesar* – six weeks' rehearsal – we would do Macbeth, with Maggie Smith. He gave me a strange look and shook his head. "See ya, Joe," he said.' About this same time Harold Clurman summed up: 'Brando has developed an extraordinary series of rationalizations to justify his actions. One, he does what he does for money. Two, acting is neurotic, anyway. Three, movies are so powerful that by staying in them he is helping the world. What he is now, is a very good actor in movies. He is talented and intuitive, has a fine sense of language, but he is not a truly great actor. On Broadway, we tend to think of him as a useless good actor – that is, one with no real interest in acting for the sake of acting, nor in acting as a social force.'

6
Two Underdogs and An Oscar

Before his stint in the Shaw play Brando had made a film which was eventually released as *The Wild One*. The producer was Stanley Kramer, and some commentators feel that Brando returned to work for him as a favour. Brando had expressed dissatisfaction with *The Men*, but Kramer now badly needed a financial success. When his deal with United Artists lapsed he was taken under the wing of Columbia by its chief, Harry Cohn, who – more than most studio chiefs – had noted the imposing achievements of some independent producers. Like the other industry executives, he did not quite recognise that the studio system was finally coming to an end; but unlike them, he did not embrace these breakaway talents with the purpose of stifling them. Unfortunately, Kramer had presented him with a series of box-office disasters. The agreement was about to come to an end and Kramer was determined to finish it with two box-office hits. One was *The Caine Mutiny*, whose proceeds went a long way towards offsetting the damage Kramer had done to Columbia's coffers; the other, which he pitched to Brando, was based on a *Harper's* magazine article by Frank Rooney about an episode in 1947 when a gang of motorcyclists had terrorized the small town of Hollister, near Los Angeles.

The first screenplay was written by Ben Maddow, who had worked on John Huston's *The Asphalt Jungle* and Clarence Brown's excellent study of racial hatred in a small town, *Intruder in the Dust*; but the credit finally went to John Paxton, best-known for *Fourteen Hours*, the study of a man who, bent on suicide on the ledge of a skyscraper, caused some hysteria among the crowds watching him below. When Zinnemann declined to direct, Kramer offered the assignment to another European, the Hungarian-born Laslo Benedek, who had made *Death of a Salesman* for him. Brando committed himself to the project before there was a finished script on the basis of the subject – the underlying violence in American society. His romantic interest in the story would be played by an unknown, Mary Murphy, who later recalled that at their first meeting he inspected her 'like a mountain lion looking at its prey'; cast as the rival gang leader was Lee Marvin, who as a supporting player saw his job 'to make the star look better than he is'. He went on, 'Then the Method came along and Brando slaughtered it for the actors. I mean, he'd go off and rub his eyes or scratch his crotch and keep everybody waiting twenty minutes and we'd all think he was concentrating. Actually, he was having a nap. But he would be secure and made everybody else insecure.' He was learning, he said, for 'Brando is not exactly a generous actor, he doesn't give. But he does make demands of you, and if you don't come through he'll run right over the top of you.' Marvin had seen him on the stage in 'Streetcar': '*Jesus*, what a star!'; on *The Wild One* he realised that they weren't reaching each other because Brando was using the Method. Marvin's reaction was to attempt his own method by unexpectedly kicking away a cigarette butt in the middle of a scene. 'He said, "You son of a bitch," and I said, "Well, up yours too, pal." And from then on, WHAM, he fixes his eyes on me, and he's boring right through me, and I don't have to act anymore, I can do no wrong. I became the cigarette butt. I love him. Whenever I watch him he just makes me *smile*.'

As preparation for the film Brando visited Hollister (though to general disappointment Cohn insisted on it being shot on the back lot) and he began to hang around in the 1953 equivalent of leather bars. In his New York days he had been a keen motor-cyclist and he drove to this set on a motorbike; but it was by watching other cyclists that he redefined his screen image, adding to *Streetcar*'s bluejeans both the heavy boots and a studded leather jacket. More than any other, *The Wild One* established Brando the rebel – though if it is read properly he is less a rebel than a mixed-up kid – the sort one hoped would be annihilated later by Stephen Sondheim's lyric, 'Gee, Officer Krupke', in 'West Side Story'.

But then the film that emerged was not the one Brando had envisaged. The Breen Office intervened. These were sensitive times, and Communist overtones were found in the subject of mob rule, as well as in the idea that the cyclists were more powerful – and in some cases, more sympathetic – than the town authorities. Changes were made to the script and Brando went ahead only under protest. His expressed disenchantment with the result belies Clurman's contention that he was not interested in acting as a social force. He said that 'instead of finding out why young people tend to bunch into groups that seek expression in violence, all we did was show the violence'. Yes, but till that time movies had offered only a stereotyped and dishonest view of violence; what was so startling here was the *gradual* way these thugs take over a town. The original title, *The Cyclists' Raid* (which Cohn loathed) is more accurate than the nebulously romantic one finally pinned on it. The British version (at least) starts with a foreword, 'This is a shocking story . . ', which exhorts us all to see that it doesn't happen again; Brando's voice cuts in, telling how this town and a girl changed his life – and that's certainly a softening-up. It was also one of the changes demanded by the Breen Office.

The motor-cyclists – the Blind Rebels Motorcycle Club – arrive in a small mid-Western town for some track races. The police move them on, and they stop for petrol in the next town. With their caps and leather jackets they're sinister in a quasi-military way, but the townspeople are friendly, even after a slight accident with an old man in a car: a brief altercation, an accusation of hooliganism, and one of the gang has to have his leg set in plaster. The gang hang around the local bar, and Johnnie, the leader (Brando), gets into conversation with the waitress, Kathie (Miss Murphy). Her dad (Robert Keith) is the town cop, and he doesn't want no trouble nohow.

They're about to blow when another gang arrives, led by Chino (Lee Marvin), an old buddy. Johnnie and Chino engage in a ritual trial of strength, watched by townsfolk only too pleased by something to break the monotony of their lives; but Chino cheeks the cop and is hauled off to jail. So his gang has a reason for staying; there's nothing to do but drink and sit around – but that's probably as much to do as there was back home. 'You don't have to go anywhere special,' Johnnie tells the girl, 'that's cornball. You just go.' They're not violent, but they're bored; they play futile games on their bikes, and above all, they drink. Tension starts when they rough-house the beauty salon of the local flirts, and when they go to the jail intent on freeing Chino. Things are hotting up in the bar, and a group of the townsfolk are banding together.

And the gangs have terrorized Kathie: Johnnie rescues her like Prince Charming – and the film begins to fall apart. They stand upon a grassy knoll, and she calls upon him to explain himself. 'You think you're too good for me,' he says. 'Anyone who thinks they're too good for me, I knock them down some time.' We'd never had any doubts that Johnnie's trouble was insecurity, a pocket-

73

Napoleon who talks of 'my boys' protectively. When the salon blonde learns the club's name, she asks: 'What're you rebelling against, Johnnie?' 'What've ya got?' is the quick reply; he has no other reply because he can't define boredom or middle-class stuffiness. He has little sense and less sensibility, and though his conversation with Kathie deviates from the hitherto realistic mood to Hollywood theorizing, Brando ensures that Johnnie remains inarticulate.

Back in town the townsmen grab him; his bike goes careering on, and a man is killed, an innocent spectator. 'Finally killed a man, eh?' says someone, a trite – if quick – way of saying that we're all responsible. The County Sheriff (Jay C. Flippen) arrives, and once the truth is told Johnnie is let off with an avuncular caution – and a rejoinder never to set foot in the town again. Before leaving (and in view of the level to which the film has sunk, we're not surprised) he goes to the bar to see the girl again.

She is weakly played, and given so many 'concern' close-ups that the film suffers. The rest of the cast is fine, and Brando is magnificent: cocky at the beginning among his own kind, he has the unsureness of adolescence among the adults at the end of the film. His long silences suggest a dumb brain trying to get its mechanism going, the mouth is weak, and the eyes shift, mirroring the master-boy mind behind. Physically, there are the itty-bitty side-burns, and the way he grooves to the juke box: because of such things, twenty years later, after a run of officers and martyred heroes, he never would be thought of as a square actor. In the 60s, when the poster craze came in, the posters of the then-podgy actor were always from *The Wild One* – while his rallying cry, 'What've ya got?' would still be reverberating, through several dozen lesser films about youthful rebels. This one was not particularly popular at the time. In Britain the Board of Film Censors banned it as likely to encourage adventurous youths to emulate its gangs. A few local councils authorised showings and in those pockets it created a sensation; but it raised little interest when the ban was lifted in 1968.

In his next film Brando emerged again from the underbelly of society, in a performance so different as to be amazing. His predecessor, the last actor to play rebels and chip-on-the-shoulder guys, was said by numerous commentators to be John Garfield; but once you've acknowledged Garfield's vitality, and a few minor changes of characterization, you're faced with an absolutely conventional performance, part soul-weary, part chin-up-and-take-it. Brando not only offered several new ways of looking at under-privileged heroes, but he played them as capable of varying moods and multitudinous thoughts and changes – all aspects of the the man all at once. His performance in *On the Waterfront* is one of the most remarkable ever recorded on film.

Because of it, the film is the most famous, and it was the most successful, of all the 'social protest' films which Brando made; it was unanimously well-received, it broke box-office records and it won a goodly number of awards. It almost didn't happen.

Like *The Wild One*, it grew from a magazine exposé – a series of articles by Malcolm Johnson called 'Crime on the Waterfront', which claimed that the longshoremen's union was controlled by the mob. Johnson was awarded the Pulitzer Prize and his pieces became the basis of a screenplay by Budd Schulberg, born into Hollywood nobility (his father had been one of its founding members) and best-known as the author of a satirical novel on that community, 'What Made Sammy Run?' Robert Siodmak was to direct the film on a modest budget on location in the East, but the project was abandoned when potential backers proved elusive. Meanwhile, Kazan planned a film with a similar setting and had asked Arthur Miller – whose 'Death of a Salesman' he had directed on Broadway – to write a screenplay. 'The Hook', as it was called, was rejected by 20th Century-Fox and then Warner Bros., but was picked by Harry Cohn for Columbia. This too was abandoned when Miller withdrew, claiming that 'the red thing' had come between Kazan and himself.

This was a discreet reference to Kazan's testimony before the Senate Committee. That was a matter which also upset Brando. He was rehearsing *Julius Caesar* at the time and Mankiewicz found him in tears: he wouldn't know what to do, he said, when he next saw Kazan, 'Punch him in the nose? Because I loved that man.' Mankiewicz – who had led the fight within the Directors' Guild against an anti-Communist witch-hunt within the industry – advised him not to side with the 'crazies'. Brando also discussed the matter with Clifford Odets, before Odets testified; he averred that he wouldn't work with Kazan again but decided 'he's good for me. Maybe I'll work with him a couple of times more. At least once.'

Another who testified was Schulberg, whom Kazan contacted in the belief that they should be friends in adversity. As a result of their meeting Kazan read the longshoremen screenplay. It was a good first draft for the film he wanted to make. The two of them set to work, and also visited Hoboken, where they intended to shoot. With Brando pencilled-in for the lead, it was turned down by every studio in Hollywood. Kazan's bankable credibility had been weakened by the failure of *Zapata* and more especially *Man on a Tightrope*, which at this point looked like one of 'the lowest-grossing pictures in the history of 20th Century-Fox' – a company which had gratuitously announced that it had dropped the picture from its schedule. That didn't help Sam Spiegel, who had committed himself to finding backing after a chance convivial meeting when he, Schulberg and Kazan were staying at the same hotel.

Spiegel was one of those entrepreneurs, not uncommon in this industry, who regarded film production as an expedient way of keeping themselves supplied with women, motor-cars and the other luxuries of life. Originally hailing from Austria, he had fled Hitler's Germany in 1933; in Britain he had produced a woebegone, cut-price vehicle for the great Buster Keaton, then on his uppers – and he had fled again, leaving a huge pile of debts. That was a fact known to John Huston, who used it as leverage when they went into partnership together. Their first film together, *We Were Strangers*, had been a huge failure in 1949 and their second, *The African Queen*, an even greater success. No Hollywood studio had been interested in that (though United Artists agreed to release) and Spiegel's wheeling and dealing in London reached new imaginative levels without, however, resulting in full funding before the highly-priced participants (Huston, Bogart, Katharine Hepburn) assembled to begin work. The story had a happy ending, but the good to Spiegel's standing within the industry was distinctly undone by *Melba*, a biography of the Australian singer which emptied cinemas the world over. He had wooed Kazan at the time he had won the Oscar for *Gentleman's Agreement*; their coming together now was providential to both parties. Kazan described him as 'the canniest negotiator' he had ever known, always coming out richer than anyone else involved in the agreement; but as far as *On the Waterfront* was concerned, worth all the grief and trouble he caused him.

These were considerable. Kazan says that he never knew what Spiegel was doing, despite the fact that he owned 25 per cent of the film. A deal was set at United Artists to star Frank Sinatra, who had just made a notable come-back in Zinnemann's *From Here to Eternity*. With Sinatra there was a ceiling on the budget of $500,000. Harry Cohn was prepared to go considerably higher than that with Brando in the lead, but Brando refused to work with Kazan (because of his testimony to HUAC) – and Kazan by this time felt that morally he owed the role to Sinatra. When

Spiegel signed Brando, Kazan gave in, because 'I always prefer Brando to anybody'. Brando was apparently influenced by the fact that he was permitted to leave the Hoboken locations at 4 pm for his daily psychoanalysis. During filming he constantly reminded Kazan that he had only agreed to work with him again because he needed to be in New York to see his analyst (who had been recommended to him by Kazan).

Apart from harsh winter conditions in New Jersey, Kazan had also to contend with Spiegel's cheeseparing production methods – cutting down on crew and on the planned locations – but he did bring it in at a total cost of $902,000 – which included $100,000 to Brando and a like amount to Kazan. Its domestic gross would be $4,500,000, making it one of the most profitable films in Columbia's history. Cohn slept through most of it when it was first screened for him, while Brando disliked the result so much that he left the projection room without speaking to Kazan. The sequence with Rod Steiger in the cab (to become famous in its own right and as frequently anthologised as Gene Kelly's dance in the rain) he found unconvincing when they filmed it and he looked back on it with dislike. Steiger, he observed, was 'one of those actors who likes to cry [so] we kept doing it over and over'. During the filming of it Steiger complained to Kazan that he was treating Brando better than he did him.

Brando got on much better with Eva Marie Saint, a television actress who had been studying at the Actors' Studio; she was offered the role of Edie two weeks after making her debut on Broadway in 'A Trip to Bountiful'. She remembered Brando's 'gentlemanly behaviour' and his 'incredible sensitivity . . . He was like an open wound. What he was never got in the way of the role he had to play. It became such a natural part of him that he didn't have to put it on . . . Actors *start acting*. But Marlon never did. He *was* Terry Malloy.'

Terry Malloy is an ex-pug, a longshoreman, close enough to the Mob because his brother, Charley the Gent (Steiger), is the right-hand-man of Joe Friendly (Lee J. Cobb), who controls the docks. Any docker who doesn't toe the line is harassed, bullied – or killed. As one of them puts it, 'You don't ask questions and you don't answer questions on the docks.' The death of one man brings about the Crime Commissioners (Lief Erickson and Martin Balsam), and it spurs the anti-corruption crusade led by a fanatical local priest, Father Barry (Karl Malden).

Terry starts seeing the dead man's sister, Edie. 'Which side you on?' she asks. 'I'm with me,' he replies. Later, 'You wanna hear my philosophy of life?' he asks, 'Do it to him before he does it to you . . . Father Barry? What's his racket? Everyone's got a racket . . . Down here it's every man for himself.' When a second man, another 'canary', is 'accidentally' killed, Terry is persuaded by the priest to confess to Edie his role in her brother's murder: 'It started out as a favour, who am I kidding? It was "do it or else". I thought they were just going to lean on him.' Because he is seen with the girl and the priest, Charley is sent to secure his brother's loyalty – but Terry has been compromised before: years before, they'd made him pull a fight at the Garden, and 'What did I get? – a one-way ticket to Palookaville. I coulda had class. I coulda been a contender.' Because of this, Charley doesn't warn him in the commanded fashion, and winds up dead.

As a result, Terry testifies to the Commission, and dockland turns against him; ignoring the contempt in which he's held, he turns up for work, and, when he isn't offered any, he takes on Friendly and the gang. Because he survives the beating-up, the men at last rally to him. It is his martyrdom and his atonement, and as the film works best as a study of awakening conscience, it is an effective climax.

The film also works as a thriller, organically constructed,

but if it is not otherwise as seriously flawed as *The Wild One*, it does fall into almost every trap lying in wait for producers and directors of reforming zeal. It is brutally dishonest; it is over-composed and over-hysterical, with too much of the action in for electrifying effect. You might wonder why, at the end, the men are so slow to support Terry when Friendly and his gang expect imminent arrest: well, public ostracism is one thing, but even more blatant is the scene where Terry's teenage chum turns on him, having killed all his pigeons, 'A pigeon for a pigeon'. Even more might you wonder about Charley's death, a harsh way to treat your right-hand-man, even as a warning to his brother – especially if the latter's as unimportant as Friendly insists. You might also be curious as to why a truck tries to run Terry down *before* he's discovered his brother's corpse; and you might also query the shot of 'Mr Big' watching the Commission on television – a device going back to Capra if not before.

The faults were generally overlooked, though later, in *Sight & Sound*, Lindsay Anderson called it 'a bad film' and made a bitter and well-aimed attack on the fascist implications of the final sequence-points which might have had more authority if he hadn't lauded at its expense a vastly inferior movie, *Force of Evil*, directed by Abraham Polonsky (who had been black-listed; Kazan, of course, was employed, successful and chic). Years later, Kazan commented that all Anderson 'had was this schematic left-wing idea about the ending', and, he pointed out, he had lived on the waterfront and Anderson hadn't.

The relentless dramatics would seem to have been Kazan's, rather than a mandate from Columbia or Spiegel; Kazan works in a coruscating style which is often momentarily stunning (as in the famous passage where important dialogue is lost under the ship's hooters) – and which is often offset by Boris Kaufman's grimy, grey photography of Hoboken across the river, with winter mists and winter steam drifting across the street; and that is offset again by Leonard Bernstein's jagged pre-'West Side Story' score, as emphatic as anything ever written for an Old-Dark-House thriller. The effect aimed at is the 'torn from today's headlines' sort of thing, which contradicts a weak-kneed preface intimating that such things happened in the past – and adding that the film 'will exemplify the way self-appointed tyrants can be defeated by right-minded people in a vital democracy'. It will not, we find, indicate how the tyrants got there, and the man who defeats them is motivated rather by love (and later, revenge) than by convictions about democracy.

Brando's performance partly obscures this, just as it obscures the fact – for all the skill of his dialogue – that he's also having to enact out the old 'a man's gotta do what a man's gotta do' philosophy (there are other ways of showing an awakening conscience than this). It *is* a performance, so carefully thought out that there's nothing of Kowalski or Johnnie. He smiles a lot, a gentle, defenceless man, but, reprimanded, he does an insolent grin, the thug's form of defence when up against forces stronger. He's unthinking rather than vicious. He rolls his pug's eyes a lot in his battered face, as in the ring, sometimes in despair and sometimes not to miss anything – and both reactions have the same root cause: he's dumb, and he knows it. His eyes are more useful than his brain. He brings into play his hands when the words won't come. And for all that, Brando is still underplaying – or at least under-reacting – in marked contrast to the admittedly convincing histrionics of Malden and Cobb. The love scenes with Miss Saint he takes in a bantering, kidding fashion, in the way we might associate with Bogart or Melvyn Douglas, but in this sombre atmosphere they seem startlingly original, and are more holding than all the wham-bam-bam.

The performance brought awards from the New York critics, and the American and British Academies (it was

Brando's third consecutive 'Best Foreign Actor' award from the British Film Academy: he had also won for *Viva Zapata!* and *Julius Caesar*). Miss Saint also won a (Best Supporting) Oscar; and the New York critics voted the film both the best of the year and Kazan the best director. These were also the pronouncements of the Academy when the Oscars were handed out. The film took eight of the statuettes in all (a record it shared with *Gone With the Wind* and *From Here to Eternity*) but none of these went to Cobb, Steiger and Malden, all competing in the Best Supporting category.

In his autobiography Kazan offers four reasons for the film's success: Schulberg, for tenacity, devotion and talent; himself, for his toughness and persistence; Spielberg, for his cunning and insistence over restructuring and rewriting; and Brando. 'If there is a better performance by a man in the history of film in America, I don't know what it is.'

He told me, 'He's the best actor I ever worked with. He contributed a lot to my films. He made me look better. He had instinctive characteristics that approached genius. I don't know what to call it. I would direct him in a scene and he'd do it better than I had hoped. He had a trick that annoyed me. I'd be talking to him, giving him directions and about halfway through he'd walk away. He'd gotten the drift of it. Something was working in his head and he didn't want any more explanation. I began to cut down and just give him hints. That scene in *On the Waterfront* where the girl drops her glove, well, that wasn't the way I directed it. She took her glove off and was going to put it in her pocket, but as it happened she dropped it. I didn't say "Cut". I was smart enough to keep my mouth shut. And Brando picked up the glove. She reached for it but he wouldn't give it to her, which was a way of keeping her close to him. What he did was something sexual – he put his hand in the glove. He did that scene so marvellously and easily. It comes from that school of acting that he was raised in, where improvisation was stressed. You start out with a certain intention but play it in any different way. He did that all the time; he was absolutely marvellous with that. He was also very handsome. He had tremendous emotional powers. He was a close friend, he used to play with my children. He used to come to the house, like a child himself. They say that artists are often like children. He's an example of one. He was naif. He never knew where he was sleeping. You couldn't find the guy at night because somebody had always taken him in. I also roomed with him for a while and he had a proclivity for dark girls. They complained that he often slept a lot. He was like a cat. If you left him alone for a minute he'd just fall back and be asleep. His body was very relaxed. He was, I don't know, a phenomenon. I've never seen anything like him. I miss him and I think about him sometimes but, well, those days are gone forever.'

7
Into Commerce and Colour

Brando's Oscar produced something like euphoria in Hollywood-watchers. In the first place, it was a just award; secondly, his good-humoured, tuxedoed acceptance speech (he seemed stunned and genuinely grateful, observing that the statuette was heavier than he expected and concluding 'It's a wonderful moment and a rare one and I am certainly indebted. Thank you') suggested that he was falling comfortably into line with tradition; and thirdly, the accolade usefully carried with it increased power. Bette Davis, handing it to him, observed that she admired him because he was a rebel, like herself. Rebel or not, no one nurtured in the place, voter or winner, is ever indifferent to the importance of Oscar, and the acumen so far shown by Brando might well grow into an influence. The public was showing an increasing tendency to go to the films the critics liked (in 1953, *Shane*, *From Here to Eternity*, *Moulin Rouge*), and the critics had liked all of Brando's films. The directors with whom he had worked – Zinnemann, Kazan, Mankiewicz, and to a lesser extent, Benedek – were the new Young Turks. With a handful of others – John Huston, George Stevens, Vincente Minnelli, and Kirk Douglas and Burt Lancaster among the actors – they were the long-awaited new leaders of the industry, not afraid of Harry Cohn, the big bad wolf, or anybody.

There was an infinitely lesser Brando film between the opening of *On the Waterfront* and the Oscar ceremonies nine months later, but it did not ruffle the climate of hopefulness, which was growing warmer all the while – despite a temporary chill when Brando announced that he was quitting films forever to return to the stage. The climate already existed when 20th Century-Fox announced that Brando had signed an agreement with them, calling for two films a year. The details were left so vague (as published) as to suggest that the studio merely had first call on his services if it came up with a project he liked. That he agreed to do *The Egyptian* in the first place is puzzling enough. The original novel was a long-winded account of people in antique times, in the manner (but without the gift) of Robert Graves; no one who has seen the film can imagine that at any stage there was a reasonably intelligent script; and the genre was one which seldom brought Hollywood any kudos. The last such at this studio, *The Robe*, had been far from a critics' favourite, but audiences were pouring in to see it. They, at least, had always shown a partiality for Biblical spectacles – and that one was also the first film in the wide screen process, CinemaScope, expected to be the saviour of the industry as patrons deserted to the small screen in the lounge. 20th Century-Fox was committed to filming all of its output in CinemaScope; the second film in the process – *How to Marry a Millionaire* – was released as Brando agreed to *The Egyptian*, and due to some spirited acting it disguised the fact that the new width favoured sets, views and spectacle more than performers. It was not the case that Brando needed a popular film after a solely 'artistic' success (a reason offered by Henry Fonda for some of the bad films he made), though he may have been attracted to a complete turnabout. He may have relished the prospect of Hollywood luxury and the huge $5 million budget after the New Jersey cold and Spiegel's pennypinching. He may have felt that the character he would be playing was an interesting one – the Pharaoh's court physician who (like most screen doctors) finds redemption after dalliance with worldly matters – the sort he wouldn't be offered again (indeed not). Bob Thomas in his book on Brando says that he took on the role for the money – $150,000, which his father needed to complete an investment in a Nebraska cattle ranch 'incorporated under the name of Marsdo, short for Marlon's dough'. (Brando Junior was not interested in handling the money he earned, and since his father's business affairs had faltered he was happy to have him take care of it.)

Within days of finishing *On the Waterfront* Brando was reading the script of *The Egyptian* with the other members of the cast – including Jean Simmons, Gene Tierney, Victor Mature, Michael Wilding, Peter Ustinov and Bella Darvi – under the supervision of the director, Michael Curtiz. Within hours he was on his way back to New York. He had not liked the way Zanuck had lectured him; he had not liked Curtiz, the role or the script; and above all, in the words of his agent, he couldn't stand Miss Darvi, whom Zanuck was promoting to stardom. Her surname was derived from Zanuck's first name and that of his wife Virginia – surely with insolence, since she was his mistress, chronologically the first of several untalented ladies whom he thrust on an uninterested public.

Affronted but assured that the contract was iron-clad, Zanuck kept the cast and crew waiting for three days. Brando's psychiatrist reported that the actor was 'very sick and mentally confused'. Equally obligingly the studio agreed to pay the psychiatrist's expenses to be at Brando's side while filming proceeded. That could not be arranged, nor were the studio's own doctors permitted to examine Brando or his medical records. The film went ahead with

the unfortunate Edmund Purdom, whose career was forever blighted by it (casting that at least did not satisfy
Ustinov, who had been attracted to the project for the
chance of working with Brando). The studio instructed its
lawyers to serve Brando with a writ for breach of contract,
demanding $2 million in damages.

It was settled quickly enough: he would do *Desirée*
instead. There was no indication that it would be a better
film than *The Egyptian* – it was a version of an equally
meretricious historical novel – but it would give him a
chance to play Napoleon. Even poor actors don't resist
such chances, even if the director was Henry Koster (who
had done little worthwhile since his Deanna Durbin pictures) and the screenplay by Daniel Taradash (and they'd
got his surname almost right). His performance gave the
film its sole claim to distinction; he has the stances, the
expressions, the appearance that we know from the icono-
graphy, and he is probably right in speaking softly but
urgently – if too care-ful-ly. Napoleon must have been
more magnetic: Brando's own magnetism had left him, as
if drained by circumstances and the rest of the cast.
Michael Rennie was a predictably wooden Bernadotte,
Merle Oberon a colourless Josephine, and Jean Simmons
a giggle-of-the-Fifth Desirée, or Daisy Ray, as the cast
would have it.

It is Marseilles, France, 1794. Daisy Ray has met a certain Joseph Bonaparte (Cameron Mitchell) and has invited
him home so that he may propose to her elder sister (Elizabeth Sellars). 'Bonaparte, what a curious name,' says her
brother. Two Bonaparte brothers arrive, and Napoleon
takes Daisy Ray into the garden while the soundtrack gives
with 'Parlez-moi d'Amour' and then the Marseillaise:
'Today', says Napoleon, 'that song is played throughout
France. Tomorrow it will be heard throughout Europe.'
But he has espoused the cause of Robespierre, and when
he falls, is carted off to prison. 'An adventurer', says Daisy

Ray's *frère*, 'that'll be the end of him.' How wrong he was! A moment later Napoleon is whistling the Marseillaise under Daisy Ray's window, but the sensible puss refuses to elope with him.

Cut to Madame Tallyrand throwing a party; Daisy Ray, mysteriously in Paris, tries to gatecrash and is escorted in by Bernadotte, whose courtesy she repays by throwing a wineglass at Josephine on learning that she is Napoleon's intended. Her voice (she keeps a diary) details his rise to power, and then there's Josephine bidding her 'Welcome to Malmaison' (with, I have to interject, much less of the imperial grace than Loretta Young once loaned to the Empress Eugenie). Over dinner, Napoleon divulges his plans for Egypt, unheeding the steady good sense of Bernadotte. Bernadotte marries Daisy Ray, who has a baby. Enter Josephine, with long-stemmed roses from her garden. 'I envy you your roses,' says Daisy Ray. 'I envy you your son', replies Josephine sadly. Napoleon becomes First Consul and then Emperor of the French ('Remember that first night he came to Marseilles?' says Elizabeth Sellars, a lady given – in this film – to stating the obvious).

So much has happened in just forty-five minutes, but the film dallies ten minutes on rehearsals for the Coronation, after which it scurries again – to the dissolution of the marriage to Josephine. 'She's only eighteen, you know, that Marie-Louise,' says someone. As in most films about Napoleon, Marie-Louise remains a distant figure; here, it is Daisy Ray beside him when he holds up the baby King of Naples to the court at Versailles. He detains her with a music box: 'This belonged to the last Austrian to inhabit these quarters. Please teach me to waltz.' Then arrive at the Bernadottes' royal messengers from Sweden, offering Bernadotte the Crown Prince-ship because he, Bernadotte, Marshall of France, is not subservient to Napoleon. Daisy Ray learns her first Swedish word ('Sköl') and Napoleon is furious. Says Bernadotte: 'I watched you juggle with the thrones of Europe . . .' adding (debatedly, the only good line in the film), 'Would you make me a greater man than yourself – by obliging me to refuse a crown?'

In fact, of course, Bernadotte was as much a pawn of Napoleon as any of his family, and his desertion of him, in alliance with England and Russia, is a matter of some fascination. The film will have none of it: it is concerned instead with whether Daisy Ray will make a good Crown Princess. There's a fairly good scene (by the standards of this sort of movie – the only scene which has, say, something of the hold of the Garbo–Charles Boyer Napoleon film) where Daisy Ray is reminded by Napoleon that as she is now royal and a foreign national she is permitted at the French court only by his tolerance.

After the Russian debacle (indicated here by a cheap montage), it is of course to her that Napoleon rushes, begging her to straighten things out with her husband. She refuses, and the next thing we know she's confiding in her diary the escape from Elba and the Battle of Waterloo. He imprisons himself at Malmaison, and it is she who persuades him to surrender: Brando's musings on his plans for Europe might just – at this eleventh hour – have got this film off the ground, but we're distracted by a hideously painted back-cloth. One is left, simply, with surprise, at a last touch of intelligence. 'When did you stop loving me?' he asks. 'I don't know,' she replies. As far as this film is concerned, most people never started.

The film was the antithesis of what was expected of Brando. His performance was well-received by the critics, several of whom thought it would have been even better with a stronger director and a more intelligent script. He himself knew better. 'I used a lot of nose putty and layers of make-up and just walked through the part,' he told Carlo Fiore; to Bob Thomas he said, 'I wasn't going to break my neck playing Napoleon in that picture. I got as many laughs out of the part as I could, and that was that.

I went to see it, expecting to be amused. But I was only depressed. It was my own fault. If I'd had any sense, I would have handled the situation better.' Cameron Mitchell, who played Joseph Bonaparte, remembered Brando's attitude on the set: 'Marlon didn't give a damn. He was fucking 20th Century-Fox. He would walk onto the set and go from chalk mark to chalk mark without the slightest show of interest. He flubbed and fumbled and fluffed his way through everything.' Said Merle Oberon, 'Marlon was very cooperative with me but not with the others. One of their complaints, there were hundreds, was that he would mumble his lines in the rehearsals, and when the scene came, he would scream at them and they wouldn't know how to take it.'

Miss Oberon, renowned as mistress and hostess but not as an actress, found Brando a willing guest for her dinner parties. At one of them he met Noël Coward, who found him 'gentler and nicer' than he expected. About this time he observed that he regretted the image created when he first came to Hollywood, which was not his fault 'to any great degree'. The disadvantages of being a movie star were cancelled out by the advantages – like having the means to travel: 'If I want to go to Europe, I won't have to scrimp and save. It's nice to be liked.' He admitted that he had not returned to the theatre because he liked making money – and he liked being in profitable movies. 'I used to bitch about how artistic standards were overlooked in Hollywood. It's still a legitimate beef. But now I can see the producer's side more clearly. You can't expect anyone to put up two or three million dollars for something that's going to lose money.'

By his own criterion, therefore, *Desirée* was a success, taking in $4,500,000 domestic, not quite enough to put it into the ten top money-making films of the year; it did better than *On the Waterfront*, and the success of both films brought Brando in at 10th in the *Motion Picture Herald*'s poll of top-drawing stars (1954). This fact had much to do with Sam Goldwyn's casting him in *Guys and Dolls*.

As a stage musical, this had opened on Broadway in 1950, an adaptation by Jo Swerling and Abe Burrows of a story ('The Idyll of Sarah Brown') by Damon Runyon, with music and lyrics by Frank Loesser, notable even among the incredibly good scores of the time. The show was a smash, and Hollywood bidding began. Paramount were so sure that they had it that they announced their cast – Betty Grable, Jane Russell and Bob Hope, with the ladies getting $150,000 apiece. Later, William Goetz (agent and sometime producer) said that Miss Russell owned half the rights. MGM bid $600,000 and Goldwyn bettered that offer by $50,000; in the end, the price was $800,000 plus residuals (not quite a record) – though Arthur Marx's book on Goldwyn says that MGM bid $850,000 and Goldwyn $1 million plus 10 per cent of the worldwide gross over $10 million. Goldwyn, once the most prolific of independent producers, had virtually ceased activity, but the success of a Technicolor musical in 1952 – *Hans Christian Andersen*, also with a score by Loesser – had given him a taste for spectaculars the whole world would want to see, supposedly representing Hollywood entertainment at its glittering best. *Guys and Dolls* was budgeted at a huge $5 million, and with a percentage of the profits agreed in his contract Joseph L. Mankiewicz was signed to write the screen treatment and direct.

Goldwyn's original choice for the gambler Sky Masterson was Hollywood's leading song-and-dance man, Gene Kelly, who later said, 'A part like Sky comes along once in a lifetime . . . I was born to play Sky the way Gable was born to play Rhett Butler.' He also needed a hit after two failures (*Brigadoon* and *Invitation to the Dance*), but as it happened he was under contract to MGM, whose corporate chief, Nicholas Schenck, refused to release him – despite Kelly's personal pleas and those of his agent, MCA in the shape of its head man, Lew Wasserman – reputedly because of an old grudge* against Goldwyn. Ironically, Goldwyn later made a distribution deal with MGM for this one film; since 1941 his films had been handled by RKO. Brando was approached and hesitated, till Mankiewicz sent him a cable, 'Understand you don't want to do *Guys and Dolls* as you've never done a musical. You have nothing to worry about as I haven't done one either. Love, Joe.' The idea of Brando as a song-and-dance man was a novel one, not least to the actor himself. He wanted to work with Mankiewicz again, and having extracted a salary of $200,000 he agreed to have a go (influenced by the fact that Robert Alda, who had played the role on Broadway, was not a trained singer either).

Frank Sinatra also wanted the role more than somewhat. When he lost it he was prepared to settle for the secondary role of Nathan Detroit – created on Broadway by Sam Levene, who in Mankiewicz's word was 'divine' in it. He knew that Sinatra would be 'terribly miscast' but gave in to his pleas, certainly aware that he was becoming a box office draw. He was adamant, however, over Vivian Blaine, who had played Miss Adelaide in both the New York and London productions. Goldwyn preferred Miss Grable, whose fame had eclipsed Miss Blaine's when they were both under contract to 20th Century-Fox – and who, though now a waning star, was far better known to cinemagoers. (Marilyn Monroe telephoned Mankiewicz to ask him for the role, but he neglected to pass the request on to Goldwyn.) When Grace Kelly proved unavailable to play the female lead, a New York mission sergeant who falls for Sky, Jean Simmons was cast. Also from the stage version came the indispensable Stubby Kaye to sing 'Sit Down, You're Rocking the Boat'.

Miss Simmons, who had charmed Brando when they

* Certainly Schenck hadn't forgiven Mankiewicz for walking out of MGM in 1944, so he drove a very hard bargain ten years later when Mankiewicz wanted to borrow Ava Gardner for *The Barefoot Contessa*.

had worked on *Desirée*, enjoyed another pleasant working relationship with him, but that between Brando and Sinatra left much to be desired – from their first meeting when, according to Carlo Fiore, Sinatra found it difficult to smile at his co-star, 'honestly delighted to meet the fabulous Sinatra'. As major movie stardom came to Sinatra and because of his many business interests, he liked to get the filming over as quickly as possible – that is, in one-take. Brando needed several and a confrontation was inevitable. It came when Sinatra was required to eat cheesecake while Brando was speaking. On the eighth take he got up, shouted at Mankiewicz, 'These fucking New York actors! How much cheesecake do you think I can eat?', and walked off the set. He later described Brando as 'the most over-rated actor in the world'. 'Poor Marlon,' Mankiewicz said to me. 'He did his best. There he was trying to sing *Luck Be a Lady* and kneeling among the chorus boys is Frank Sinatra. And Marlon knew that Frank was there and Frank comes out with a single of that same song which sells two million copies. So there was no love lost there.' During filming Brando complained to the director about Sinatra's singing of one of the other songs: 'He's supposed to sing with a Bronx accent. He's supposed to clown it up. But he's singing like a romantic lead. We can't have *two* romantic leads.' Mankiewicz agreed with him, but did not think the tact for which he was noted would extend to telling Sinatra how to sing. He advised Brando to tell him himself. 'It's not *my* job to tell him,' Brando said to Fiore. 'It's the director's job. I'm never going to work with Mankiewicz again.'

These differences were not reflected in the press releases, which were smug even by Goldwyn's own self-inflated standards. The world's screens had been heavy with adaptations of much-loved Broadway musicals (*The King and I* was the most recent) and Goldwyn's was bound to be the best. In the event, money or something was over-lavished: the film seemed interminable and fatally lacking in spontaneity. Mankiewicz had rewritten chunks of the book, and as in earlier films, showed a marked indulgence for his own words; the songs were packaged between endless Runyonesque conversations. His direction was prosaic, except in one sequence, where Sky takes Sarah on a jaunt to Havana and it briefly finds the correct verve. Most fatally, someone had decided on a stylized, representational New York, an unsuitable setting for Runyon's urban fairy-tale, which needs the clutter and clatter of a real, large, dusty, city.

The score and the stars did the salvage work. Miss Simmons received the best notices, for mingling gravity and an irrepressible gaiety as a serious girl unwillingly falling in love. Miss Blaine was praised again for her chorus-girl of genteel vulgarity, but Sinatra, in an over-sized Homburg, only registered when he sang. For whatever reason, Sinatra is overshadowed by Brando, despite the fact that the latter's three songs (two solos and a duet with Miss Simmons) revealed him as no great singing shakes (Decca issued a 45 rpm extended-play of Brando and Simmons; Sinatra's commitments to Capitol prevented a full soundtrack album – though Sinatra's importance to Capitol was such that he could have brought the soundtrack there had he wanted to). Brando 'acted' his songs, and otherwise assumed without effort the character of Sky, insolently aware of his own sex-appeal, casually cunning and dandy-smart. Miss Simmons's singing voice was only marginally better, and their scenes together sometimes reflected a hint of amateurism which added, rather than detracted, from their charm. Brando later said that they had enjoyed making it, 'not having to be perfection, just doing a good days' work'.

Audiences at least were impressed. As the film played its dates throughout the following year (1956), it wound up second biggest attraction at American cinemas (following *Giant*). At the end of 1955, Brando made another appearance in the *Motion Picture Herald* poll of exhibitors, at 6th. Ahead of him, of the actors, were James Stewart, John Wayne, William Holden and Gary Cooper, and in a poll held by *Box-Office* magazine some months later, Holden was the only actor in front; in other words, with the exception of Holden (and his versatility had never been a byword), Brando was the best possible bet for any producer who needed a young star actor.

It is not surprising that MGM were excited when he expressed an interest in another film of a Broadway success, *The Teahouse of the August Moon*, which he had seen four times on the stage. He thought it very funny and he approved of its theme – stated succinctly and using a later expression, that Coca-colonization was not in the best interests of the natives. Dore Schary, head of production, commented, 'If Marlon had wanted to play Little Eva, I would have let him.' What Marlon wanted to play was Sakini, Japanese interpreter and Okinawan houseboy – played brilliantly on Broadway by David Wayne, a Hollywood quasi-star who had already been announced as the star of the film version. Schary had assumed that Brando wished to play the American captain, a role promised to Gene Kelly but eventually assigned to another contract player, Glenn Ford, whose relaxed, genial on-screen presence increasingly belied – as stardom arrived, after fifteen years in films – his off-screen tantrums. Trouble was inevitable. 'Glenn Ford is a precise guy who gets in there and does his job,' said Edward Dmytryk, who would direct Brando a couple of years later in *The Young Lions*, 'Marlon took so long that by the time he was good Ford was all worn out and terrible. You couldn't work that way. They had a real row on that.' Matters were not improved by the fact that Ford was getting a modest fee while MGM were paying Brando a princely $300,000 plus $21,000 per week if the film went over schedule, with the right to work only eight hours a day and with only two weeks either side of shooting for fittings, stills, post-synching, etc.

Schary liked and understood talent. As the unexpected chief of production at MGM after the downfall of Louis B. Mayer, one of the founders of the company, he felt obliged to encourage some of the independent spirits he had worked with when he had been a producer at RKO. He now created or permitted a situation which would in time cripple most of the major studios. Of course, if it had not been Brando it would have been another star – and, anyway, in the past five years, as the studio system crumbled, the stars' demands had encroached on the studios' prerogatives. These could be traced back to the teen-years of this century, when Mary Pickford and Chaplin discovered that their popularity was such that the executives would accede to their every wish. Since then the contracts drawn up gave the studios great power and the players very little – whatever their popularity. But the days of the long-term contract were ending and the studios were competing for the box-office draws. Brando's standing was by now so enormous that it was a coup for MGM just to have him on the lot. Schary had heard rumours of his playing around and delaying shooting on *Desirée*, so he asked for an assurance that the film would be brought in on time. That given, he agreed that Brando should be financially compensated if the studio or another individual should cause delays. It was simple, then, to agree to other requests, all asked and granted in gentlemanly fashion.

In view of the quality of those who had directed Brando (with the exception of Mr Koster) it seemed reasonable that the actor should select the director of *Teahouse* – and Daniel Mann suited MGM too, for he had recently given the studio a commercial and critical success with *I'll Cry Tomorrow*; nor would there be any argument when Brando suggested that the screenplay be written by John Patrick, who had written the Broadway original (from a novel by Vern Sneider), since Patrick was an experienced screenwriter with two very big recent hits (*Three Coins in the*

Fountain and *Love is a Many Splendored Thing*) to his credit.

Filming was not fun. Louis Calhern, Mark Antony's Caesar, whom Brando revered, died and had to be replaced by Paul Ford – giving, incidentally, a beautiful comic rendering of military incompetence. Brando and Ford constantly tried to upstage each other – Ford because he was unsure whether Sakini wasn't the more showy role, and Brando because he feared that audience sympathies would be with the American captain in the first place. Mann called them together and told them that they were 'just creating additional problems to what is already a difficult picture. Now why don't we quit this silly childishness and get down to business?' – which decreased Brando's already diminishing regard for him. Rain constantly stopped location-shooting in Japan and after a month the unit was transferred to the MGM back lot at Culver City.

The result is only a mite less depressing than *Desirée*. As soon as the credits are over and Brando turns to the audience you know that the rest of it isn't going to differ much from what went on on the boards of the Music Box. The play had won a Pulitzer Prize and the New York Drama Critics' Circle award – also, presumably, it had delighted millions – so MGM and Mann offered it infinite respect.

One didn't go to comedies at that time expecting smart or funny dialogue, and the most this one offered was a bumbling charm; the least was some poor colour and much expendable talk. They'd used CinemaScope, and the long takes only served to emphasise the staginess of it all. The humour was supposed to spring from the contrast between the efficient and sophisticated Americans and the primitive but resourceful villagers who, led by Brando as Sakini, continually outsmart and outwit them. It wasn't an original idea, but Patrick's screenplay had an agreeably sharp eye for certain military personnel. The whole enterprise involving

Sakini and woefully incompetent Captain Fisby (Glenn Ford), 're-habilitating' a native village, is the brainchild of a malignly stupid colonel (Paul Ford) who lives by the book, and it does offer certain pleasures. The colonel's discovery that they've thrown away the book, that Fisby's countenanced a brandy-still among the cottage-industries as well as a teahouse, is predictable, but none the less funny: he wanted to leave the army a brigadier, he tells Fisby, but now he'll be lucky to leave it a private; he wanted it for his wife – 'Fisby, you've broken the heart of a proud woman.'

The film should have ended there, but Fisby, earlier said to have personally delayed victory by a year, has to turn out to be a success; and he has to have a parting with Lotus Blossom (played by Machiko Kyo, whom Western audiences knew from Kurosawa's *Rashomon*), which takes on all sorts of spiritual resonances, East isn't West, vice-versa and all that. In a pinewood setting left over, I imagine, from *Seven Brides for Seven Brothers*, they try for magic: they don't get it, or whatever they're after (it can be done, cf. Renoir's *The River* and Ivory's *Shakespeare Wallah*, both of which managed something about Westerners confronted with the East), and the comic mood is shattered. No one had tried to re-create this *Teahouse* for the screen; whatever the vigour and self-sufficiency promoted by Brando's earlier films – and they had been thought influential – Hollywood had become timorous, with no higher ambition than to set down replicas of successful Broadway theatre.

Brando's role was subsidiary to Glenn Ford's, and it's a tour de force of characterization. Having got the make-up right, and, I'm assured, the correct accent for an Okinawan speaking English, there's no acting to do: Sakini is sly and lazy, adept at stone-walling, and that's that. It was the first of his screen performances not to be universally praised. I realise that that is a huge generalisation, but his notices till *Teahouse* were impressive. His versatility was a by-word among reviewers, but some of them carped on this occasion. He looks 'synthetic' said Bosley Crowther in *The New York Times*, 'too elaborate, too consciously cute. His Sakini is less a charming rascal than a calculated clown.'

'It's a shame,' Brando said to Edith Van Cleve, 'I'd hoped that at least some of the magic of the play would have come across on the screen.' It was his ninth film and yet another disappointment.

8
Two Officers and Gentlemen

While the public flocked to the *Teahouse*, those who hoped that Brando would transform American films did not entirely despair, for he had formed his own production company and ambitious plans were afoot. He said: 'I've made enough money to live comfortably the rest of my life, so my main concern is not with making money. I would like to make a cultural contribution and help some of the big social problems of our day.' He made that statement in 1957, while struggling with various projects he hoped to produce. Before looking at them, let us glance back to some other plans, and, for the record, to his first well-publicized romance.

In the autumn of 1954, it was announced in France that he would marry Josanne Berenger of Bandol, a resort on the Riviera; they had met in New York, and romance hastened when he visited her in the Midi. The world's press carried pictures of the engaged couple smiling at the cameras, but after much mystification and prevarication the wedding was called off, because, it was said, the prospective groom thought the prospective bride spoke too much to the press. The photographs, incidentally, show a new Brando, grinning shyly at the camera like Joe Doakes; she doesn't look like a movie star, either, which may have been part of the attraction.

That Brando was a Francophile was witnessed by another French film project, when, after completing *Desirée*, he was interested in *L'Amant de Lady Chatterly*, to co-star Danielle Darrieux and Leo Genn, directed by Marc Allégret. He would, of course, have played the gamekeeper, but even though he offered to take a much reduced salary, the producers still couldn't arrive at that (the role was played by Erno Crisa).

About the same time Luchino Visconti wanted him for his romantic melodrama, *Senso*, and he sent him the script; but his producers preferred Farley Granger, 'the up and coming star to launch' – an odd decision, since Granger's days as a Hollywood star were almost over. In 1954 Warner Bros were jubilant when he consented to play the title-role in one of the prize properties of the decade, *Mister Roberts*, as played on Broadway for several years by Henry Fonda, who was considered to old for the film version; while Fonda debated whether to play the older role of the ship's doctor the producer, Joshua Logan, signed John Ford to direct: and Ford insisted on Fonda. In 1955 Stanley Kramer announced that Brando would co-star with Cary Grant (once the most vocal of Brando's critics) and Sophia Loren in *The Pride and the Passion*, a tale of the Peninsular War: Kramer had to make do with a miscast Frank Sinatra. He was also 'definitely set' for *Heaven Knows, Mr Allison*, as was, at another point, Clark Gable; the role was finally played by Robert Mitchum. At RKO Howard Hughes conceived his Genghis Khan epic for Brando, *The Conqueror*, but when MCA claimed that Brando's schedule was busy the unfortunate John Wayne was recruited. Some sources say that Brando turned down the lead in two of Kazan's productions, *Baby Doll* and *A Face in the Crowd*; I imagine it is true, although Brando's name was never linked with either project in the trade press. Kazan would have been far too canny to risk being publicly snubbed by Brando.

He may also have been first choice for roles eventually taken by his imitators – say, the boxer Rocky Graziano in *Somebody Up There Likes Me*, which Paul Newman inherited from James Dean after the latter was killed when he crashed his Porsche. In view of the durability of Newman's career, it should be borne in mind that he took three or four films to find himself, and that in combining a demotic manner (despite extreme good looks) and intelligence, he was following rather than imitating. Dean was another matter. He was younger and with much less acting experience than Newman. He made his first film, *East of Eden*, under Kazan's direction, and he hero-worshipped Brando.

He imitated him on and off screen, pestering him via his answering services for a meeting. When they finally met at a party 'he was throwing himself around', Brando told Truman Capote, 'acting like a madman. So I spoke to him. I took him aside and asked him didn't he know he was sick? That he needed help?' He recommended an analyst to him, of which he said, 'At least his work improved.' Asked about Dean's performance in Kazan's film, he said 'he's wearing my last year's clothes and my last year's talent'. Later he considered doing the narration for a documentary on Dean, partly because his friend Wally Cox was involved with it, 'Maybe not, though. I get excited about something, but it never lasts more than seven minutes. Seven minutes exactly. That's my limit. I never know why I get up in the morning.'

Perhaps that was what was wrong with his having his own production company. Kazan has said of himself after *On the Waterfront* that he could tangibly feel the power he wielded in Hollywood – not the power to command, but to work where he liked, with whom he liked, on what he liked. Brando probably felt the same when he set up Pennebaker Productions, named after his mother (who had died of a heart attack in 1954). His father, who had been unwisely investing his earnings, was nominally the company treasurer but actually, says Fiore, 'a paper shuffler, doing minor chores in the office'. The other partners were friends of Brando: George Glass, whom he had met while making *The Men*; Walter Seltzer, also a press agent; and George Englund, an actor friend with no meaningful credits. MCA gave advice and chose Paramount out of several studios willing to put in finance – in the hope of getting Brando's services for non-Pennebaker productions. Pennebaker's first film was to be 'significant', but from the start Brando left the decisions to the others. None of them had any experience in producing a film. Finally there was announced *To Tame a Land*, based on one of Louis L'Amour's best-selling Westerns, with Robert Parrish directing and Brando as star and director. For these functions he would keep 85 per cent of the profits (Hollywood gasped: but hadn't a lesser star, Robert Mitchum, just got 75 per cent for a minor effort, *Foreign Intrigue*?). Due to script troubles, it was cancelled a year later, in 1956. The second project was also scrapped – after, again, much anticipatory publicity from Paramount: an adventure story about a United Nations research worker who disappears in South East Asia. The film would contain a fair amount of propaganda for the UN Technical Assistance Programme, and would be filmed on location through the area, with a script by Stewart Stern, produced by George Englund and tentatively titled *Tiger on a Kite*.

In 1956 Brando and the Pennebaker team went on a fact-finding mission to the area, accompanied by the photographer Herbert Leonard; it was to conclude in Tokyo just four weeks later (because Brando was to begin *Teahouse*), which seems a short while to see so many places, including Singapore, Hong Kong, Manila, Jakarta and Bangkok. Leonard says that Brando was mobbed everywhere and that he loathed it. In Jakarta, President Sukarno laid down the red carpet and greeted Brando with 'Well, how's ya love life?' In Bali, where he and Leonard fled and booked in under pseudonyms he was recognized by a horde of American tourists. In Bangkok they went to a nightclub 'and he took a liking to a singer and sent me over to ask her to our table for a drink. She refused. I said, you know he's Marlon Brando, don't you? She said sure, but it's still no. Brando was really peeved. She was very attractive – not a piece, you dig. He finally won her over and for three days in the hotel they never left the room. When we left she was in tears at the airport, hanging on this wire fence, fingers through the mesh like one of those war pictures. She gave me a book of Buddhist prayers for him.' In this case it would not be true, as has been reported, that Brando pined for Anna Kashfi, whom he had left behind in the States and whom he was soon to marry.

In 1955 Brando had optioned a story about a baseball player who wore spectacles, 'Man on Spikes'. In 1957, three more projects were announced: *Ride Comanchero* (later called *The Comancheros* and *Comanchero*), in which Brando would play a Mexican, in a story set towards the end of the last century; *Hang Me High*, which he would produce only; and *The Spellbinder*, for which he had reputedly signed Errol Flynn. One of the more persistent Pennebaker projects was *A Burst of Vermilion*, a Western which Brando himself was writing, but that got nowhere. 'It was a fancy title, born of an inspiration so childish that Hopalong Cassidy would have cringed in embarrassment. It was Marlon's idea to have his gang of bank robbers and murderers tie blood-red scarves around their necks that would snap in the wind,' says Fiore, who made the point that it was hardly in the robbers' own interest to proclaim themselves murderers. It would work cinematically, Brando replied. In 1958 the title *Guns Up* first appeared. That eventually became *One-Eyed Jacks*.

As each project stalled and with his money being swallowed in script development, Brando was forced back into working for others – though with the concession that Penne-baker would be credited with William Goetz (returning to this field) as one of the two producers of *Sayonara*. Warner Bros distributed, but it was not they or Goetz who was the guiding spirit but Joshua Logan. When he and the novelist James A. Michener had worked on 'South Pacific' he had suggested, meeting in the Tokyo Foreign Correspondents' Club, a modernized 'Madame Butterfly', set during the post-war American Occupation of Japan. Michener would write the novel, which could become a Broadway show; but it didn't, for when the book was published in 1954 it became a bestseller – and Logan was on the verge of switching from Broadway to Hollywood. His *Bus Stop* and *Picnic* were both big successes; mean-while Paul Osborn was writing the script for the film.

Brando originally turned it down (so did Rock Hudson, but it is unclear whether that was before or after Brando first read it; Hudson chose instead to do *Something of Value* which, unlike *Sayonara*, was a failure at the box-office). Several factors made him change his mind: it had some points to make on racial intolerance and the ending would be changed to suit him, showing that an inter-racial romance could have a happy ending; the protagonist would become a Southerner, which would permit him to do *that* accent and suggest a bigotry behind his upbringing; the chance to return to Japan, which he had enjoyed both during the location work on *Teahouse* and an earlier visit to perfect his Okinawan accent; and a salary of $300,000 plus a percentage, with Warners picking up the tab for his entourage. This last extravagance became a *sine qua non* of the big stars' demands when they really gained control, but it was still rare at this stage. 'Ordinarily we wouldn't put up with it,' a Warner executive told Capote. 'All the demands he makes. Except – well, this picture just *had* to have a big star. Your star – that's the only thing that really counts at the box-office.'

An additional factor in Brando's signing his contract was the gentle way the bulky Logan picked off the dead leaves of a plant when they were discussing the project in Logan's East River apartment; this apparently proved that he could entrust his talent to him. He did not share Logan's admiration for the script; it was pure soap opera, Fiore assured him and Brando agreed, remarking that he was only doing the film for the money. He wasn't, after a few days, doing it with any respect for Logan. Logan enthused about him: 'Marlon's the most exciting person I've met since Garbo. A genius. But I don't know what he's like. I don't know anything about him ... I've never worked with such an inventive actor. So pliable. He takes direction beautifully, and yet he always has something to add.' Brando's enthusiasm for this relationship was rather different: 'I give up. I'm going to walk through the part, and that's that. Sometimes I think nobody knows the difference anyway. For the first few days on the set, I tried to act. But then I made an experiment. In this scene, I tried to do everything wrong I could think of. Grimaced and rolled my eyes, put in all kinds of gestures and expressions that had no relation to the part I'm supposed to be playing. What did Logan say? He just said "It's wonderful! Print it!"'

These remarks were made during a long evening's conversation with Truman Capote as that gentleman made his progress from *enfant terrible* and boy sensitive of American letters to the malicious alcoholic socialite of his later years. He had arrived in Tokyo in the company of the British photographer and designer Cecil Beaton, who made a note in his diary of seeing Brando at the airport: 'He has lost his looks in ten years, looks like a heavy-set businessman, podgy hands, a Guys and Dolls hat. But his behaviour is all that could be desired, a courteous, cooperative, good-humoured, but quiet and restrained smile, a tongue flip, an occasional reminder of his embarrassment at giving spontaneous performances for camera and microphone.'

The two men were there as friends of the Logans and the Goetzes (that is, Beaton was a chum of Irene Mayer Selznick, who was Edie Goetz's sister). They were both homosexual and two of the beautiful people, that is men of achievement moving in the best society – the sort to be attracted to the handsome, brilliantly talented, bisexual Brando. He must be lionised and then cut down to size. The evening Brando spent with Capote he thought merely social. In 1963 Brando told Beaton, 'He told me he was not going to do a *Sayonara* piece. He'd arrived too late. He told me a person very close to him had committed suicide and I kind of went along with that.' Brando told another friend, 'The little bastard spent half the night telling me his problems. I figured the least I could do was tell him a few of mine.' He had only himself to blame, since Logan had warned him under no circumstances to talk to Capote (which perhaps is why he did so); and Logan, to be doubly sure, told Capote that Brando would not be good copy since he was taciturn to the point of silence. At all events, Capote engaged Brando's sympathies and got from him an extraordinary account of self-revelation by plying him with vodka. In his article Capote says that Brando handed him a large vodka; he does not say that he brought a large bottle with him. Towards the end of the evening Brando spoke about his mother: 'I thought if she loved me enough, trusted me enough, I thought, then we can be together, in New York . . . She left my father and came to live with me. In New York, when I was in a play. I tried so hard. But my love wasn't enough. She went back. And one day I didn't care any more. She was there. In a room. Holding on to me. And I let her fall. Because I couldn't take it any more – watching her breaking apart, in front of me, like a piece of porcelain. I stepped right over her. I walked out. I was indifferent. Since then, I've been indifferent.'

These days we are accustomed to the revelations of

the famous, but in 1957 it was virtually unparalleled for a movie star to speak so frankly to the press; and this was not for a fan magazine but for the *New Yorker*, perhaps the most prestigious magazine then in any country in the world. Capote has a snide word or so for Fiore;* he has Brando sneering at the possibility of returning to the theatre; and he paints him as a complete egomaniac: 'The voice went on, as though speaking to hear itself, an effect Brando's speech often has, for like many persons who are intensely self-absorbed, he is something of a monologuist – a fact that he recognizes and for which he offers his own explanation. "People around me never say anything," he says. "They just seem to want to hear what I have to say. That's why I do all the talking." '

Brando knew soon enough that an account of the convivial evening would appear in print, since Capote bragged to all and sundry that Brando had spent five whole hours in the confessional with him. Brando wrote to him – in a letter Capote claimed was illiterate – to tell him that he could say what he liked about him and begging him to delete his references to other people (on Jay Kanter: 'He does what I tell him'). Only absent, it seems, is something that the *New Yorker* would not in any case have published: Brando's admission that he had slept with a mutual friend, one of many men to have that privilege – for, he said, he wasn't homosexual but had obliged several men who were crazy about him. The article, entitled 'The Duke in His Domain', appeared on 9th November and Capote wrote soon afterwards to Beaton, 'I had a telegram from the Logans telling me how much they "loved" the piece. What a pair of hypocrites!' Professionally, the worst the article did for Brando was to have the industry look askance for bad-mouthing the project on which he was work-

* He decided to call him Murray in the article for undisclosed reasons; we do learn that Fiore called Brando 'Mar' which perhaps implies the simplicity of their relationship.

ing. Fortunately, the *New Yorker* did not have a large circulation. It was also hard not to agree with his description of the film. He had sat through twenty-two hours of script conferences, he said; Logan had encouraged him to 'rewrite, Marlon, write it your own way' – and he had done so, the 'whole damn script. And now they're going to use maybe eight lines.' So: '*Sayonara*, I love it! This wondrous hearts-and-flowers nonsense that was supposed to be a serious picture about Japan.'

The subject matter was basically serious – the American military in Japan, their fraternizations, and the obstacles which the USAF authorities put in the way of mixed marriages. It was strictly partisan (doesn't the whole world love a lover?) and already outdated (the regulations had been relaxed, the Japanese GI brides were already arriving in the States), but it did, for whatever reason, conform to Warner Bros long-standing policy of expounding liberal virtues.

Brando played Major Gruver, suffering from combat fatigue in Korea, and sent to Japan to be near his fiancée, Eileen (Patricia Owens), the daughter of General Webster (Kent Smith). Reluctantly and rashly he agrees to be best man at the wedding of an airman, Kelly (Red Buttons), to a local girl, Katsumi (Myoshi Umeki), and when he himself falls in love with a Japanese actress, Hana-ogi (Miiko Taka), he espouses the cause of mixed marriages. This results in plenty-trouble with his fiancée's family, and when he fails to persuade the general to countermand an order posting Kelly home to the States, Kelly and wife carry out a suicide pact. Because of this, Hana-ogi gives up Gruver, but (the reversal of Michener's ending) he persuades her to marry him.

The film was well-received in the US but elsewhere – certainly in Britain – the critics confirmed Brando's own opinion. Its main value was its picture of American servicemen abroad, done with an authenticity which was almost unchallengeable. For the rest, it was a long (very: almost 2½ hours) romantic wallow, with love and yearning all over the place. As in his two previous pictures, all else gave way before the director's determination to be passionate, visually striking and significant always and all at the same time. Verily, cherry blossoms are pretty, and the whole bright package deserved the title-song (by Irving Berlin, no less). Other than that, only Brando's presence gave it any relevance. His romantic interest, Miss Taka, had had no previous acting experience. Audrey Hepburn had turned down the role rather than submit to the required make-up. While Warners searched Japan, Hawaii and other places, Miss Taka – a salesclerk from Seattle, working in Los Angeles; and Miiko Taka is the name the studio gave her – presented herself for a test. That was apparently good, but she does resemble, in more ways than one, a block of wood. Brando, however, manages a more than passable impression of a man in love. The role was conventional, and he knew it; he gave one of his least showy performances as this mild, somewhat droll Texan (in the book, a Westerner), suggesting kindnesses and considerations only hinted at in the script and otherwise ignored by the director.

Sayonara opened in December 1957, to be followed five months later by *The Young Lions*, which was again well-received by most of the press, and the public went to both films: both wound up among the dozen big financial successes of the year, and Brando trailed only Glenn Ford, Elizabeth Taylor and Jerry Lewis in the *Motion Picture Herald* poll of exhibitors. As it happened, 1958 would be his best year professionally since he won the Academy Award: it was also the last good year for a very long time. *Sayonara* was his tenth film, and would mark his fifth Oscar nomination – but that would also be his last in a long while.

Privately, things did not go well. In October 1957, he

married an Indian actress, Anna Kashfi. At least, she looked Indian, and presumably Brando thought she was, for the marriage was over almost as soon as you could say Joan O'Callaghan – her real name, as revealed to the world by her proud Welsh parents the day after the wedding. In riposte she claimed to be illegitimate, born in Calcutta in 1934, but that her mother had married Mr O'Callaghan two years later. Brando had first set eyes on Miss Kashfi in October 1955 in the commissary at Paramount, who had taken her on for a small role in *The Mountain*. The reader will have noted in passing a preference for dark-skinned or Oriental partners – the best known of which, so far, were two minor actresses, Movita, the Mexican whose only large role had been as Clark Gable's island interest in *Mutiny on the Bounty*, and the Puerto Rican dancer Rita Moreno (who would later become a fairly important name in films). Brando, anyway, asked A. C. Lyles (who was working on *The Mountain*) to effect an introduction – but Miss Kashfi had apparently never heard of him and was not impressed with what she saw. That afternoon Brando asked a Paramount publicist to arrange a date, but the lady wasn't interested; she did agree to go out with him when he telephoned her a few days later, for he promised to bring along a chaperone – who turned out to be George Englund. When Kashfi apparently learned of Brando's reputation vis-à-vis women she refused to see him again. He renewed his efforts two months later, when she decided to sleep with him out of curiosity. The result, she claimed, was pure Stanley Kowalski: asked whether he intended to rape her, he replied that that was 'just an assault with a friendly weapon', but what followed was 'a well-rehearsed, polished performance, selfish, without warmth or naturalness'. As a suitor he left much to be desired, appearing and disappearing at will; there were also serious quarrels – and most of this is protractedly retailed in Fiore's book and her own, 'Brando for Breakfast'. There was no love lost between the two of them, partly because she considered Fiore's interest in her husband unhealthy and in that respect she considered that Brando's relationship with the French actor Christian Marquand 'displayed an affection toward each other that far overreached the usual expressions of friendship.'

Fiore also undertook marriage, but that was to quickly expire when he left his bride at home to take trips with Brando. On one of these Brando met the Eurasian actress France Nuyen; during the courtship he was also seeing Miss Moreno. With everything else, Miss Kashfi can hardly have envisaged a marriage such as ordinary people have, and it endured less than a year. Kashfi says Brando took Miss Nuyen to their mansion home to meet her and the baby, but the last straw came when her death was mistakenly announced on the radio. It was in fact her maid who had drowned in the Brando swimming-pool but Brando's disappointment, on arriving home, was so palpable that she moved out. They were legally separated in September 1958 and divorced in August 1959, with Kashfi charging mental cruelty and getting half-a-million dollars in settlement plus $12,500 in child support. A son, Christian Devi – named for M. Marquand – had been born in May 1958. Years later she said of his father: 'He wasn't a considerate husband or lover. I was young and immature and fascinated by [him] because he was a movie star'; the marriage, she said, died of boredom on both sides. On other occasions, she said that Brando was vindictive towards the women he had loved, and that he was the most egocentric man that ever lived.

The wedding pictures showed him with his hair dyed blond for *The Young Lions*, in which he played a German army officer. The film was based on Irwin Shaw's novel, a book very conscious of its own importance – a three-pronged tale of one German and two Americans, tracing their fates through the 1939–45 War. It was purchased by

Al Lichtman, whose prior moments of Hollywood glory had been as salesman for Adolph Zukor and, for a while, president of United Artists. He had arranged with 20th Century-Fox to release and finance – to $2 million, which was not a large budget for a piece requiring hundreds of locations throughout Europe. It was to be cast with the studio's contract players, including Tony Randall, but when Edward Dmytryk agreed to direct he suggested a higher budget and more impressive casting. He thought of Montgomery Clift, whom he had just directed in *Raintree County*. Clift told his agent, Jay Kanter, that he wanted to do it, and Kanter decided that with Brando as co-star they might strike box-office gold. Brando was interested in playing the German provided that he was made more sympathetic. In any case Kanter asked for him and got script approval plus $200,000, which was less than he had been paid for *Sayonara*, but it would conclude the two film commitment he had made to the studio as settlement of their suit over *The Egyptian*.

Kanter, or at least MCA, then informed Lichtman that there would be no deal if Randall was not replaced by another of the company's clients, Dean Martin – who had made only one film since breaking up with Jerry Lewis, *Ten Thousand Bedrooms*, a box-office disaster of such eloquent proportions that there were no further offers. Bob Thomas says the decision was left to Clift, who would have most of the scenes with whomsoever played the role, and he wouldn't be confident with the less experienced Randall – but then, both Clift and Brando were friends as well as clients of Kanter (it was he who telephoned Anna Kashfi, the night that she left home, to say that Brando had taken an overdose; she returned to the house to find him grinning at her). Neither actor made public comment when the matter was first aired in *Show Magazine* a few years later, but Martin did: '. . . all I did was let my agents know I'd like to play it. There's nothing wrong with that. It's done all the time in this business.'

Years later George C. Scott was to comment – after mentioning that Clift reached his 'zenith' in this film – 'It was sad that those two young actors couldn't have had a great actor with them in that . . . then the picture would have been unbeatable.' He went on to say that America's three greatest actors were Brando, Clift and John Barrymore – the latter an odd assessment, since he could only have seen him on film, where the legacy is of ham. Brando agreed on that issue; he placed Barrymore with Paul Muni and Chaplin, though on another occasion he cited Muni, Tracy and Cary Grant. However, asked whether he had any idols among actors he named Robert Donat. He used the words 'admire' or 'admirer' several times, but concluded '. . . and I respect Laurence Olivier'. Of Clift, he once observed that he looked 'as though he had a Mixmaster up his ass', but by this time he respected him – and was trying to get him to join Alcoholics Anonymous. He once told him, 'In a way I hate you. I've always hated you because I want to be better than you, but you're better than me – you're my touchstone, my challenge, and I want you and I to go on challenging each other.' Clift became a burnt-out case long before Brando; neither went on to play Hamlet, Lear or Macbeth. Nor did they, except in one scene, have to challenge each other on the set of this movie.

The most notable quality of Shaw's novel was its irony, and that was retained in Edward Anhalt's screenplay, a synthesis of the experience of war in best-seller terms. On those terms it is entertaining (as Brando expressly hoped when considering it: 'They say in Hollywood if you want messages you go to Western Union. People are not interested in the message picture, but entertainment. I believe a combination of both is possible and essential, particularly in the international exchange of ideas.') It revives much better than *From Here to Eternity*, based on a better book, with a better director (Zinnemann), and considered at the time to be much superior. Once you get used to being hurtled back and forth between the German and the Americans, the incidents prove lively; and Dmytryk keeps things running smoothly from myriad and varied locations.

Brando plays Christian Diestl, part-time ski-instructor who's discovered spouting pro-Nazi sentiments to an American girl (Barbara Rush). She provides the link with the Americans, Whiteacre (Martin), a Broadway singing-star (in the book, a writer), and Noah (Clift). They are both about to join the army, but Noah meets a girl, Hope (Hope Lange), and the film dallies on her father's prejudice when he learns that Noah is a Jew. The action reverts to Christian, and not a moment too soon; last seen as an officer in occupied Paris, he's in Berlin on an errand for his friend and commander, Hardenberg (Maximilian Schell), delivering a gift to his wife (May Britt). She leaves him in her flat to dine with a general, and returns to find him drunk. The subsequent sexual fencing is splendidly done by Brando: she is so 'forward' that he is embarrassed, silent, not looking at her, seemingly abstracted. The director, Dmytryk, once observed that Clift was the clever one, and seemed not to be, and that Brando was stupid and pretended not to be: but Brando's playing here is more original than anything Clift ever did (in life, most people can't take overt sexual overtures, at least not from your best friend's wife; I can't think of another movie hero thus fazed).

Brando also brings something original to his next sequence, with Hardenberg in the desert, behind enemy lines, preparing to mow down a small British unit: both men go about the task with exhilaration, caution and wonder. Later, when they come across a survivor, Christian, less cold-blooded, refuses to shoot him; and Brando's expression as he waits for Hardenberg's shot is as enigmatic as anything Garbo ever managed – part contempt, part smiling embarrassment, part the conceit of a man who thinks he understands humanity. After that, his smug Nazi, beautifully and correctly accented, is less interesting: he is an idealist with wrong ideals reduced to impotency and despair. No one seems interested in the later, disillusioned Christian – including Brando himself, despite his insistence that the character of the book be softened.

Reverting to the Americans, the film gets mealy-mouthed about anti-semitism in the army. Noah gets picked on (just as Clift was, earlier, in *From Here to Eternity*), and we have to assume it's because he's Jewish. He's called 'dog-face', and his sadistic captain hurls away his copy of 'Ulysses'. Whiteacre gets posted away for pointing out that the man is being victimized, but Noah still gets beaten to a pulp and stuck in the jug. Coming out, he finds his old enemies have clubbed together to return his stolen money and to replace the book; and as the sadistic officer has also been exposed, you have to conclude that the army isn't so bad after all.

The film is charged with this sort of elementary drama. The reason that *From Here to Eternity* now fails is that the observation in the book was from life, not from other books; Hollywood bowdlerized and conventionalized it. In the four years between these two films, censorship was relaxed, but Shaw had written precisely the sort of second-remove stuff which Hollywood understands best. You don't want to throw-up when the Jew becomes a hero (rescuing one of his erstwhile torturers), because it's exactly what you expect. As for the final scenes, the opening-up of the concentration camp, I think we should be grateful to any movie that treats that subject honourably. We are still contending with Shaw's heavy irony, but one senses the indignation of the film's makers at this point, and their awareness of their limitations. There is an odd look, a look of seriousness, on the faces of Noah and Whiteacre as they refer to the 'ovens' – after which they run across Christian and shoot him down, just in time for Noah to return to Brooklyn and Hope.

Martin acts with a fatcat smile which suits his interpretation of the role; Clift is as sympathetic as he was in *Eternity*; and Schell is good as the career officer. It is possible that he and Brando were hoping to say something about the lack of humanness, the lack of humanity that one finds in many Germans, but, clearly, this wasn't the film to do it. If so, it would be indicative of Brando's complete complicity in a role, because one of the reasons that Christian was softened for the screen was that Brando did not want to make a point of the Nazis being solely responsible for the war; and, probably, he did not want to see Clift and Martin get all the sympathy that was going. Sam Peckinpah, who worked for a while on *One-Eyed Jacks*, spoke much later about Brando in that film: 'Strange man, Marlon. Always doing a number about his screen image, about how audiences would not accept him as a thief, how audiences would only accept him as a fallen sinner – someone they could love.' Brando held a similar view of Christian, and he was anxious, at the end, that his dead body be spread-eagled in the manner of the Crucifixion, but Clift, in the only scene they shared together, violently opposed the notion and it was dropped. 'Because of the structure of the story,' said Dmytryk, in a further comparison between the two actors, 'they never appeared together on the screen except at the end and by then the character Brando was playing was dead. But, thank God, Monty never had to work with Marlon. It would have killed him. He disapproved so highly of the way Marlon worked. And he was absolutely right. They could never have worked together. It would have been impossible. The difference between the two was that Clift prepared for his role weeks ahead of time . . . Monty was best, just as Spencer Tracy was best, on the first or second take, because he was ready by that time. He had worked on the scene in his mind literally for weeks. If he didn't get it in one or two takes he would begin to get mechanical and had to stop and go off and do something else. He'd come back to it later when he was fresh.

'Marlon on the other hand was completely different. When I first knew I was going to work with him I asked people what he was like and they said he'll go fifty, sixty, seventy takes, and they'll all be terrible. And suddenly, on take seventy-one, something happened and it's great.' On another occasion Dmytryk said, 'He told me after we had finished *The Young Lions* that it was the best working relationship he had had since Elia Kazan, who is his spiritual godfather. But we had a test of strength before the film began. This is not uncommon with certain types of actor, but it has to be faced and got out of the way or the film will suffer.' Chronologically, Dmytryk was the first of Brando's directors to speak of the difficulties of working with him. Joshua Logan, diplomatically, only hinted at these (and he was bearing in mind, perhaps, Brando's letter of apology to him over the Capote piece – sent at the behest of MCA – saying that he hadn't then realised how fine a director he was): 'The greatest natural talent of our time. A special sort of man with a special sort of possibilities. He can act anything. His complex is that he thinks everyone wants to put him down. He hates authority. He'll defy anyone with power – producers, directors, writers, politicians. He has only confidence in those who are poor and anonymous.' Professionally, this would become increasingly evident, and self-destructive. At this point so much was expected of him yet Peckinpah's remark is revealing. 'Like all actors,' said Shelley Winters, 'Marlon wants to be liked.' Like all stars, perhaps. In the days of *The Men* and *Streetcar* Brando didn't give a damn whether audiences liked him.

9

Travail: One Minor, Two Major

Pennebaker eventually became involved in film production, partly out of need for cash, but not in any major
way. Glass and Seltzer were associated with Troy Films,
the independent company formed by the producer-director
Michael Anderson, in making *Shake Hands With the Devil*,
a tale of the 'Troubles', filmed in Eire in 1959 with James
Cagney, Don Murray and Michael Redgrave. Pennebaker
was also one of half-a-dozen production companies involved with Anderson's equally mediocre *The Naked Edge*,
a thriller starring Gary Cooper and Deborah Kerr, released
after Cooper's death, which gave it a fillip at the box-office
since the public wanted to see their old favourite for the
last time. *Paris Blues* also boasted a clutch of producing
companies, none of whom could have been proud of the
result. Pennebaker may have been more instrumental in
getting this off the ground than in Anderson's two films,
since it had been announced a couple of years earlier as a
vehicle for Brando. Its appeal to him was obvious, as its
leading characters were black and white jazz musicians
working in Paris (which in the film consisted mainly of
blow-up photographs): but he changed his mind, despite
Marilyn Monroe's apparent agreement to do it provided

he was her co-star. The unfortunates who replaced them were Paul Newman and Joanne Woodward, with Sydney Poitier: Martin Ritt directed – and combinations of two or more of these four talents would do some vastly more distinguished work. United Artists released all three, and only in the case of the Cooper film were they rewarded.

Paramount, meanwhile, found Brando in no hurry to make his first Pennebaker picture for them. He had, however, found the property which would be its basis, 'The Authentic Death of Hendry Jones' by Charles Neider. It was submitted to him by Frank P. Rosenberg, who had produced some run-of-the-mill movies for 20th Century-Fox and Warner Bros. It took him seven months to get through to Brando, but the actor agreed to the script only two days later. That was by Sam Peckinpah, at that time writing television Westerns, but it was not, as these things go, the one used – that, after rewrites by various hands, was credited to Calder Willingham, the author of *End As a Man*, and Guy Trosper. Stanley Kubrick, hired as director on the strength of his first important film, *Paths of Glory*, became exasperated at the endless script conferences; the break with Brando came when he objected to the casting of Brando's friend France Nuyen in the Chinatown sequence (later cut from the film). He left 'by mutual consent' and 'with deep regret because of my respect and admiration for one of the world's foremost artists, Marlon Brando'. He was not entirely sorry to go, since his experience till then had demonstrated that only one individual could have autonomy on the set. According to James Mason (whom he directed in *Lolita* some years later), 'Ultimately [he] had to give up on the Brando film because he figured that life was too short. Brando, it seems, was not one to make snappy decisions. But in all other respects Kubrick had nothing but praise for him. Aside from his talent as an actor he had, according to Kubrick, great theatrical intelligence and on the spur of the moment could improvise an entire plot development or an impressive exchange of dialogue.' These gifts he now put at the service of Brando the movie director – and Paramount tore its collective hair out as he proceeded, in the name of perfection, to go out of control.

There were endless re-takes, hold-ups for the right climatic effects, delays while he decided what to do next. The budget, originally fixed at $1,800,000, went to over $5 million, and the actual shooting extended to over six months. Trouble didn't cease when the cameras stopped turning: the first cut lasted over five hours. One hour was chopped out without great difficulty, but Paramount was no more interested in a four-hour film than a five-hour one: it came out finally at two hours twenty minutes. The company's trepidation was somewhat alleviated by the world-wide interest, and the ease with which the publicity department could get news coverage.

Brando's Western: *One-Eyed Jacks*. (The title was inaccurate: 'You're a one-eyed jack around here, Dad, I seen the other side of your face,' Brando says to Karl Malden, but Malden was the *only* character who wasn't what he seemed, who could be accused of duplicity.) He had insisted that the film was a frontal attack on the clichés of the genre – but even the most respectful critics told him that it wasn't. His performance was: you'd have to go back to William S. Hart to find a Western hero so lacking in heroic qualities – though it was precisely the contradictions of Hart, 'the Good Bad Man', which had attracted audiences. Brando was undeniably a hero, but he was also vain, vicious, cunning, sentimental, and, whether intended or not, rather stupid. Brando was perhaps confused between the performance and the film. He exists, therefore the film exists, and they are one and indivisible. The esteem accorded him justifies the film, but he neglected something in his performance, often a matter of brooding Napoleonic silences in close-up. For the first time he seemed to be repeating himself. The director's fascination with his leading actor often looks like megalomania.

The film, like its hero, was vain, vicious, cunning and sentimental, and you could say beautiful and perverted as well. It borrows from John Ford (the town fiesta, the sandstorm), and from Japanese cinema (the beguiling silences, the seascapes), and, like *Viva Zapata!* meanders from the realistic to the romantic and back. Its self-indulgence, rare at the time, would be echoed and exceeded in scores of lesser films before the decade was out, so that the symbolism of Brando's use of himself now seems tentative. Reservations remain about the sadism, the first confirmation of Brando's Messiah-complex – but that got more extensive workings-over in later films over which he nominally had less control. Here, at least, his whipping by Malden could be justified by the fact that Brando had fallen for his step-daughter – and it gave him a motivation to keep his vengeance at white-hot pitch.

The film is built around revenge, and it's a good motif for a Western. Rio (Brando) and Dad Longworth (Malden) are bank-robbers stranded in the desert with one horse. Longworth goes for another and doesn't return; Rio surrenders to his pursuers. Longworth, in fact, had good grounds for not returning – he knew it would be hopeless: but when they meet again, he lies and says there were no horses available. By this time, he's respectable, over the border, the sheriff of Monterey. Rio arrives, bent on revenge, and also to rob the bank with three companions – the Mexican (Larry Duran), who had been his jail companion, and two drifters (Ben Johnson and Sam Gilman). In self-defence, he kills a drunken reveller who had been pestering a woman, and Longworth, who had welcomed him, if gingerly, not long before, horse-whips him and runs him out of town.

Now: Rio's action should have made him the hero of the hour – there were enough witnesses; and as an old pal of the sheriff, he might have been immune from justice. So here's a credible dilemma being handled in conventional movie manner so that the plot can function. Longworth does have reasons for wanting Rio out of the way – he has betrayed him, he has betrayed the Code of the West (it doesn't matter that Rio knows of his past: so do the townsfolk). As the film proceeds, Longworth – though played in Malden's usual smug, vacillating way – becomes even more dastardly, and Rio even more noble. His faults are played down, though at the end, he betrays the Code and shoots Longworth in the back (as did Robert Taylor in the 1941 *Billy the Kid*, which also talked much of the Code and also attempted a compendium of all Western myths).

The bank raid goes wrong. Because of the girl – Longworth's wife's niece (Pina Pellicier, a Mexican 'discovered' for the film, and a suicide some years later) – Rio has opted out. The Mexican refuses to accompany the other two, and they kill him (with overtones of racialism). They proceed alone and bungle it: one is killed, and so is a small girl. The sheriff rounds up Rio and leads the townsfolk in refusing to believe his innocence. The West was a place of rough justice; and though Monterey is picturesque, and civilized by the standards of other towns, you can almost smell the blood.

For all its romanticism, this was the first Western in fifty years to broach realism: squalid girls in empty, run-down bars, the men in duds like those of the photographs of the period (1880). There are few characters in any Western (till Peckpinah's, later) as wholly despicable as the deputy (Slim Pickens), a rube-like yokel who guards Rio and spitefully ridicules him. The two bandits, though first discovered when one of them is manhandling a whore, may well be homosexual; and the girl is exactly the sort of grave, meek thing to attract the sort of man Rio is. There is, in fact, so much in the movie that is good that one would like to see the footage left on the cutting-room floor.

Well, not everyone. For *Esquire* Dwight MacDonald found it 'such an egregiously self-indulgent film. The character that Mr Brando has been playing for years now has never had such an uncorseted exposition, doubtless because Mr Brando was here his own director.' *Time Magazine*'s anonymous reviewer was another who thought – astonishingly, in my opinion – that Brando had played this role endlessly before, though I find it easier to accept Hollis Alpert's view, in the *Saturday Review*, that the 'performance is fierce, moody and flamboyant by turns (and is basically a series of variations on the kind of acting he unveiled as Stanley Kowalski)'. Few critics regarded this as an exceptional Western, and Brando didn't help Paramount, either, by describing it as 'a potboiler'. Equally and typically perverse, he also said 'It is not an artistic success. I'm a businessman. I'm a captain of industry – nothing less than that. Any pretension I've sometimes had of being artistic is now just a long, chilly hope. *One-Eyed Jacks* is a product just like that – a news item. News makes money, not art. Movies are not art.'

It was touch and go whether this news item would make money. At the box-office it performed respectfully but not outstandingly – and that was what was needed for Paramount to get a return on its investment. The domestic gross of $4,300,000 needed to be at least twice that before the red ink in the ledgers disappeared. It did quite well abroad and, via eventual television sales, earned back its cost. Although Brando's debut as a director was decreed promising (it was more than that) it is a fair bet that he was never asked to direct again. Little more was heard of Pennebaker and his plans to produce, as if, having given birth to a monster, the effort had depleted him for life. On the other hand, his much-publicized self-indulgence on another film would make his antics on this one look like small potatoes.

Between the two came a smaller-scale film which was released before *One-Eyed Jacks*. This was *The Fugitive Kind*, with Pennebaker partnering Martin Jurow and Richard A. Shepherd in a venture which United Artists would distribute – the film of a play by Tennessee Williams. It had started out as 'Battle of Angels', his first full-length play; after a disastrous out-of-town opening, it had been abandoned – by all except Williams, who was wont to re-work material. The new version, much changed, was called 'Orpheus Descending', and the leading roles were fashioned with Brando and Anna Magnani in mind. Williams rewrote it at least twice when Brando complained that his role was unplayable . . . but he thought, in any case, that 'she would wipe me off the stage'. Directed by Harold Clurman, the play was done on Broadway with Maureen Stapleton and Cliff Robertson, but a run of only two months did not seem to presage Hollywood interest. Jurow, however, had been Magnani's agent and knew that she wished to make another American film – partly because the first, *The Rose Tattoo* (based on a play by Williams), had been a huge success and the second, *Wild Is the Wind*, a great failure. A third might indicate whether she had a future on that side of the Atlantic, and this particular venture had a co-starring part for Anthony Franciosa, who was her lover both in *Wild Is the Wind* and in life. Williams continued to dicker with the material, and Meade Roberts was brought in to write the screenplay, now called *The Fugitive Kind*. It was to be directed by Sidney Lumet, who had established a reliable talent since coming from television two years earlier.

Brando needed money: his resources had been depleted by Pennebaker and Kashfi both, and since the role had been his before it had been Franciosa's Jay Kanter advised the producers that he was prepared to discuss it. He was also prepared to discuss a salary of $1 million, although that seems to have been the idea of the producers, who thought they were getting better value with Brando than 20th Century-Fox was getting with Elizabeth Taylor* (for *Cleopatra*). Brando said yes with alacrity (temporarily abandoning the editing of *One-Eyed Jacks*) and the signora does not seem to have minded. That was where the trouble started. She dropped Franciosa and then was disconcerted to find that Brando did not wish to take his place in her life.

Williams commented that the stars 'engaged in a clash of egos never again equalled'. Quite early in the proceedings she made clear her fury that Brando was getting top billing, even in Italy. Lumet wanted to rehearse, but she thought that that would dissipate her spontaneity – and that was in increasingly short supply as Brando found his way into the role in take after take. She accused him of distracting her on the set, of speaking his lines slowly when he should have been speaking fast and vice-versa. But Lumet told *The New York Times*: 'I thought Marlon was brilliant in that movie. His scenes with Joanne Woodward contained some of the best acting he's ever done. But it's no secret that Anna Magnani was a problem; she had arrived at a sad state in her life and none of us could help her. That great talent had a great problem, and it was vanity. Suddenly, she was worried about the way she looked. The whole staging had to be shifted, and there were things Anna literally refused to do. But Marlon was Herculean – very giving – and yet he bore the brunt of the blame.' On another occasion Lumet said that she loathed acting in English and the more emotional she became the heavier her accent: eventually she had to re-record at least 50 per cent of her dialogue.

* Taylor's salary for *Cleopatra*, announced a few months earlier, in November 1958, made headlines because it was the first million dollar salary. It was also pure hype. It was only $125,000 for 16 weeks' work, but it did carry a percentage and expenses, plus $50,000 for every week it went over schedule. Since it did, considerably – and partly because of her shenanigans – she did eventually earn well over $1 million.

Lumet – who as a young actor had replaced Brando in *A Flag is Born* – enjoyed working with him: 'He's extraordinarily knowledgeable about his own instrument. And like all people who are, he therefore knows that his talent and ability have to be put into place. Marlon works in a fascinating way, by a process of elimination, constantly questioning why a point couldn't be made this way or that way. Primarily what he's doing is eliminating any other possibility of how to commit himself, it's thrilling to watch it. And it's thrilling to argue with him, and help him to channel that extraordinary motor into the place that the script demands.' He did not say that at the outset Brando tested him as he had tested Logan, by acting against the meaning of the text. Lumet passed the test.

Miss Woodward, in the third leading role, did not agree with Lumet: 'I hated working with Marlon Brando – because he was *not* there, he was somewhere else. There was nothing to reach on to.' She liked neither his performance nor Magnani's – and 'I wasn't awfully crazy about my performance.' She was judging these from a rough cut, which she left abruptly after bursting into tears. She has never been able to bring herself to watch the finished film. She has missed therefore one of the better films based on Williams's material, but as far as Brando is concerned no one can blame him for being wary of it.

His role was that of a drifter, Val Xavier, a strolling guitarist who had been run out of every town he'd ever played in. He lands in a Mississippi town called Two Rivers, and gets a job in the general store, run by Lady Torrance (Magnani). He settles down, and they fall in love, a matter suspected by the husband dying of cancer upstairs. Val is simultaneously sought by Carol Cutrere (Woodward), of the town's first family, but because of dipso and nympho tendencies as much of an outcast as he. The husband, Jeb, learns that Lady is pregnant by Val, and he sets fire to the confectionery parlour she and Val had built.

She shoots Jeb and he dies; and the sheriff and the towns-folk drive Val into the fire with the hosepipes. Later, in the ashes, Carol finds his snakeskin jacket.

It began, strikingly, with Brando listening insolently to his enemies, heard but unseen. His power in this prologue pervades the subsequent events, imbuing the character with something more than Williams had written into it – the quintessential Williams hero nevertheless, glowering, idealistic-disillusioned, oddly quixotic, possibly bisexual. Brando's excellence was equalled by Magnani, Miss Wood-ward and Miss Stapleton (now playing the sheriff's wife), three others not conforming to the standards of bigoted society, pitilessly mouldering. The conclusion, however, was not positive: Williams still hadn't got the thing right.

The peripheries of the tale are as over-heated as its centre, but, like most of Williams's work, it is not as absurd as its outline. His stuff is not easy to film: the melodramatic essentials, the sexual exoticism, the poetic yearnings must be rendered exactly and appropriately. Kazan had succeeded twice, compellingly (*Streetcar* and *Baby Doll*), but other directors, before and after *The Fugitive Kind*, either over-heightened Williams or steel-filed him down. John Huston was to find the right approach with *The Night of the Iguana*, and Lumet found it here: the exact boldness, the exact black-and-whiteness. Both judged the extents to which the photographer (here, Boris Kaufman) could load the screen and the players the dialogue. It may be a matter of chance: Lumet's direction was effusive, with too many hints, ends dangling, and the evil of the play now merely implied; but the effect was of some modern myth, its curling edges unfamiliar. It had not been filmed, incidentally, near the Mississippi, but in Milton, near Poughkeepsie in New York state, given a little clever art direction. The public was not comfortable with the film; the reviews and attendance were on the poor side of modest. Producer Shep-herd later said that United Artists got huge advances from exhibitors on the strength of it being 'a Marlon Brando-Tennessee Williams package' but there was no further income. (Ten years later Lumet returned to Williams and with a screenplay by Gore Vidal filmed his drama, 'The Seven Descents of Myrtle', even more successfully, in my opinion, given that the material is even more lurid, even more intractable; the stars were James Coburn and Lyn Redgrave; whether under the title *The Last of the Mobile Hotshots* or *Blood Kin*, it was an even bigger box-office disaster than *The Fugitive Kind*.)

The failure could, of course, be rationalized. *The Fugitive Kind* had been in standard screen ratio and black and white. The public was having enough of that in the living room; it had certainly turned out to see Brando in splashy Technicolor wide-screen spectacles. Yes, MGM had heard of Brando's antics on the set of *One-Eyed Jacks*, but talent – especially of that order – was a law unto itself. He would be granted artistic control over another multi-million dollar epic, a refloating of the Bounty, the studio's old warhorse of 1935.

The original *Mutiny on the Bounty* had won an Oscar for the Best Picture way back then, and had been enormously popular; there had been a number of reissues. The decision to remake it – at the suggestion of director John Sturges – in Technicolor and wide-screen was taken from necessity rather than zeal (if either quality is at a premium in Hollywood): MGM needed a box-office blockbuster. In 1950 when the studio's finances were foundering, they had thought back to their big success of the early Talkie era, a jungle adventure called *Trader Horn*: they had not remade it, but they had made something very much like it, *King Solomon's Mines*. In 1958, another bad financial year, studio executives had noted the money pouring into Paramount as a result of its remake of a Silent success, *The Ten Commandments*: MGM followed suit, and the new *Ben Hur* wiped out the studio's deficit. A record eleven Oscars helped re-establish Metro's old image as the mightiest of the studios, and though the revenues from *Ben Hur* were still healthy in 1960, there was an understandable urge to see whether lightning would strike twice. To an extent the studio's future was at stake, for it had been saved on several occasions only by a reissue of *Gone With the Wind*. *Ben Hur* would seem to have the same reissue potential, but there was little or none in the old black and white library (the studios had started hiring these out to the rival television; no one foresaw that one day new or newish films would be shown in that medium); it would be as well to have a third guarantee against insolvency if again times were hard, and thus a second sortie of the Bounty mutineers was decided upon. The production was assigned to Aaron Rosenberg, despite the fact that the first two films he had made for the company had flopped; prior to that he had had ten successful years at Universal, where a number of large-scale Westerns had given him the sort of experience to get the Bounty to the South Seas and back. In fact, he was to have produced MGM's co-production venture with Cinerama, *How the West Was Won*, but there were second thoughts on that; he threatened to sue, and was offered HMS Bounty instead. The budget was eventually set at the dangerously high $10 million, but for that audiences would be getting an extended tour of Polynesia – and throughout the 50s Cinerama's giant travelogues had run for years in those cinemas equipped to use that process. They had begun tiring of them, but this time the sweeping panoramic views would be accompanied by a tried and true tale, plus a major star or so.

On the principle that for the biggest pictures you get the biggest stars, however unlikely, Brando was approached – again, the idea was that of Sturges – to play either Clark Gable's old role, that of Fletcher Christian, leader of the mutineers, or that of Charles Laughton, the villainous and wronged Captain Bligh. He turned down both suggestions (unlike Laughton, Olivier, Bette Davis and the other few movie-stars working in traditional actors' fashion, he was not really interested in playing a real villain), and he refused the film again when he read Eric Ambler's script. Each time MGM cajoled him, their terms became more generous; in their anxiety to get him, they promised him a good proportion of the earth, if not the moon. He eventually indicated that he was not much interested in the voyage of the Bounty, but he was drawn to the fate of the survivors on Pitcairn Island. He had re-read the original novel by Nordhoff and Hall, and was fascinated to learn that the mutineers, instead of finding happiness in their Pacific paradise, had killed each other off. In his own words, the mutineers 'had one moment of glory, when they rose up and conquered tyranny' and yet what happened 'presented a microcosm of man's situation throughout history: the struggle of black versus white, of the urge to create and the urge to destroy. If man cannot find happiness on an island paradise, where can he find it?'

Rosenberg, in his own words, 'made a deal agreeing to give him consultation rights on that [the last] part of the picture'. Brando's salary would be $500,000 against ten per cent of the gross, plus $5,000 a day overtime if shooting went over schedule. Brando agreed that the subject required a British director, and approved Carol Reed on the strength of such films as *The Fallen Idol* and *The Third Man*. (When he first met Reed he showed less interest in this project than in making a film on Caryl Chessman, the rapist who after innumerable stays of execution had recently gone to the gas chamber in San Quentin; Brando was one of many to spend the all-night vigil outside the prison that night, when a reprieve was expected in the name of humanity.) Whether or not Reed chose Trevor Howard to be Captain Bligh isn't known, but Reed had already directed Howard several times and knew his range – recognized in Hollywood after many American-backed films of little consequence because of an Oscar nomination for *Sons and Lovers*. It was Reed, anyway, who telephoned him from Los Angeles to offer him the part.

Filming was due to begin in Tahiti in October 1961. One of the first priorities was to find a local girl to play Fletcher Christian's romantic interest. Many were tested, and a nineteen-year-old hotel-worker was selected, to be called Tarita simply on the film's credits. She particularly pleased Brando, who in real life duplicated their on-screen relationship. The replica of the Bounty, due to arrive from Nova Scotia in September, did not turn up – partly due to two fires on board – till December, by which time Reed had shot most of the scenes which didn't need it. More permanently absent was a finished script: the one Ambler had written had been reworked by Borden Chase and William L. Driscoll – and though the final credit went to Charles Lederer, many other hands had been at work. And that, in this case, was where the trouble seems to have started. Without a final script, Reed considered it his pre-rogative to avoid filming those scenes which showed Bligh in a much more favourable – i.e., to 60s sensibilities – light than the 1935 version. And that was a view, given the old film's success, adhered to by the MGM brass back in Hollywood. Brando, without a final script, was having second, third and fourth thoughts about the in-terpretation of Fletcher Christian – which led to Howard and Richard Harris, in the third lead, having to re-play scenes with him which in most cases they thought bore no relation to what had happened before and what would ensue in the next scene. About the time the Bounty finally hove into view, Brando decided that he wanted to switch roles and play the botanist (in which role Richard Haydn was cast) – though this has been denied. Relations between Brando and the rest of the cast began to deteriorate. Howard, a consummate professional, found it difficult to work with an actor who was wearing ear-plugs so that his

concentration would not be impaired – so that he sometimes did not know when the scene was over. According
to Howard's biographer, Vivienne Knight, 'when he
[Brando] did appear for work he lost his lines and would
mumble his way through an unheard number of takes. He
even resorted to having his lines written on pieces of paper
which were attached to the costumes of the actors with
whom he was playing a reverse shot.'

Throughout all the dissension Reed drew on twenty
years' experience of directing major talents: that is, he kept
calm and cool-headed. But he had begun to dislike both
Brando's interpretation of Christian and that in the script,
also evolving, of Captain Bligh. He wanted to resign but
was sacked instead, in February 1961, after MGM had
recalled the whole unit to Culver City because the rainy
season rendered shooting on location unfeasible (and that
is another in the chain of mistakes made on this film, for
no one had given much credence to the Tahitians' claim
that this is what would have happened). Reed was also ill
with gallstones, but it was Rosenberg's expressed opinion
that his progress on this film was such that shooting would
drag on interminably. Little, as they say, did he know. A
successor was found in Lewis Milestone, who had made
some fine films, and many bad ones, since the one for
which he would always be esteemed, *All Quiet on the Western Front* in 1930.

Because of that film, and its pacifist sympathies, Brando
was pleased to be working with him. Reports differ as to
whether Brando was pro-, con-, or neutral about Reed's
leaving, but it was soon apparent that Milestone and
Brando had opposing ideas about the relative importance
of star and director. Milestone believed that a director
directed and an actor took orders; he was not disposed
towards Brando's technique, which was to get, well, into
the right mood. By the time they returned to Tahiti, at the
end of March, their confidence in each other was diminish-

ing. Brando had become convinced that he was making yet another film of which he would be thoroughly ashamed. He firmly believed that its success or failure depended entirely on him – and given Howard's skill and eminence (in relation to the contributions of Gable and Laughton to the original film), I'm sure he was right – at least from the point of view of the American box-office. Milestone did not think so, perhaps because of his record – which he is unlikely to have regarded as being as qualified as it was. Shooting continued under conditions which made Reed's tenure seem like a pussy cat's picnic. In 'The Celluloid Muse' Milestone spoke of the experience: 'I felt it would be quite an easy assignment because they'd been on it for months and there surely couldn't be much more to do. To my dismay, I discovered that all they'd done was a seven-minute scene just before they land in Papeete ... Brando swears that he had nothing to do with Carol Reed's departure; that was a matter between Reed and the producer ... During my first two weeks on the film Brando behaved himself and I got a lot of stuff done – especially with sequences like the arrival in Tahiti, when I could work with the British actors. I got on beautifully with Trevor Howard, Richard Harris, and the others; they were real human beings, and I had a lot of fun.

'Then the trouble started. I would say that what went basically wrong with *Mutiny on the Bounty* was that the producer made a number of promises which he subsequently couldn't keep. It was an impossible situation because, right or wrong, the man simply took charge of everything. You had the option of sitting and watching him or turning your back on him. Neither the producers nor I could do anything about it.

'Charlie Lederer wrote the script from day to day. He would bring it on the set in the morning, then they would go into Marlon Brando's dressing room and lock themselves up there till lunchtime ...

'After lunch, they came out. By then it was about two-thirty and we hadn't shot a scene. You had the option of shooting it, but since Marlon Brando was going to supervise it anyway, I waited until someone yelled "Camera!", and went off to sit down somewhere and read the paper.'

There were other hazards as shooting dragged on – illnesses and accidents (a canoe of Tahitian extras was dashed against the reef, with one man killed and many wounded), while the re-shooting of the local people welcoming the *Bounty* proved a nightmare as Milestone attempted to match the existing shots. The actor, already known as Never-on-Monday Brando after enjoying his weekly day off with the local population, might not appear till eleven, while the British cast waited in uncomfortable clothing in the tropical climate; he had demanded and got a speedboat to bring him to the location – and just two weeks from the end of shooting chose to move house (this was one of Milestone's beefs) at a cost to the company of $8,000. With actor and director not speaking, Brando went into endless debates with the writer and producer – when *he* wasn't in desperation doing Milestone's job, till his relationship with both also collapsed. Milestone reckoned that Brando's behaviour had 'cost the production at least $6 million', while right to the end Brando blamed all the troubles on the failure of MGM to provide a final, usable script. Whatever the nature of his conduct, he had been granted that control over the ending. It was his chance to send a message to humanity, and he was not going to let it go. According to Richard Harris one ending was shot in which he, Harris, died in a blazing boat. Brando refused to work until it had been abandoned; he explained to Harris, 'I'm the star and the star must have the best scenes.' An ending agreeable to all had not been shot when the unit left Tahiti for the second and last time in the summer. Deliberations on this matter continued till October, when Milestone finally decided that enough was enough. He walked away from the unfinished film, 'a bloody mess' in his own words, admittedly a quarter of a million dollars richer but convinced that he would never be offered work again. The production shut down – a whole year after shooting had commenced – and no one knew whether it was to start up again. There was no agreement on any of the endings written or shot: executives and editors shuffled what was available while film-makers of the calibre of Billy Wilder and Ben Hecht advised. Brando's intransigence on the matter was reckoned to have cost the production another $2 million, and he and Rosenberg were no longer on speaking terms – till, that is, July 1962, when Brando saw a rough-cut and observed that he liked it – except for the ending. Since the entire MGM brass was in agreement on that matter, Rosenberg gave instructions to film yet another ending, the twelfth, accepting Brando's offer to waive his $25,000 overtime fee for two weeks' shooting – though, on examination (see below) that was not as generous a gesture as it may have seemed. There was no question of Milestone returning, and Brando accepted as his substitute the writer-director George Seaton – whose conditions included the stipulation that his name was not connected with it.

Milestone might, in fairness, have acknowledged that Brando's methods were opposed to his own. Later, John Cassavetes said that when Brando was allegedly difficult it was because he was 'unsatisfied, often justifiably, with some aspect of the project he's on – the director, the script or whatever. But when those things are right, when people deal with him honestly, there's no one better – ask any actor.' Brando was not, after all, the first actor to subject the crew to his vagaries: in the late forties, for instance, at the height of their popularity, Bing Crosby disappeared to play golf, and Humphrey Bogart only filmed after lunch, using the morning for rehearsals and his jug of martinis; in the sixties, Gregory Peck liked only to film in the mornings. But none of these or other actors attracted the hostility that Brando did, which says much about his conduct. No one on the *Bounty* film had a good word to say for Brando, including Richard Harris: 'The whole picture was just a large dreadful nightmare for me, and I'd prefer to forget both as soon as my nerves recover from the ordeal.' Gordon Jackson, who had a supporting role, observed that Brando was one of those actors 'with a special kind of magic' but 'the film was hell. I was on it thirteen months, six in Tahiti, seven in Hollywood and in that time I think I said "Aye, aye, sir" twice.'

Trevor Howard once told me that he never discussed Brando, but years later he was frank with Clive Hirschorn: 'The problem on *Mutiny on the Bounty* was Brando. I think he took a positive delight in ruining the picture and almost bankrupting MGM. He didn't take to me at all – which was fine. What upset me was how unprofessional he was – never knowing his lines and having to read them off "idiot" cards, as we call them. I think I can honestly say that I've never met an actor who took so little pride in his work as Brando.' At the time he did tell *The Saturday Evening Post*, 'The man is unprofessional and absolutely ridiculous.'

The *Post* was in trouble. Its circulation was over 20 million but as less than a million of these were news-stand sales its owners, Curtis Publishing, had to chop down a number of trees for every issue: but these subscriptions had been gained at offering cut-rates, so the average cost of every copy was fourteen-and-a-half cents on a cover price of 25c. Consequently every issue of the magazine chalked up a huge loss, sustained by bank loans. Four full colour pages of advertising would have put it back into profit, and so the old cosy image was abandoned in search of a more dynamic image. An attack on Hollywood's golden boy provided a good start, and the assignment was offered to Bill Davidson, who was still smarting because Brando had 'killed' (as it was his right to do) a full-scale interview with him some years earlier. The *Post* article he titled 'The Mutiny of Marlon Brando' and Milestone's comment helped to provide the subtitle: 'Six Million Dollars Down the Drain'. Milestone provided much else in the piece, which neglected to find any good in Brando's conduct. The *Post* added an editorial, bracketing Brando with Elizabeth Taylor because of *Cleopatra*: 'For their separate but equally extravagant performances we think the two would be perfect castaways. Why not send them both to bountiful Tahiti, equip them with one movie camera apiece, an unlimited supply of film and an eternity in which to produce definitive and epic motion pictures of each other?'

Infinitely more than the Capote piece this would permanently damage Brando's career – and that at the box-office of the film, if audiences decided that its star was a public nuisance. The cost now stood at $20 million, twice the original estimate – and his original salary had been augmented by estimates varying from $750,000 to $1,250,000 (it was after the *Post* piece appeared that he agreed to do the new ending for nothing). Brando himself claimed the cost was $12 million: the inflated figure took into account overhead charges, including $500,000 for the story, owned outright by the company. The new head of M G M, Joseph Vogel, stated that the article was 'gravely unfair' – while at the same time soliciting information from Milestone which would enable them to take legal action against Brando (as 20th Century-Fox had done with Taylor, taking her off salary during production for alleged misconduct). Milestone would not oblige, but neither would he agree to testify on Brando's behalf if the latter took the case to court; he told him he would tell the truth. At the same time – October 1962 – Brando wrote Howard 'a long, long letter' describing his frustrations and suffering on the film, and his hurt at Howard's comment to the *Post*: Howard was apparently 'amazed' to receive it. In January the following year Brando sued Curtis Publishing for $5 million.

It was, alas, impossible to see the film without thinking of Brando's sulks. It turned out to be surprisingly good, but it never became the duel, the battle of giants required by the subject, a prolonged clash between hero and villain.

It starts well. Bligh (Trevor Howard) is a salty-looking man; it is his first captaincy, and he makes it clear that Christian (Brando) was not his first choice for First Officer. He refers to him as 'a career fop', and Christian irritates him by referring to their voyage as 'a grocery errand' – they're being sent to the South Seas by the West India Merchants to collect sprigs of breadfruit trees, with the idea of feeding the fruit to the slaves in the West Indies. Christian is a fop indeed, supercilious and smirking. Their first clash occurs when Mills (Richard Harris) is accused by a crew-mate of stealing cheese: Mills confesses that he acted at the captain's command, but Bligh refuses corroboration. He is a petty tyrant; he flinches when told that the men have a complaint, and when making absurd commands his look is furtive. He tries to go round the Horn to Tahiti, against advice, but is forced to turn back – Christian has countermanded his orders. The actual mutiny occurs because he has insisted on restricting the water supply (for the breadfruit plants), and put it, literally, out of reach. As a result, one man is keelhauled, another drops to his death from the water jug and another goes mad after drinking sea water. It is Christian's compassion in offering the man water which brings Bligh's wrath on him, and thus to blows.

It doesn't matter how much of this is based on fact: these are strong situations, and both Brando and Howard are outstanding actors. But just as the film's publicity played up Brando and part-ignored Howard, so does the film, and that is one of its weaknesses. Their best exchange is when Bligh observes that Christian is motivated by only one thing – contempt; and Christian replies that he tries not to let his private opinion conflict with his duty.

Howard is not so much fun as Laughton was, nor as loathsome, but his Bligh is much more a flesh-and-blood being, a blunt, instinctive navy man.

For Gable's straightforward hero, Brando offers a man of complexity. Despite the permanent sneer, he commands sympathy from the start – and that is partly because his parody of a British aristocrat accent is done with wit; it is excessive and amusing. During filming he and one English actor, playing a small role, were inseparable despite – it seemed to observers – having nothing in common. The actor was therefore hurt and astonished when Brando brutally rejected the suggestion that they meet again when shooting finished. Simon Callow in his book 'Being An Actor' cites this instance as a 'chilling' example of the ruthlessness of actors, 'for coming out of Fletcher Christian's mouth, is that hapless English actor's accent'.

But if Brando gets his inflections correct, the voice is too 'light'; it's rather the voice of a poseur. He finally gets gummed up when he has to say to the native girl, the King's daughter (Tarita): 'My name is Fletcher Christian.' He can't avoid it being ridiculous. After two hours you're so sick of the accent and the mannerisms that he thinks characterize the British aristocracy that you long for Clark Gable, so that even if they'd given Howard more footage they would never have been equals, eagles both; and as a silly man who becomes a hero under duress it is quite wrong for this particular film.

For what the film is, is spectacle. There is nothing wrong with an attempt at profundity, but Brando's earlier reluctant heroes were part of weightier events. The scenes at sea – billowing sails and scrubbed decks, seascapes and twilights – are infallible film material. The Polynesian islands are magnificently photographed, and as a roadshow spectacle the scenes of native dances, native rituals and native fishing are entirely apt; the screen throbs, and no matter that it's all extraneous to the plot. But when this *Mutiny* goes on the jungle princess kick, halfway through, it sags, earthbound and ghastly. For all I know, Christian was ordered back because the king's daughter had taken a fancy to him, but it rings false, reeking of pre-Griffith two-reelers. Indeed, apart from the mutiny itself, the second half strays into muddy waters. The Court of Enquiry which exonerated Bligh is disposed of in three minutes. Twenty minutes or more are allotted to the settling on Pitcairn – a superfluous business with Christian muttering: 'I put it to you, we shall never find contentment on this island.' In the ending used (and it was a compromise one; the first, Ambler's, couldn't have been worse), he proposes to sail back to face the music, but his men loyally burn the *Bounty*: after trying to recover his sextant, he dies from burns. It concludes in bathos, and although Brando was not, finally, responsible, it is probable that without his participation a more simple and appropriate ending might have been found. (In fact, Christian was murdered two years after landing on Pitcairn by a native he had brought from Tahiti: to have told this truth would presumably have meant either a racial slur or showing Christian in a bad light.)

Both the film and Brando's performance were favourably reviewed. Said Bosley Crowther in *The New York Times*: 'Where Trevor Howard puts wire and scrap-iron into the bulky, brutal character of Captain Bligh, making him really quite a fearful and unassailable martinet, Mr Brando puts tinsel and cold cream into Christian's oddly foppish frame,' but he goes on to find him 'truly electrifying' during the mutiny itself, and 'thoroughly reasoned and mature' in the aftermath. MGM's hopes rose but sank again as business dropped off: with a domestic take of only $7,400,000 (*Variety*'s figure; other sources claim $9 million) that was little enough for a much-publicized picture shown at reserved-seat prices. In financial terms it was the worst flop in MGM's history; and it had no re-issue potential.

The 1985 re-telling of the tale, *The Bounty*, did even more spectacularly badly, returning only $3,500,000 on a $25 million investment. It might have been predicted, since in the changed conditions most people knew the earlier two versions from frequent television showings. The story was so familiar that almost certainly it wouldn't have been remade had not David Lean wanted to, and in the event he left the project as costs rose – though they were finally much less than for the version he planned. Robert Bolt's script was retained, if pared down; and the New Zealander, Roger Donaldson directed. Of the three versions, it is the one to see. It has the strong homosexual undertones which Brando meant to imply, when Christian (Mel Gibson) takes advantage of the unspoken crush he knows Bligh (Anthony Hopkins) feels for him: wanting to be back midst the Polynesian pleasures and fearful of the voyage back round the Horn he pushes his luck too far. In a moment of blind panic, he defies Bligh and the mutiny is suddenly upon him. The fates of the two men have then to be dealt with in cinematic and dramatic form – and they are. It is a pity that Brando, Rosenberg, *et al.*, didn't have Mr Bolt to guide them.

10

The Decline Begins

There was a script around at the time by Robert Bolt which Brando might have done – and indeed was wanted for. Since *On the Waterfront*, Sam Spiegel had produced another Oscar winner, *The Bridge on the River Kwai*, directed by David Lean; they were now planning *Lawrence of Arabia*, with a screenplay by Bolt. Brando was endlessly wooed, but chose to do *Mutiny on the Bounty* instead. Lean wasn't sorry, for he considered that Brando had become a star performer, with everyone dancing attendance, which wasn't what Lean wanted. Spiegel told the press: 'When I made *On the Waterfront* with Marlon he was magnificent. Now he has become a tortured person and in turn a tortured actor. He no longer trusts himself or his psychiatrist and it is beginning to show in his work. He would have been impossible for Lawrence.' This seems ungracious, to say the least, since he had been announced for the role. It was taken by a young British actor, Peter O'Toole, whose film career accordingly took flight. The film itself enjoyed a popularity with critics and public which far exceeded anything Brando did in the next decade.

Fortunately for him, the reviews of *Mutiny on the Bounty* silenced some of his critics. There were many in the industry and the press who felt that he and Miss Taylor should be run out of Hollywood – along with Marilyn

Monroe, whose lateness caused hold-ups and finally cancellation of *Something's Gotta Give*. It would be some years again before the outside world heard of his being difficult on the set – but then, he had a lawsuit pending to prove that he wasn't. And if his career was in jeopardy he would have had sound advice from the good people at MCA – except that they were now quartered at Universal, which was where Brando now berthed, very quietly.

MCA had become the most powerful talent agency in the business, putting together deals to unite its clients; from there it was not too great a step to become a television producer, but the two interests were in conflict, according to the government's anti-trust laws. MCA was given the option of dropping its clients or its television shows, and it chose to keep the latter, as the more profitable. In 1962 MCA Television managed to acquire Universal Pictures, attempting to regain its old eminence after a decade of turning out run-of-the-mill action movies. Lew Wasserman, the former head of MCA, was now the production chief and Jay Kanter a senior executive. They had no difficulty in welcoming the talents of Pennebaker and acquiring from the company the rights to *The Ugly American*, the best-selling novel by William J. Lederer and Eugene Burdick which Brando and George Englund had purchased themselves for $100,000. The price paid is reputed to have included the assets of Pennebaker, estimated as worth a million dollars: though some sources say that the deal wasn't done till a year later, after Brando had made two films for Universal. Similarly it has been said that he did not sign a term-contract with Universal till after *The Ugly American*, but it would seem that that was the first of a five-picture deal for each of which he would get $270,000 against a percentage. At this stage it was to his advantage for the industry to see that his old colleagues had such faith in him that they wanted a long-term commitment – and for the industry to know that he was working harmoniously with an inexperienced director, Mr Englund.

1. The young Marlon Brando on his arrival in Hollywood

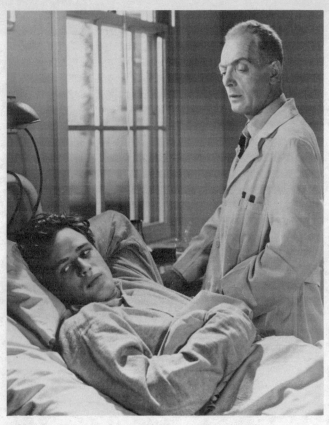

2. Brando's first film *The Men*: with Everett Sloan as the understanding doctor

3. *A Streetcar Named Desire*: the pose that launched a
thousand T-shirts

4. Pictured during a break in filming on the set of *Streetcar*: with Vivien Leigh and Kim Hunter. Vivien Leigh had pleasant memories of the filming, after initial suspicion she and Brando got on well

5. (*Inset*) *Viva Zapata!*
6. *Julius Caesar*: Brando as Mark Antony haranguing the crowd

7. *The Wild One*: a posed still of Brando and the girl,
Yvonne Doughty

8. and 9. *On the Waterfront*: still Brando's most famous performance and perhaps his most impressive. *Above* The girl is Eva Marie Saint who, like him, won an Oscar for her performance. *Below* Showing his parents around the film set

10. Marlon Brando as Napoleon in *Désirée*

11. (*Left*) Playing a Nazi officer in *The Young Lions*

12. (*Below*) Brando as Fletcher Christian in the infamous 1962 *Mutiny on the Bounty*

13. (*Above*) A scene from *Bedtime Story*, a romantic comedy starring Brando, David Niven and Shirley Jones
14. (*Below*) Disguised in *The Appaloosa*

15. Miscast in Chaplin's *A Countess from Hong Kong*, with Sophia Loren: 'it shouldn't have happened to anyone'

16. A magnificent performance in *Reflections in a Golden Eye*: Brando and Elizabeth Taylor – after she has whipped him in front of their guests. The film flopped in the US but was widely acclaimed in Britain

17. Renaissance! He won an Oscar for his portrayal of Don Vito Corleone in *The Godfather*, one of the most successful films ever made, but refused the award

18. In *Last Tango in Paris* in this scene with Catherine Allegret

19. Deliberate sabotage? Marlon Brando with Jack Nicholson in *The Missouri Breaks*

20. (*Above*) $3.7 million for
12 days work as Superman's
father

21. (*Right*) Another disguise
for *The Formula*, but the
film did not work

Englund – who directed only one further film, *Signpost to Murder* – does only a fair job on *The Ugly American*, managing some moments of alarm amidst the general inertia. To everyone's credit, it's on an important subject – and there were few enough of those to be experienced in the other movies released in 1963. Stewart Stern tries in his screenplay, but what no one can buck is the nature of the political arguments set forth. In some quarters, the film, like the book, was greeted as a hard-speared attack on American foreign policy – and it does provide a sweeping, if confused, indictment of American interference in South East Asia between the Korean and Vietnam wars. The level of argument is specious: it nestles around a journalist (Brando) chosen as ambassador because his wartime buddy Deong (Eiji Okada, a fine Japanese actor chosen on the strength of his performance in *Hiroshima, Mon Amour*) has become a nationalist leader, but who may or may not be a puppet of the Communists. The country is a fictitious one (though the locations were done in Thailand), a democracy under a king; a 'Freedom Road' is being built through the jungle to open out its natural resources. There is much bloodshed because the Communists – whether 'inspired' from China or Russia – wish to destabilize the area; and in the end the ambassador gives a press conference to explain that his good intentions and misreading of the situation are (it is implied) actually what constitute American policy in the area. All these years later, the movie industry is not too happy questioning America's involvement in the affairs of other countries, or – for this is the film's secondary theme – the struggle for influence of the US and Russia, one using money and the established government and the other arms and the malcontents who, usually with reason, dislike the way the country is being run.

Englund and Stern present these problems with the subtlety of soap opera, which may also be said of *Etat de*

Siège and *Missing*: but those films of Costa-Gavros are made with a passion which this torpid piece lacks. You are left with Brando's portrait of the ambassador, a decent but obstinate man, anxious to do good but going about it so naively as to bring about the destruction of his friend – and, of course, his own disillusionment. It was a new departure for him; he acquired a moustache for the role, and a pipe and spectacles, and was smoothly urbane – at least, in his public persona. In the scenes with his wife (Sandra Church) and Deong, he played it doubtful and dishevelled. It was a typically astute way of playing a public man, but when you see him here in tails and silk hat you are reminded of Cooper, Tracy, Gable and the other actors of the 30s who might regularly wear such togs. Brando in authority singularly lacks their humour, their sense of absurdity. Like his Fletcher Christian, it's showy on the surface, with nothing to get to grips with underneath.

The film was moderately successful, and the star's metamorphosis from noisy, temperamental star back to serious actor was duly noted. His performance gave further credence to the theory that he could play anything, and admirers were further heartened by the announcement that his next film would be a comedy, *Bedtime Story*, directed by Ralph Levy, from television, at Universal, with Pennebaker listed as one of the co-producers.

Universal had been turning out a series of vaguely salacious comedies with players like Doris Day, Rock Hudson and Tony Curtis. Both Day and Curtis had had scorching successes opposite the veteran Cary Grant – *That Touch of Mink* and *Operation Petticoat* respectively – and *Bedtime Story* was originally envisaged as a vehicle for Grant and Hudson: but when Brando intimated that he wanted to do a comedy Universal jettisoned Hudson. Grant declined the co-starring role. The name of Stanley Shapiro appeared on most of these movies as producer and/or writer, and he functioned on this one as both, sharing the screenplay credit with Paul Henning. It was somewhat more abrasive than the others, and it would have been better still if they'd speeded things up and done some pruning – notably in the sequence where David Niven explains that he robs for philanthropic reasons and we visit said reasons.

Niven was Brando's own choice for co-star, and has one of his best roles. They play con-men. Niven has class and works the Côte d'Azur, where the chickens to be plucked are wealthy American women who think he's an exiled prince needing funds for his people. Brando is an army corporal stationed in Germany, and his victims are fräuleins who think he is starving to pay for his grandmother's operation. It is only suggested that Niven beds his victims; Brando is cruder, and prepared to shed his uniform on any pretext. Demobbed, he meets Niven on a train, and fancies settling in his playground. Twice, Niven ships him out, till he learns too much and forces Niven into taking him into partnership. They continue to 'take' rich broads, with Niven posing as a prince till he's engaged to them, after which he introduces his idiot brother, Prince Ruprecht, who is Brando. They split, and for a while the piece zips along, cross and double-cross, as inventive as any of the thirties comedies on which it is modelled (there's a high point, believe it or not, when Niven crashes a whip down on Brando's supposedly paralysed legs); but then it goes slack and fizzles out, with Brando marrying an heiress who turns out to be a beauty queen (Shirley Jones).

The slapstick is similarly misjudged: Brando buried in the sand with a seagull on his head, Brando in a runaway wheelchair. Brando takes the script literally. Told he's crude by Niven, referred to by him as 'an uneducated, maladjusted army corporal' and by Niven's aide as 'an ape', his performance embodies each of these aspects, perhaps because he's too complete an actor to ignore them. His comedy technique, otherwise rudimentary, is at his best when he's being fastidious – giving his sad little spiel to his girlfriends, offering advice to the more experienced Niven. Niven is quicker and much more debonair, but it is a complementary performance: the script has made sure of that.

Brando's next commitment was at 20th Century-Fox, for Aaron Rosenberg, who had left MGM after *Mutiny on the Bounty*. As far as the studio was concerned, Brando was no longer the box-office star that he had been at the time of *Desirée* and *The Young Lions*, but it was still a coup to have him on the payroll. As far as Brando was concerned, he was delighted to work with Rosenberg again, since his suit against *The Saturday Evening Post* was to come to court. He suggested Trevor Howard for an important guest appearance, and agreed to the casting of Keith McConnell, who had also been in *Mutiny on the Bounty*. If he, Brando, had been such a bastard, why had these three people chosen to work with him again? The case was settled out of court – in Brando's favour, according to Howard's biographer, who says that only after agreeing to the picture did Howard realize that he was being used.

The title was *Morituri*, which had a screenplay by Daniel Taradash based on a novel by Werner Jörg Lüdecke, to be directed by Bernhard Wicki. Brando was finally working with one of the European directors he so much admired, but that wasn't why he was making the film. 'Sometimes I need the money,' he told an interviewer who visited the Catalina locations. 'It is like a car and the oil dipstick. You look at it once in a while, and find you need oil. Well, every so often I look at my financial condition and I find I need money, so I do a good-paying picture. You see, I have three households to support and I pay alimony to two women.'

This did not mean that Brando would be merely an employee. According to Taradash, there were endless script conferences at Brando's home, when he, Wicki and Rosenberg would invariably wait a couple of hours for the star to appear – and which would dissolve into a discussion of how Brando's character would react: 'His idea of rewriting was how would Marlon Brando act in the situation.' The rewriting continued on the set – done by Brando and his cronies, who included Wally Cox, playing the ship's doctor; also according to Taradash, 'Bernhard told me that Marlon went completely to pieces at the studio. At one stage, Marlon actually ordered Bernhard off the set.' A troubled shoot was not helped by some unexpected moves by the star so that he was within sight of his idiot boards. Nor by Mr Howard, who would shout gleefully whenever he had a sympathetic listener and much to the mortification of Brando and his entourage, 'It's like *Mutiny on the Bounty* all over again.' Since Howard had only one important scene (at the beginning) it had been written so that he would dominate it, but during filming Brando found some gramophone records and other props to fiddle with; some rewriting was done so that the scene no longer belonged to Howard, who didn't really seem to mind.

Brando was playing a German named Crain, a pacifist blackmailed by British Intelligence (in the person of Howard) into working for the Allies. Posing as a member of the Gestapo, he is to board a German cargo ship, and, in due time, disarm the scuttling charges so that, in evading capture, the captain can't sink it. (The Allies want the cargo – rubber.) Crain's adventures on board are considerable: the only real Nazi is the First Officer, whose help he has to enlist. The Captain (Yul Brynner) is anti-Nazi and therefore wary of Crain; two officers who board the ship – with a Jewish prisoner (Janet Margolin) – are suspicious and wire Gestapo headquarters.

This is a good cliff-hanging plot, tense enough, and, as melodrama, attractive enough; its statements on Nazism, if unremarkable, would be worth repeating any time. Brando's own prerequisite, that a movie be more than a mindless entertainment, was reasonably fulfilled; among didactic thrillers there were many more didactic and less thrilling – like another shipboard drama which came out in 1965, Stanley Kramer's *Ship of Fools*. I mention that, because *Morituri* was mauled by the press, and it seemed to me then, and since, a decent entertainment – worth a dozen *Ships of Fools*, which Mr Bosley Crowther of *The New York Times* listed as one of the ten best pictures of the year. There are fashions in these things, and neither Brando nor the director were in vogue. Wicki had been much praised for *Die Brücke* when it was shown in the States in 1961, but he collected no roses when he directed *The Visit* for Fox in 1964 – though it had seemed to me that he had done a good job on that against almost insurmountable odds. Similarly, he gave a raw edge to the placid movie conventions of *Morituri*, setting up a conviction where the dialogue provided none. He was inestimably aided by Brando: with little character to work on, he again did an excellent German accent and conveyed with ease the tensions of the saboteur. The initial reaction was so poor that Fox hurriedly retitled it *The Saboteur, Code Name 'Morituri'*, but it still didn't do much business.

For his next role, Brando returned to Sam Spiegel. Spiegel's productions were not, or were not intended to be, mindless. He tended to like class subjects, usually with a literary flavour – this was his first production since *Lawrence of Arabia*. He also made a habit of using praised and/or expensive talents. His first choice for the male lead was his Lawrence, Peter O'Toole, who was under contract to him – and he threatened to sue when O'Toole didn't see himself in the role of a Texas sheriff. His second choice was Robert Redford, who preferred the smaller role of the convict. His director was Arthur Penn, from television and Broadway, at that stage the veteran of only three films, the critically-admired *The Left-Handed Gun* and *The Miracle Worker*, and one flop, *Mickey One*. Penn's later work – which would include *Bonnie and Clyde* – shows him to be the best director Brando worked with since Mankiewicz and Lumet. Penn found the experience rewarding: 'But there were some scenes that Marlon Brando improvised that were quite remarkable. It's a shame we can't see them, and run the two versions side by side. You'd be amazed! The scenes are the same as in the released film, only he would do them in a most extraordinary way. Changing the dialogue, perhaps . . . It was, though, an experience I never had before. Clearly, I was watching the best actor I had ever seen in my life!'

Perhaps it was because he improvised that the credited screenwriter, Lillian Hellman – working from a play and novel by Horton Foote, best known for *The Trip to Bountiful* – asked for her name to be removed. However, there is no question that they all regarded it as something more than roaring melodrama. It is of the species small town drama, Southern variety. At first you think of King's Row, but later descend to Peyton Place, with the expected cross-section, and how they react to the news that Bubber Reeves (Robert Redford) has broken jail. Most affected is his wife, Anna (Jane Fonda), who's having an affair with his friend Jake (James Fox). Jake is the son of Val Rogers (E. G. Marshall), and Val is Mr Big around these parts. He's the bank manager and its owner, he builds the hospital, he appointed the sheriff (Brando). He doesn't know about Jake and Anna, but he knows that Jake doesn't like him ('Jake! Stop running away from me'). Then there are the two vice-presidents: Damon Fuller (Richard Bradford) and Edwin Stewart (Robert Duvall). Damon has curly grey hair, and he's smooth, man, smooth; he's having an affair with Edwin's trampy wife (Janice Rule), while his own (Martha Hyer) gets sodden with alcohol.

Bubber, meanwhile, has reached town and is hiding in a used-car lot. He sends his friend Lester (Joel Fluellen) with a message to Anna, but Lester is black, and when he's found lurking near her room, Damon and two equally drunken cronies want to lynch him. The sheriff takes Lester into jail for safe-keeping, while he waits for Jake and Anna to bring Bubber in for a fair hearing; but Val wants Jake back with him, and to get him he has to get from Lester where Bubber is. He tries to bribe him, and then beats him up – while Damon and buddies are beating up the sheriff. Val rushes to the dump, followed by Damon and cronies, the bloody sheriff and the whole town. Hooligans throw flames into the dump; someone spills a petrol-tank. The sheriff saves Bubber from the mob – but he's shot the next morning on the steps of the jail. The sheriff and his wife (Angie Dickenson) drive away to a new life, and, we trust, a more wholesome environment.

Movies about small-town corruption have been around since we were all in short trousers, but the trouble with this one is that it's small-minded; it lays blame all round (even on Bubber's mother, for making him what he is). It never suggests causes or reasons – but then, these movies never do. Val, the man who can 'buy' everyone, is only pretending to be the villain; as for Damon and his cronies, they're just small and mean, hating niggers and beating up the sheriff. They're drunk, too; and one of the best things about this movie is its implicit picture of a boozy Saturday night. You'd have to go back, coincidentally, to *The Wild One*, for a like cinema portrait of booze, boredom and heat.

Penn handles the glimpses of parties and bars well, and the mob in action – the climax at the dump – is excitingly done; but the film never comes to life. It's one of the three interesting Brando films of the sixties, but it's a far cry, even, from *On the Waterfront*. It's always a movie, looking like other movies; you'd swear the town had been standing on the back-lot since vacated by the Hardy family. The actresses are always that; and there is a middle-aged couple (Henry Hull and Jocelyn Brando) who walk the streets, commenting like a Greek chorus, and they're ludicrous.

Then there's the script (no wonder Miss Hellman repudiated it). The relationship of the father and son is so hackneyed as to be laughable. *The Chase* offers a footling analysis of the difficulties of the South, but once you're into lynching and like matters (the murder on the jail steps is even more serious) you can't without great skill remain within the conventions of melodrama. It might have been more convincing without the constant over-emphasis – of which the beating-up of the sheriff is the worst example. It's an unlikely happening, even if Damon and company hope the Big Man will protect them; and only in a movie could Brando be so blood-boltered and still walk.

He was not the first or last actor to make a speciality of screen suffering (Gary Cooper suffered severe rigours in most of his serious films of the fifties), but when it's as gratuitous as here some speculation is inevitable. As he's beaten to a pulp, you wonder whether he's not attempting allegory (not the least of which might be an actor's persecution by his following); it's difficult, otherwise, to understand what attracted him to the role. He's not too interesting in it, as if he was marking time now that he had turned into middle-age, too old for heroes and rebels, too young for character parts – yet he has always been a character actor. This role could have been played by any no-longer-young star, by William Holden or Gregory Peck, and he relies for the most part on the personality tricks which are their stock in trade. He does, however, make the sort of gestures they would never think of – examining at length the palm of his hand, running his pipe across his forehead; and he does in the end manage a portrait the way they never could – a prickly, awkward man, somewhat tainted by corruption (Rogers got him appointed) and uneasy about it. What integrity is left surfaces at the end, but meanwhile he's disenchanted not only with the town but with his wife. He's tired, a little dandyish, and given to violent outbursts. The film is packed with fine actors, and he dominates it.

American critics who hadn't seen through *Ship of Fools* (there are other examples, but why get depressed thinking of them?) saw through *The Chase*, and it did little better elsewhere. Brando realized that he needed a good film to regain his ascendency, for he shortened the odds, and for the next three years made two films a year – the first time he had worked as intensively since 1953. His second film in 1966 was *The Appaloosa*, and there is little to say about it.

It was made at Universal, and directed by Sidney J. Furie, a Canadian-born director who had arrived in Hollywood after a career in Britain and one big success (*The Ipcress File*). They didn't get on. Furie said: 'He's disorganized. No discipline at all. A procrastinator. One little scene that should have taken us a few hours to film took ten days. Every day he had another complaint – his tummy ached, his head ached – you should have heard the moans. What a performance! Then he'd be searching for his lines. Anything to procrastinate.' Years later the two men met in London and Brando apologized by saying, 'It takes me a long time to get to know people. I thought you were a phony, a liar, a dirty double-crosser. I discovered you've got the great visual sense of the good directors.' He suggested doing another film together: I do not know what Furie replied, but behind his back he said, 'Never!'

Brando's quarrels with Furie were the first outside indications of professional discord since *Mutiny on the Bounty* (he had got on notably well with Arthur Penn), and if it's of interest at all, it's because the film was a common or garden horse-opera, the sort of thing you'd imagine they'd saunter through. *Time* magazine made just that point: instead, their critic pointed out, 'Brando handicaps himself with a fiercely concentrated acting style more suitable for great occasions. He seems determined to play not just a man but a whole concept of humanity.'

Such ambitions have their rewards. Brando's brooding power brought something, an extra dimension to this tale of a loner set on revenge. With a Mexican accent and poncho, he played the Mexican-American who is constantly harassed and humiliated by a bandit general (John Saxon); when the bandit steals his horse – the appaloosa of the title – he sets out to even scores; at the climax, single-handedly, he takes on the whole gang. Even if there were echoes of earlier Brando films and performances, and even if this was, again, a role a fair number of Hollywood actors could play, he was able to create a tension which ran rings round his contemporaries. He was 'heavy' enough to fit into Mr Furie's grandiloquent designs, and into the beautifully photographed, autumnal, border country, in itself impressive enough to require a big actor for counterbalance.

The reviews were carping. The film had pretensions above its station, but the combination of Brando's presence and a strong plot made for a good entertainment movie – and Universal sold it that way. To most people it was just another movie, and the time for 'just another movie' was passing. The title wasn't helpful. In Britain they changed it to *South West to Sonora*, which was hardly more appealing. We were – for the first time in years – already anticipating his next film.

It promised to be a film *hors serie* – for it was written and directed by the one creative film-maker to whom few then would deny the word genius: Charles Chaplin. Chaplin had left the United States in 1952, just after he had finished *Limelight*; he was persona non grata with the State Department, and, for equally foolish reasons, with most sections of the industry. He had made one film in the interim, in Britain, *A King in New York*, in 1957; it was made without the usual industry backing, and Chaplin wouldn't permit it to be shown in the US. In 1966, the industry decided to make up with Chaplin and atone for the years of neglect.

A year earlier Chaplin had seen Sophia Loren in *Ieri*,

Oggi e Domani. As a result he dusted off a screenplay he had written thirty years earlier as a vehicle for his then-wife Paulette Goddard* and Gary Cooper. He took it to Jerome Epstein, with whom his sons had worked in Los Angeles, and Epstein became the film's official producer. They had a script for the woman regarded as the most beautiful in films; they might as well try for the best actor. In 1957 in an interview Chaplin had been asked which contemporary actors he admired, and he had floundered, 'There is one young actor . . . he played in – what was that film? – something to do with a streetcar. M . . . M . . . Marlon Brando. I saw him in a film about paraplegics and there was a moment in that when he'd been given some bad news. I watched the way he handled that scene and I thought this man has something.' Epstein knew that Brando's friend Jay Kanter had become the head of Universal's producing team in Britain – where the piece would have to be filmed, since Chaplin had no intention of returning to America. Universal announced with pride that one of its British films, *A Countess from Hong Kong*, would be the product of the world-famous and ageing prodigal son. He was being given that complete authority that he had enjoyed, since 1920, as his own boss, and carte blanche in the matter of leading players. Loren and Brando accepted without reading the script; according to her, 'Brando was half-asleep, or pretended to be' during their first meeting with Chaplin.

Filming did not go well. 'In all fairness,' says Miss Loren in her autobiography, 'he was certainly not suited to the role . . . uncomfortable in it, he gave up on it soon after we started. He didn't feel right in it, and to make matters worse, he and Charlie didn't get along. There was no chemistry between them, no interplay, no carefree clim-

---

* Although she was accepted throughout Hollywood as his wife, after a reputed wedding at sea, it was later reported that the ceremony apparently had never taken place.

ate to encourage the inspiration and invention that comedy needs; they knocked heads, and day by day the atmosphere on the set grew worse.' Chaplin insisted on acting out every gesture. Sympathising with Brando was Gloria Swanson, a survivor of Chaplin's own era; after visiting the set one day she reported, 'You see why actors find him difficult. This is a simple scene and he's making much ado about nothing.'

Brando himself thought he was going 'raving mad': 'I was wanting to go to Charlie and say "I'm afraid we've made a horrible mistake".' He buckled under, and meekly took instructions, until he realized, perhaps, just how bad the film was going to be. In an effort to salvage something, he began to question some of Chaplin's commands, and shooting finished in hostile compromise. Chaplin later spoke disparagingly of him, but made no reference to his inability to learn lines. The publicity was so intense that gossip about the differences between them was rife: but many a good movie had been forged in mutual dislike.

The film's opening, in London, in January 1967, amidst more publicity, continued its so far triumphal progress in the world's press – till the truth was revealed in all its painful nakedness: the film was a bomb. The critics had only themselves to blame: whatever Chaplin's powers as a young man, *Limelight* in 1952 had been proof enough that they were failing – but you wouldn't have known it from reading the reviews. The Chaplin myth was upheld, through *A King in New York* in 1957, further, awful proof of a declining talent; and if the critics refused to reveal the truth, it is hardly likely that Chaplin himself was aware of it. But the industry is cautious: did any of Universal's executives take the trouble to see either film? – and if any of them read the script of this one, why didn't the shareholders sue for criminal negligence?

One might speculate – anything to postpone a discussion of the film itself. A sentence or two will suffice: we will console ourselves with Miss Loren's beauty, and let it return, hopefully, to oblivion. It must have been old hat when Chaplin first thought it up – a stale comedy set in that playground of countless old movies, the ocean liner. Miss Loren was a White Russian countess of doubtful past who stows away in Brando's cabin; he was a wealthy diplomat who compassionately hides her, despite the fact that he has an important new ambassadorial post and is planning a reconciliation with his wife (Tippi Hedren). The dialogue was compounded of platitudes ('At this moment I'm very happy. That's all we can ask for') and archaisms ('You're just a common harlot'); wheezes included Miss Loren hiding in various cupboards and Brando scampering around without his trousers. There were jokes about seasickness and a rough-and-tumble climax in which Miss Loren, now loved by Brando, has to marry his compliant valet (Patrick Cargill). The stars caved in under the monotonous tread of the direction. Neither is a natural comedian, but Miss Loren was willing and high-spirited. Brando, having failed to find any humour in the script, played it straight; he's tried to give the man a character, or at least a distinctive way of walking, sitting, moving about, without finding any charm. Not surprisingly, they've both wilted long before the end of the picture, but they remain amiable towards each other and the audience. Their good will was not reciprocated.

At first the public refused to believe the critics. It was one of those films which starts the week well but is playing to empty houses by Saturday. By all accounts, Chaplin by this time believed that he was the only important filmmaker in the whole world: so he was incensed by the reviews, unprecedented in his long career. The critics, he said, were 'bloody idiots'. He was prevailed upon to cut twelve minutes (from 120 to 108 minutes, including almost all his own footage, in a cameo as an old steward), but it fared equally badly in the United States.

11

Off Screen and One Very Good Film

Two or three years earlier, Sophia Loren had talked of her first meeting with Brando: 'Shortly after I arrived in Hollywood Marlon Brando decided to introduce himself to me. He just walked into my dressing-room and prowled around, staring carefully at each of a number of original paintings which I had hung on the walls. After a long pause he turned and looked at me and sadly shook his head. "You're sick," he told me. "Emotionally disturbed." I asked him what made him think so. "Tell me," he said, "did you choose these paintings yourself?" "Yes, but what has that got to do with my being sick?" "Everything," Brando said. "The mere fact that you picked those particular ones clearly shows your state of mind. You know something? You're suffering. Deep down you have a secret emotional wound." "Well, never mind," I told him. "At least, I keep it secret. What a pity more people don't do the same."'

Brando's off-screen behaviour, ignored or overlooked during the late fifties, got more press coverage than his films in the years after *Mutiny on the Bounty*, soon revealed as the watershed of his career. He was just another movie-actor, involved with battles with his ex-wife over the custody of their child; involved in various romances which, to be sure, he didn't want publicized; and involved with political and humanitarian causes in the name of Civil Rights. His conduct, in fact, made him an object of derision to what later became known as the Silent Majority, and a subject of interest or indifference to the more radically-minded.

The custody battles, and Brando's appearances in court, were clearly an embarrassment to him – as were interviews given by Miss Kashfi, and occasional articles by-lined by her, including 'Marlon Brando Is Out to Destroy Me – and He Will' (published in *Photoplay* at a time when he had temporary custody of the boy). In 1963 he went on the 'David Susskind Show' on television in an attempt to answer the riles of the gossip columns, and he said: 'I have two children growing up in this community and I think they deserve protection as do their mothers.' The custody trials lasted on and off for fourteen years, with accusations of physical violence, of kidnapping and of course unfit parenthood. Brando in court seems to have been what he sometimes wasn't on the film-set – a model of probity. He could be amusing, as when a judge spoke of his rumoured eccentricities and Brando asked whether these could be listed so that he would see what he could do about eradicating them.

It is not surprising that his other children have been so completely shielded from the press that accounts vary of their names, at least where his second marriage is concerned – and that is a matter no more straightforward than the first. He met Maria Castenada when he was making *Viva Zapata!* Reports differ as to whether she had a small role in the film (she isn't listed in the credits), but she was an actress – and as Movita had played Clark Gable's lady in the first *Mutiny on the Bounty*. As Movita Castenada she played another Polynesian in *The Hurricane*, returning to her native Mexico when the offers grew fewer. She was, however, back in Hollywood doing supporting roles in 1950, a handsome woman still in her early 30s; as merely

Movita again she had another in *Dream Wife*, made around the same time as he made *Julius Caesar* – at which time she left him, unhappy that he would not commit himself to marriage. They were married secretly in 1960, it was revealed during one of the custody battles with Kashfi; a son was born the following year called either Sergio or Michael or Meiko, and a daughter, Rebecca, six years later; but when the marriage was annulled in 1968, Brando declared that neither was his, which was strongly denied by their mother. As if he didn't have enough trouble publicly with the women he married, a Filipino dancer slapped a paternity suit on him in 1963. A blood test soon disposed of that, and Brando kept characteristically quiet about the rest of her revelations.

Tarita Teriipaia was only nineteen when she was cast opposite Brando in *Mutiny on the Bounty*. She never acted again, perhaps because she became a mother the following year. The boy is called either Simon or Tehotu; he was joined by a sister, Tarita Cheyenne, six years later. Between the two births Tarita apparently complained of neglect and went to live in Paris. According to some sources she regrets not being married; according to others, they are married under local law – that of Tahiti, for they lived on the atoll some thirty miles north of Tahiti which Brando bought while on vacation in 1963. This atoll, Tetiaroa, consists of thirteen islands, some of which Brando has developed – a hotel, an airstrip – for tourists, partly to provide an income for this family. On one of them he raised lobsters and studied marine ecology, reading books on Eastern philosophy and politics. According to whim, he welcomed uninvited journalists, but: 'Privacy is not something that I'm merely entitled to,' he once said, 'it's an absolute prerequisite.' He preferred to live in Tahiti between movie assignments and public engagements, but maintained a house in Beverly Hills (which had once belonged to Howard Hughes and was appropriately guarded like Fort Knox).

According to *Time* magazine, Brando is 'famous for his sometimes tumultuous off-screen romances', and from the same source comes this glimpse of the private Brando: 'What little is known of his true nature comes from a handful of his friends and associates. By their testimony, he is intelligent, warm, charming, compassionate, humorous and unpretentious, as well as undisciplined, boorish, gloomy, supercilious, cruel and downright bent. About the only thing everybody can agree on is that he is a prankster.' It is known that many of his affairs ended traumatically for the young ladies concerned, but with the exception of Miss Kashfi, none of them has so far made the details known to the press. In private life he is a tremendous mimic, and an amusing talker; his put-down of Miss Loren's paintings could be one of the deadpan jokes he enjoys. He can be disconcerting in conversation, when his sole object is to discover the real motives of the other speakers, and he remained intensely quick to spot, and expose, phoneyness of any kind. His sympathy with the underdog led him into the Civil Rights movement, though some sources suggest that he is atoning for his fame, or the way he earns his money.

His interest in Civil Rights developed in the fifties, and in 1961 his signature appeared in an ad in *The New York Times* soliciting funds for Martin Luther King and the Struggle for Freedom in the South; other signatories included Eleanor Roosevelt, Harry Belafonte, Van Heflin, Nat King Cole and Elmer Rice. The text was sufficiently critical of police behaviour during a recent incident that the mayor of Montgomery, Alabama, tried to sue the paper for half-a-million dollars. He made appearances for the Civil Rights movement when he thought his presence might be useful, or just add weight to other show business personalities equally incensed; and one remembers his involvement with the Caryl Chessman case. He is known to have recommended black artists within the industry, and in 1964 hired a black secretary. That year he became interested in the plight of the American Indian, and, as with Civil Rights, gave financial help; and he spoke against apartheid in South Africa at the Central Hall in London. That was a public meeting, only partly full (his own appearance was unpublicized); a friend who was with him told me that backstage Brando was in tears contemplating how little he could actually do against that iniquitous cause.

There were fewer reports of film offers which came to nothing. I know only of *The Man Who Would Be King*, which John Huston had first planned in the early 50s for Clark Gable and Humphrey Bogart. In 1966 he revived the idea for Brando and Richard Burton and then for Brando and Peter O'Toole (it was finally made in 1975 with Sean Connery and Michael Caine). Visconti had considered him for *Il Gattopardo*, but preferred Laurence Olivier, who turned it down; it was made with Burt Lancaster. Ten years later Visconti wanted him to play the Baron de Charlus in *A la Recherche du Temps Perdu*, but the project was postponed and then cancelled. He had probably had first crack at every major male role in the late 50s, but this had changed by 1967.

It was not entirely his fault. At least two of his films had been unjustly handled by the press; *A Countess from Hong Kong* shouldn't have happened to anybody. The plum parts were now being offered to Paul Newman – ironically, in view of those accusations that he imitated Brando. Newman was the first to admit that Brando was the superior actor and despite the fact that his wife – Joanne Woodward – had disliked working with him he tried to do so on several occasions. One was *Butch Cassidy and the Sundance Kid* in 1969: Steve McQueen was originally set to play Butch with Newman as Sundance. McQueen walked out when the director George Roy Hill suggest they swap roles – and there was general agreement that Brando should be approached to play Sundance, 'but they couldn't locate him' according to Hill, 'he was off somewhere painting himself black'. It was a pity: that film had the sort of success which Brando now badly needed. In 1967, the following at least were all considered bigger stars than Brando: Lee Marvin, Sidney Poitier, Steve McQueen, Dean Martin, Sean Connery, John Wayne, Richard Burton and James Coburn. For the first time in a while Brando was pleased to step into another man's shoes.

These belonged to Montgomery Clift, then in such an advanced state of alcoholism as to be virtually unusable; but his co-star was Elizabeth Taylor, and she wanted Clift. The film was her idea; she had wanted her husband, Burton, to direct, but Clift was not amenable. The film would reunite the producer and director of *The Night of the Iguana* (in which Burton had starred), respectively Ray Stark and John Huston. On that occasion, as I've mentioned, Huston was able to control the style needed for Tennessee Williams – and Carson McCullers was a soul-sister in both talent and life to Williams. She had written *Reflections in a Golden Eye* in 1941, but its hothouse of adultery and perversion would never have been sanctioned by the Breen Office, now abolished (briefly: because exhibitors were demanding bolder fare, to win back those cinemagoers now happily staying home with television). Huston accepted to work with Clift, though he had had a poor experience of handling him on *The Misfits* and a worse one – leading to lawyers' offices – on *Freud*. However, Clift died before filming begun, and Miss Taylor (with Mr Burton's concurrence) approved the substitution of Brando, who accepted second billing for the first time since *A Streetcar Named Desire*.

He had qualms about the role, according to Huston. He flew to see him in his home in Ireland, saying that he was 'unsuitable'. Huston asked him to read the revised script, but instead Brando went for a walk in a thunderstorm: when he returned he had decided to do it. In his autobiography Huston chose not to discuss working with Brando, but perhaps the cinematographer Aldo Tonti spoke for him when he said 'He impressed us all with his quiet professionalism and discipline. He was first on the set, punctual and sober. No fuss. When Liz Taylor appeared she was late and followed by a trail of assistants, fans, the more the better. Brando was serious and couldn't stand fawners and camp followers and fans.' Brando offered his opinion of her some years later – in a roundabout way – when he spoke to *Ciné-Revue*. He detested Richard Burton, he said, 'He's an idiot. How do you admit that someone who began his career so well now spends his life running after that nut he's married to?' The remark is self-revealing in two ways, since Miss Taylor fought studio opposition in order to have Brando in the film. She had also put at his disposal her chalet in Switzerland so that he could introduce his children to the delights of that country. As a gesture of thanks he flew to New York to accept on her behalf the New York critics' award for her performance in *Who's Afraid of Virginia Woolf?* We have, incidentally, Burton's consideration of these two talents: 'Elizabeth is terribly like Marlon Brando who, I think, is the best actor America ever had. She has the same qualities I would use to describe Marlon: slow-moving, quiet, with a suggestion of infinite power.'

As for Huston, there is no doubt that he admired his talent, for in his book he says at one point that he considered Robert Mitchum 'an actor of the calibre of Olivier, Burton and Brando'. He says merely that Brando claimed he had been brought up with horses, but turned out to be so terrified of them – as was the character he played – that Miss Taylor was affected, and she was an excellent horse-woman. Huston writes, 'I remember he once said, "If you care about it, it's no good." Meaning you've got to get into a role, to the point that you're no longer acting.' Huston was satisfied with Brando's performance (and with the others) but he does not take a long paragraph to describe the pleasures of working with him – as he does with Mitchum, Bogart and Miss Taylor.

Because of her tax situation, the film was shot in Italy although set in the Deep South – but some preliminary locations were done in New York State and Long Island. Huston delivered a Technicolor print suffused in a golden glow, an experiment which everyone at Warner Bros. disliked: one wholly in Technicolor was substituted when the film failed to find a public during its first few days in New York.

It opened in six months after the Chaplin film, and failed just as totally. It opened in Britain another six months later, to an overwhelmingly favourable response from critics and public. Huston observed later: 'It's only now' – 1972 – 'beginning to become appreciated. More and more people . . . mentioned [it] as one of my better films. And I quite agree.' Maybe in the States its baroque quality seemed dated – and certainly the novel is faithfully followed in the screenplay by Chapman Mortimer and Gladys Hill. Both they and Huston have gone about their task in confident fashion.

Reflections in a Golden Eye begins (and ends) with a line from the first paragraph: 'There is a Fort in the South where some years ago a murder was committed.' Huston sketches in this army installation – the barracks, the captain's lecture room – and moves on to the married quarters, furnished in appropriate impersonal taste. It is a mellow, lingering autumn: sunlight dapples the woods where riders canter, and a soldier lurks in the bushes. One recalls that when Huston handled similar materials – *The Night of the Iguana* – he set his misfits just as firmly into their equally real and beautiful setting. Mrs McCullers used a plangent prose to deal wth her subject, a muted quadrille for two army couples.

These are the Pendertons, Leonora (Miss Taylor), and

Major Weldon Penderton (Brando). He is cold and prissy; she is uncomplicated, and she despises him. She is having an affair with Colonel Langdon (Brian Keith), whose sick wife, Alison (Julie Harris), is disliked by the three of them, living in a half-fantasy world with her Filipino houseboy, Anacleto. The soldier in the bushes, a Private Williams, has a crush on Leonora and takes to keeping vigil in her room at night, fingering her clothes; while, independently, the Major gets a fixation on him which at first he diagnoses as hatred. He follows him about, and when he sees him creep into the house, he thinks it is to visit him. He sits waiting, facing up to something he has been afraid to confront; and when the soldier goes past him to his wife's room, he takes a gun and shoots him dead.

The book delves only into the actions of these people, allowing but glimpses into their motives. They're set down, like flies in amber, basically pathetic. The things we remember most – that Alison has cut off her nipples with garden shears, that the Private rides 'bare-backed and bare-arsed' as Leonora puts it – are risible businesses for the cinema. Huston doesn't seem to have recognized the difficulties. The scene where Leonora whips her husband in front of the guests (which isn't in the book, and one might question its intrusion) works because he cuts at once to Anacleto gleefully reporting the details to Alison. He makes details tell – Alison's mute acceptance of the home to which she is committed, Leonora's boast that she can get away with murder because the C.O. dandled her on his knee as a baby. The film retains the gentle (and Jewish?) Captain Weincheck, who reads Proust and listens to music with Alison. Huston regards them all with non-maudlin compassion.

And he works in humour wherever possible: Leonora's trite, flighty remarks, the Major's pompous speech about the virtues of army life, 'a man's life among men'. It is the humour which saves the film as a film, which separates it from the book. The book is an elegant charade; the film draws on its fantasy for something more down-to-earth. It offers a more tangible army camp than did Mrs McCullers, and it poses its eccentrics more firmly in that world.

The focus inevitably shifts, offering three inter-related studies: the sick wife and her fawning houseboy; the illicit affair between the Colonel and the Major's wife; and a petty military man facing up to the fact that he's homosexual. And also, of course, the strange Private, but except for one telling, brief, scene in his barracks – where we learn that he doesn't 'relate' to his fellows – he is little more than an ikon.

With one exception, Huston has drawn extraordinary performances from his players. The exception, expectedly, is Miss Taylor, who pouts, primps and grimaces, and can't be stopped. In the book Leonora is stupid, but she's not vulgar. Miss Taylor *looks* vulgar, the huge breasts, the hair either piled high or tied back in a bandana, and it wouldn't matter if only she'd stop for a minute, but she's always busy. Apart from a certain voluptuousness she doesn't appear to have understood the character. Huston allows Zorro David (as Anacleto) to overdo things; he's not 'camp' in the book but the humour is well-judged – and we see him through the Colonel's eyes. Brian Keith projects bemused virility, and it is only later – sodden drunk, or wanting Anacleto in the army to make a man out of him – that you realize he's as stupid as Major Penderton. As for Miss Harris, she comes closest to the character in the book.

Brando. This is the most difficult role. Mrs McCullers didn't understand* how it is that an officer, in his forties, starts to lust after an enlisted man – though, via his fixa-

---

* However, life imitated art when some years later her husband discovered that he was homosexual. His immediate response was to plan his suicide, which despite Tennessee Williams's amused advice, he managed two years later.

tion, she works well at it. The film makes a couple of mistakes: through a window, we watch the Major take out a postcard of a Greek male statue, and later he applies rejuvenating cream. These are jejune touches (though not out of character). Beyond the fact that it's repressed, we can only speculate about the Major's homosexuality; and Brando's is an astonishing study of sexual repression. It is the definitive study of the man beneath the uniform – practising with barbells, composing smiles in a mirror, revelling in his own tiny authority. In his own home, he is nothing; he manages to be curt with others, but his sexual frigidity, he suggests, well reaps the humiliation he accepts from his wife. He's a coward, he's self-important. After his horse had bolted, as he whips her his face is a vivid exposition of fury, of surprise, of affront – that the horse dared treat *him* so; it's the face of a spoilt child after his first spanking. Note also Brando's expression as he waits for the soldier – the tension one finds in Buñuel's shoe fetishists, the terror of an individual irrevocably committed to some sort of foolish or forbidden licentiousness. Both sequences are indicative of how much Brando dares – as he dares again in the 'English' accent he lays over the Major's Southern one. He manages, still, to lose words – which is why he was still accused of mannerisms – but you only have to see him set his head, his build and his facial muscles into the self-conscious stance of a little martinet, to realize how magnificent he can be when the conditions are right. Much thought went into this performance, and when you consider how badly it was received in his homeland, it's no wonder that he lost interest in his career – or so his next films would suggest.

It was not wise, however, to add Huston to the list of first-class directors with whom he chose not to work again. In 1971 Huston offered him the role of the over-the-hill boxer in *Fat City*, which was to become one of the best of his later films. The meeting broke up with Brando saying that he would need a couple of weeks to think the matter over: after much time and no word, Stacey Keach was signed. 'Some time later,' says Huston in his book, 'I heard that Brando was upset about being passed over.' It isn't clear whether the meeting took place before or after Brando began *The Godfather*, but it was certainly before it had opened: in any case, by that time Brando's career was in such bad shape that a second good film could only be of benefit.

12

Four Failures

Brando's salary for *Reflections in a Golden Eye* had been
$750,000 plus $7\frac{1}{2}$ per cent of the gross (it did not break
even) – thus he had at least retained his fiscal position
among movie stars. Julie Andrews, Sophia Loren, Miss
Taylor and perhaps half-a-dozen others were said to be
getting $1 million, but there was every indication that
highly-paid stars were failing to attract the public. Some
successful films were listed as flops because they didn't
recover their costs – of which astronomical salaries were
often a major part. In April 1968, *Variety* examined the
recent track records of several well-paid stars and deduced
that at least ten of them were not worth the salaries they
were currently being paid. The ten included Glenn Ford,
Tony Curtis, Yul Brynner, Rock Hudson, William Holden,
James Garner, Anthony Quinn, Natalie Wood – and
Brando. In each case, *Variety* looked at the total receipts
of their last six films: in Brando's case these amounted to
$9.6 million, or a paltry $1.6 million per film. *Variety*
itself didn't draw the analogy, but the article was nearly as
deadly as the exhibitors' infamous list of 'box-office
poison' stars in 1938. Many of these names were 'saved'
because the relation of star to film had changed, and many
of the certified top-drawing stars were also turning out
occasional flops. *Variety*'s inference was clear: these stars,
and some others, had better reduce their salaries if they

wanted to stay in business – and even then, they might not weather the storm. Brando probably would, the piece concluded, because he was regarded as '*the* American actor'.

No public announcement was made of his salary on his next two films, but the second was of obviously low-budget, and the other comprised what amounted to a guest appearance. As there were several other names in this project, and as he was instrumental in setting it up, it is probable that he worked for expenses and a percentage only. The film was *Candy*, adapted from a satire on pornography by Terry Southern and Mason Hoffenberg which had originally been published in France, in English, under a pseudonym. It became a cult book, an underground best-seller, and as the decade became more permissive it came out in the US and Britain. The idea of filming it also originated in France, with Brando's old friend Christian Marquand, who wanted to abandon acting to take up directing. When Brando agreed to appear in it, Marquand had no difficulty in setting up a French–Italian co-production (though set in the US it was filmed in Italy). Brando persuaded Richard Burton to play one of the other roles, about which time a Hollywood company – Selmur Pictures – became the third co-producer. Other names joined the cast – Walter Matthau, James Coburn, John Huston, Charles Aznavour, and the title-role was played by Ewa Aulin from Denmark, who at least looked okay as the naive teenager who wonderingly services several sex-starved men.

This was not – in 1968, at least – a likely subject for a film. The screenplay by Buck Henry altered the original, and was even more tasteless – except that words like 'tasteless' become meaningless in the context of *Candy*. It was meant to offend; it was meant to shock (there was a long sequence with blood splashing around a surgeon operating) and also to titillate. It was meant to amuse, but it had about as much wit as a hand-painted bedpan; it might have been assembled by a group of retarded and self-consciously daring adolescents. It diminished the reputation of all concerned, with the possible exception of Mr Matthau, who did his sequence with an expression of dour pessimism. Brando almost atoned for his back-stage role by twenty minutes of impeccable impersonation – which, unfortunately, came towards the end of the film, and thus the only reason to sit it through. Renata Adler in *The New York Times* summed him up: 'Marlon Brando, as a Jewish guru (the film has an ugly racialism and arrested development, frog-torturing soft sadism at its heart) is less unendurable, because one is glad to see him on the screen again.' The film itself reaped vile opinions, and after initial curiosity died at the box office.

The other film, *The Night of the Following Day*, was made in panic by two men who badly needed a successful film. The other was Jay Kanter, whose British productions for Universal had been financially and artistically disastrous. One of the executive producers was Elliott Kastner, who had initiated the project – originally to star Yves Montand. When Montand changed his mind Richard Boone was contacted – and he was compliant when asked to do a lesser role, but with co-star billing, when Kanter told Kastner that they could probably get Brando. Although, as I said, no announcement was made of Brando's salary, it has been said that one or other of these gentlemen remembered his commitment to Universal – which meant that he could be had for what was theoretically much less than his current fee, that is, one commensurate with a modest film. Also coming cheaply was the producer and director, Hubert Cornfield, a *maudit* talent whose cult thriller, *Pressure Point*, had done such poor business that it brought him no further assignments. The leading female role would be played by Brando's ex-girlfriend, Rita Moreno, who had not been inundated with movie offers since winning a Best Supporting Oscar for *West Side*

Story. And the film itself would be of that sure-fire genre, the thriller: 'When in doubt, make a thriller with comic moments,' Carol Reed once advised an aspiring director. Perhaps the trouble here was that they omitted the comedy.

Cornfield also wrote the script, with Robert Phippeny, from a novel by Lionel White. I do not know whether the novel was set in France, but the film offered no reason why these American crooks should be there, other than to provide an atmospheric setting – the marshes where they live, and the nearby, almost desolate, village. The teenage girl they kidnapped was played by Pamela Franklin; they were Brando, Moreno as his wife, Richard Boone and Jess Hahn. There were imitations of emotional disturbance – the wife drugged herself, Boone was a sadist and child-molester – and the plot was carefully plotted till it fell into the crooks-fall-out formula and ended by being a dream. Brando, hair dyed blond as the brains of the gang, was accused by several critics of self-parody, and by others of having little seeming interest in the proceedings – charges from which it would be difficult to exonerate him. He tried to get away from cliché by playing the ringleader as a man of moods, withal concerned for the girl's welfare, but it was his least rewarding work since he had entered films.

His concentration had once again been less than a hundred per cent, which didn't entirely surprise Cornfield, who had noted at their first meeting that Brando had said that they would make a little money together rather than a good film. He found Brando very polite then, but the amity between them did not last. 'It wasn't fun directing him,' Cornfield said. 'Working with Marlon *sucked*. Direction is a collaborative effort. Marlon gave me no collaboration. He would ignore me. We would argue again and again.' At one stage the arguments were so bitter that Boone took over direction.

The result did not enthuse Universal's executives, who shelved it for over a year. In the US it was booked into second-run houses and in Britain it was released as the lower half of a double-bill. Because it starred Brando some critics reviewed it, but it says much about the way his career had evolved that few commented on the fact that Universal regarded the film as a pre-ordained failure.

Before it came out it seemed that relief was at hand. It was announced that Brando would star in *The Arrangement*, which Kazan would direct from his own novel. The book is confessedly semi-autobiographical, about a Madison Avenue executive in mid-life crisis, reflecting on his adultery as he moves towards a nervous breakdown. Kazan hoped to 'bring him back from some bad outings'; he had seen him little since *On the Waterfront* and reflected on something Brando had said to a mutual friend, Clifford Odets, in 1963: 'Here I am, a balding middle-aged failure ... I feel a fraud when I act ... I've tried everything ... fucking, drink, work. None of them mean anything. Why can't we be just like the Tahitians?'

Warner Bros had expected Kazan to cast Brando, but they fought that with a vehemence which 'shocked' Kazan. He was told to look at *The Countess from Hong Kong* and *Reflections in a Golden Eye* with a view to confirming their opinion of him. That was, as he told Brando, 'First, that you'd become terribly heavy and second that you were just "going through the motions" now.' Kazan reasoned that he could get a performance from Brando as he hadn't given for years – though he told me that he was impressed by his work in Huston's film – and that a reunion would be strong at the box-office. Then the Black Rights activist Martin Luther King was assassinated and Brando found that he couldn't go through with the role. He telephoned Kazan for a meeting at his house and was waiting as Kazan parked his car; he broke the news and escorted him back to it. Kazan drove away in confusion. He remembered in his autobiography, 'It was a few hours before I re-membered that he was one hell of an actor, and although his feeling for King was certainly sincere, the depth of emotion he projected came as much from his talent as from his sense of tragedy. Then I began to get mad. We were already making the man's hairpieces, for chrissakes.'

A few days later the man announced that he had retired from the screen to devote his life to Civil Rights. Friends intimated that he might reconsider his decision if offered material likely to help the cause – and Kazan cast Kirk Douglas in his place. This actor had this to say – to Roger Ebert – on the matter: 'There is something sad and dramatic about the disintegration of a talent. At the start, Brando was the best. And now . . . well, it was a damn shame he had to miss with Kazan . . . The two of them, together again. But after Kazan talked with Brando, he felt Brando wasn't quite with it . . . didn't have the old enthusiasm . . . but, hell, I don't want to get into that.' The inference that Kazan might have preferred Douglas to Brando will not be lost on those who know that that actor is not noted for his modesty – and may he be consoled with that, for the film failed with both press and public. I think the final word on the subject may be with Sheilah Graham, who wrote that Brando reneged on his agreement to Kazan not only because 'he wished to devote his time to meaningful films, but because he was afraid that if he failed with Kazan there would be nothing left'.

He was, in fact, shortly solicited for a film which would make a direct statement on the White's exploitation of the Black; it came from Italy, from Gillo Pontecorvo, best-known outside Italy for *Kapo* and *La Battaglia di Algeri*. Pontecorvo was, clearly, one of the politically-committed young Italian directors: *Kapo* (1959), though not really a good film, was compassionately composed towards the victims of Nazi concentration camps; the other film, which we know as *The Battle of Algiers* (1966), was a superb and scrupulously fair account of the revolt which finally pushed the French out of Algeria. It was the best sort of propaganda film-making, for Pontecorvo, despite his fairness, made no bones about where his own sympathies lay.

The script he submitted to Brando was by Franco Solinas and Giorgio Artorio, from a story concocted by them and him (presumably it was in English; the credits did not list an English translator or adaptor). Once Brando agreed to do it, Pontecorvo asked Alfredo Grimaldi to produce, on the strength of his experience of an American major distributor and an American star – respectively United Artists and Clint Eastwood, for Grimaldi had been the producer of the second and third Westerns which had made Eastwood a world name. Those films had made a lot of money for United Artists, who surrendered to Grimaldi's pleas for Brando – and a salary of $750,000 was agreed: but they thought him so much of a box-office risk that they would only put up two-thirds of the film's three million dollars budget. There was talk of Sidney Poitier co-starring, but Pontecorvo thought his face too 'civilized' for the role of the black peasant leader, and he used an amateur, Evaristo Marques, discovered in Colombia, where the locations were to be shot. They were begun in Cartagena, in uncomfortable heat, and with, in Pontecorvo's own words, 'thousands of extras who had never seen a camera before. Marlon was not helped by this atmosphere of noise and confusion which obviously affected his nerves (he wears wax earplugs on the set and can't bear to catch an eye-line behind the camera). But this was the price we had to pay for shooting the film live . . .'

At first Brando was extraordinarily helpful to Marques, but in those conditions he found it difficult to work with an untried amateur – and one who spoke only his native language. Pontecorvo communicated with him by signs, while Brando understandably wanted him replaced. It was over Marques that their relationship first began to deteriorate. Brando called Pontecorvo a dictator, objecting to the endless takes: 'If he wants a purple smile from me and I give him a mauve smile, he continues ordering me to smile until he gets exactly what he wants, even if I get a dislocated jaw in the meantime.' Pontecorvo later spoke about him: 'At the beginning, Brando was very happy to make the film, and very co-operative. Then he began to interfere. He got more and more angry because he said I was taking his creative space. But I was European, not American, and not used to allowing stars to dictate a film.'

He went on, 'Still, I don't resent Brando. He once said to me: "When I do a scene I am like a bird in the hand of a peasant, trembling!" I would say he is more like a Stradivarius – you can get from him any kind of nuance you want, providing you have the right technique to do it. He has a twofold power. The first thing is that he looks extraordinary. And he has the ability to change like a chameleon. Both qualities make a star. But together they make a great star – one of the greatest of all time, in fact.'

The quarrels became bitter enough for Brando to believe that in that climate his health was at risk. His doctor agreed with him and at great cost Grimaldi transferred the unit to Morocco, where filming limped to a troubled close. There were more to come: the Spanish government objected to the title, *Quemada*, which suggested that the colonial system on trial was Spanish – and when that government had last indicated its displeasure with an American film touching on a Spanish subject (*Ride a Pale Horse*) it not only banned it but also for several years other films produced by Columbia. So the Portuguese version of the word was used, *Queimada!*, since Portugal was by no means a lucrative market.

Brando was Sir William Walker, an English gentleman sent to Queimada, a Portuguese colony (so called – Queimada means Burn – because fire was once used to quell a native rebellion); his mission was to foment revolt among the natives because the British government wanted an end to Portuguese monopoly in the sugar trade. He chooses a dockside porter, José Dolores (Marques), for his foil, by provoking him and then involving him in a robbery. The robbery forces Dolores to kill Portuguese soldiers – and become an enemy of the State; after which it is not difficult for Sir William to persuade him to gather other disaffected portions of the black population about him and lead them in revolt. At the same time, Sir William works his wiles on a liberal, Sanchez (Renato Salvatori), persuading him that it is his Christian duty to assassinate the governor. Dolores assumes the leadership of the country, but after his rebel army and ineffectual government have brought the country to ruin, he's persuaded to resign and Sanchez becomes governor. Sir William leaves for home. Ten years later he's sought out, this time by the British Royal Sugar Company: Dolores, still living by the revolutionary precepts taught him by Sir William, is continuing to create unrest, and he is hired to bring the country back to peace – that is, commercial prosperity. The country is now a republic, and Sanchez is still governor. When he realizes that he is a pawn of British commercial interests, Sir William manoeuvres a plot to unseat him and has him shot. The British agents combine with the corrupt Portuguese officials and their black army to rout out Dolores: Sir William gives him a chance to escape but he prefers to die a martyr. Sir William prepares to depart, his job done; on the quayside he is approached by another dock-porter, who stabs him.

As a tract, the piece is, if not original, at least ambitious, though you might pertinently ask what the Italian writers and director know about British or Portuguese colonialism in the late eighteenth century? (In fact, its flailing aim is indicated by some origins: secret government intervention on behalf of sugar interests is characteristic of the American colonialization of Hawaii, and the rest of the plot mirrors events in French Hawaii.) They may feel deeply about the indecencies and abuses of the colonial system, and their indignation is just – except that this film always seems like an *exercise* in indignation. We know about corruption, about heroes becoming martyrs, about petty tyrants – they're old screen material (much of this is *Viva Zapata!*, with Dolores as Zapata, Sir William as Fernando): the best of this movie is when it gets closest to history to show how commercial interests were allowed to predominate. Sir William is woefully misconceived: first he's on this side, then on that, a spokesman for both the British government and the natives, a man caught between his job, his own guile, and a lingering idealism. Outside his role as spokesman, the little we learn of him, and it's after the ten year gap, is that he's been blackballed from his club; a real fallen hero, he's found fighting in a low pub. Brando plays with the same accent he used in *Mutiny on the Bounty*, but little else – he never seems to get the measure of him. There is some play made over his confrontation with Dolores – a love-hate relationship or something similar, but it goes for nothing. It was courageous of him to take on the role; perhaps with closer co-operation between actor and director, there might have been more cohesion.

At the same time, it fails as an action movie. In the old days, with a film thus full of inconsistencies, of plot-angles dropped, of irresolute changes of mood or tempo, the thing to do was to make it move so fast that the audience didn't notice: but Pontecorvo lingers, with native marches, scenes of revelry and butchery. They're prettily photographed, but fatal to the film's impact. There's a nice feeling for the ambience of equatorial islands, and why not? Pontecorvo's expressed wish was to combine action and polemic, which he had done, flawlessly, with *The Battle of Algiers*. This was a ham-fisted effort.

It opened in Italy in March 1970, but was received so damply throughout Europe that only a miracle – a rave notice by an influential critic – could help it in the US. United Artists retitled it *Burn!* when it opened there towards the end of the year with twenty minutes of the footage shorn. It went as unregarded as *The Night of the Following Day*. Its failure is one reason Pontecorvo has not made a film since; another was that he was scarred by his difficulties with Brando. He added: 'You know, for five years he refused to speak to me. Then he wanted to make his film about the American Indians, and he asked me to direct it. We spent twenty days in reservations near Wounded Knee, and it was a fascinating process. But the money could never be found.'

With the failure of *Queimada!*, Brando's professional life reached its lowest level, a depth undreamt of in the palmy days. The life of an actor cannot be all roses – at various times, Clark Gable, Gary Cooper, James Cagney and Cary Grant were considered washed-up; Charles Laughton had spent years in silly films in roles unworthy of him – as, around this time, did Trevor Howard and James Mason. A decline in popularity is almost inevitable with ageing, but Brando was a comparatively young man – he was only 46. We thought he could have gone to the moon, or as Rod Steiger put it more realistically: 'He could have done anything, *anything*, however difficult or uncommercial, on the screen and taken the critics, the industry, the fans with him, But he didn't choose to. I don't know why.'

He did choose to: *Queimada!* could be termed 'difficult and uncommercial', but even in its final faulty state it was more interesting than most films. He chose with consistency what he hoped were solid entertainment movies with some message and a good, not too showy, role for himself. Of his failures, only two were out-and-out bad movies, *A Countess from Hong Kong* and *Candy*. *The Chase* and *Queimada!* were both of two seemingly doomed breeds: the former a demonstration of the pitfalls lying in wait for earnest talents tackling social injustice within the Hollywood system, the latter the latest of a series of imbroglios involving European creative talent and American stars and American money. Only *The Night of the Following Day* was a pot-boiler. *Morituri* and *The Appaloosa* were entertainments unfairly dismissed; the reception afforded *Reflections in a Golden Eye* in the US is a matter for pathologists. Some critics continued to take Brando seriously; it was the lesser ones who slapped him down, like teachers reprimanding the brightest boy in the class because he'd become swollen-headed or wasn't trying hard enough. The fans remained curious about his work even when they didn't bother to go and see his films. Steiger had become a bigger star than Brando, reckoned more bankable by the industry; George C. Scott, like Steiger, hadn't the Brando asset of film-star looks, but he also was more in demand. James Mason observed that Scott was probably the No 1 star in the US 'now that Brando had presumably conceded and retired. Brando has made such a balls-up of his career.'

Certainly after *Queimada!* Brando chose badly. Sam Spiegel was convinced that he was the only actor with the magnetism to play Rasputin in *Nicholas* and *Alexandra*, and David Lean was considering him to play the role Robert Mitchum eventually played in *Ryan's Daughter*. In both cases – to simplify slightly – the talents involved were too imposing to be worried about an actor considered a box-office risk; and he would not, in any case, be required to 'carry' the film. It is believed that Lean said no to him, and he said a definite no to Rasputin. Instead, he accepted a script sent to him by a young British director, Michael Winner, but even with his acceptance Winner was turned down, in his own words, 'by every American company and every British company'. Winner did eventually get backing, with the connivance of Jay Kanter, freed from Universal, Elliott Kastner and Alan Ladd Jr. Winner and Brando took no salary, anticipating the eventual profits. After almost a year on the shelf and a screening at the 1971 Venice film festival, it was bought by Avco-Embassy for $650,000, and then, probably, only because Brando's 'comeback' in *The Godfather* was expected to restore him to his further glory. Although made in Britain, the film got no bookings there till *The Godfather* fever had started in the US.

At all events, Winner's acquisition of Brando was a coup. In ten years of making features his most notable qualities had been persistence and a gift for self-publicity, neither of which disguised the fact that none of his films was of a quality to suggest why an actor even of Brando's reduced calibre should want to work with him; while he himself was disliked by almost everyone who had ever worked with him. With Brando, he did not feel his customary compulsion to be rude, and they got on: years later, when the director John Boorman asked him who had been his favourite director, Brando chose – to Boorman's astonishment – Winner. He rationalized it thus: 'Winner told me that I was a great actor and he wasn't a great director. So I could do as I liked.'

Later, Winner said, 'I saw a side of him you don't often see. He was cheerful, dedicated, and worked for no money. The whole film was financed by a rich man [and it cost] a fraction of what Brando usually gets for his salary alone. He was very loyal to it. He made them delay *Godfather* while he did my picture. He insisted on eating with the crew to prove he wasn't a snob, yet he drove around in limousines with an entourage. Curious contradictions in his character.' At the same time Winner put it another way: 'Marlon Brando likes a lot of jokes on the set, surprisingly. He's delighted to be gagging around ... able to perform quite seriously a few seconds after being involved in hilarious humour ...'

The film concerned, *The Nightcomers*, was unfortunately no joke. It was based on the sort of conceit usually found on the BBC's Third Programme or in the Christmas competition pages of the weeklies. Michael Hastings wrote it: an investigation into the proceedings at Bly House before Miss Giddens arrives – an extension of 'The Turn of the Screw' (filmed almost a decade earlier, as *The Innocents*). It was a prologue posing as the thing itself, a six-minute event dragged out to ninety-six.

The guardian (Harry Andrews), is uninterested in both the house and the children, leaving them to the care of the housekeeper, Mrs Grose (Thora Hird), the governess, Miss Jessel (Stephanie Beacham), and the valet-cum-handyman, Peter Quilp (Brando). Quilp is an untidy, drunken, Irish yarn-spinner, and the children, with nothing else to do, are influenced by his shabby, nihilistic view of the universe; their outlook on life is further perverted when Miles spies on Quilp and Miss Jessel at their love-making – consisting mainly of what the small-ads call 'bondage'. The children begin to taunt and persecute Mrs Grose; and when Miss Jessel tires of Quilp and plans to leave they murder her. Miles confesses the crime to Quilp before shooting him with an arrow.

Apart from the impertinent assault on the ethics of Henry James (can you imagine him so graphically chronicling these sado-masochistic sex-games?) the film doesn't have a modicum of understanding about English country-house life seventy years ago. Even if 'bullshit' was a common epithet then, it's unlikely that even the uncouth Quilp would use it before a lady, even his mistress in bed; it's even more unlikely he'd say 'fart' before children. Even if this Quilp is a self-confessed rebel (is that what attracted Brando to the role?), his conduct is idiotic. He would never have been kept on by guardian or housekeeper – tieless and long-haired, he even turns up at the funeral of the children's parents dressed like a tramp. Photographs of the period give a lie to all this: he might have found employment as a corporation dustman, but never as a groom (let alone a valet).

Brando's performance was like the film – without bite,

without point, without atmosphere (the film was prettily photographed in cold winter sunlight, but is never so sinister as the summer gardens were in *The Innocents*). He seems to have been influenced by his work in *The Wild One*, where he also played a misfit and a layabout, but – at least – in that film it was fascinating to watch him work through his inarticulateness to express his thoughts. Here, he varies between loquaciousness and moody silences. As in *Last Tango in Paris*, later, he seemed bored by everything, even the bed-antics. Still, Winner says the film gave him 'far and away the most personal satisfaction in recent years'. He didn't say whether Avco-Embassy got back much of their money.

13
Renaissance

The Godfather saved Brando's bacon; and it brought him back to the sort of superior Hollywood product in which he had made his name; it was also his first work in the US since *The Appaloosa*. The story of the filming was itself news. Paramount had been offered it as a script by Mario Puzo, an unsuccessful novelist; they told him to turn it into a novel, and they'd finance him the while. The novel became a best-seller, having got some good notices – and if I may digress for a moment, after the film came out, its publisher wrote to *Variety* complaining that every reviewer had referred back to the novel and described it as trashy. I checked a piece I had written on the film before seeing it: I had called the book 'meretricious', and I'll stick. It was sensationalist and both over- and ill-written. It did give a vivid picture of an incredible kind of private enterprise, where men lived dangerously, unsure of their friends and expecting imminent death.

Even as the novel was selling, Paramount failed to see that this would be a major film. The studio had had a failure with a previous movie on the Mafia, *The Brotherhood* (with Kirk Douglas) and the failures of two expensive musicals, *Paint Your Wagon* and *Darling Lili*, meant that they were looking for low- or medium-budget projects. Despite the book's period setting Paramount insisted that the film be set in the present day, assigning a $2,500,000 budget with locations in St Louis. To produce they selected Albert Ruddy, with no movie experience as such, but as producer on the television series 'Hogan's Heroes' he was accustomed to getting things done with economy and speed. For similar reasons the direction was offered to Richard Lester, Costa-Gavras, Richard Brooks and Peter Yates, all of whom turned it down. Robert Evans, the head of production, then thought of Francis Ford Coppola, regarded in the industry as a failure – partly because his three films had not performed up to expectations (though no one seeing them – *You're a Big Boy Now*, *Finian's Rainbow* and *The Rain People* – could doubt that he was an imposing talent). Coppola was Italian-American, a not unimportant consideration with this material, but there was a bigger one – he also had some excellent screenplay credits, including the one which had won the Oscar for *Patton*: for Paramount was not happy with the screenplay Puzo had been writing.

While Coppola worked it over, the studio had a big success with *Love Story*, and since the book continued on the best-seller lists he was able to persuade the bosses that the movie should be in period, with a budget of just over $6 million. They scoffed at Puzo's suggestion that Brando should play the family head, Don Corleone, but his other choice – on the thesis that only a great actor could play his fine creation – Laurence Olivier, was uninsurable. Among the actors being considered were George C. Scott, Rod Steiger, Ernest Borgnine and Richard Conte – though I can't help agreeing with Marlene Dietrich, who said, 'Why didn't they ask Eddie Robinson?' This was after Brando was cast, ('too slow' was her prediction of his performance): she was of course referring to the greatest of screen gangsters, Edward G. Robinson, who was also uninsurable – though he was to play one last leading role (in *Soylent Green*). Coppola now sided with Puzo on the matter of Brando, and approached him. Paramount demanded that

Brando submit to a screen test, assuming he would refuse and so put an end to the matter. Coppola had no intention of asking an actor of Brando's experience to test, but suggested bringing a camera to his home to see how the make-up would look; accompanying him was Salvatore Corsitto who had a small role in the film. The scene they acted out impressed Paramount's executives, who agreed to Brando – but then they were getting him at bargain basement price.

Brando said that he *thought* he was getting $250,000 plus a percentage, but the usually reliable *Variety* said it was a percentage only. However, *Show Magazine* published a run-down of ownership so complete as to indicate that it is the true picture: Paramount had 84 per cent, Ruddy $7\frac{1}{2}$ per cent, Coppola 6 per cent and Puzo $2\frac{1}{2}$ per cent, with Brando on a salary of $50,000 'for making the movie and a sliding percentage of one per cent for each sum it moves to after the cost of the film is realized. He too will wind up a millionaire.' Since Paramount also promised him $100,000 if he would cooperate with publicity we may assume his claim to be quite accurate.

Paramount so loathed Brando's work on the first day that they tried to see whether Kazan was available, in the belief that he was the only director capable of handling him. 'From location in Manhattan and Sicily rumors of Marlon Brando's uncooperativeness and Coppola's ineptness reached the industry,' reported one magazine. Here are some more attributable quotes from the participants themselves: 'The pressure was incredible. Paramount acted like it was the first movie ever made. And do you know who was the greatest tension reliever of all? Brando. The guy was fantastic' (James Caan). 'The tensions on *The Godfather* were terrific. There was talk of [Coppola] being replaced after two weeks ... If the film had a fault, I think it was that Coppola was too soft – added to which Brando never likes to show the seedy side of any character he plays' (Robert Duvall). 'Brando as a young actor was terrific . . . Paramount didn't trust Coppola so they hired a standby director to follow him in case he fucked up. The Mafiosi were putting the movie down, but their very members were playing parts. Brando kept repeating that the head of the Mafia was no worse than the head of Dupont' (Duvall again). 'Brando wants to do what you want, but he wants people to be honest and not try to manipulate him' (Coppola). 'Everyone advised me to assert myself with him and say, "Now, Marlon, I'm the director, you just act." That would have been suicidal. I could understand how he got his reputation because his ideas were so bizarre, so apparently crazy. Yet without exception every one of his crazy ideas I used turned out to be a terrific moment' (Coppola). 'It was unbelievable the way he aged in the picture. And it wasn't just the make-up. He did it from inside. He's incredibly inventive' (Al Pacino), 'I felt that Brando really cared for me personally, and that acceptance was a great thing for me' (Pacino). 'I know Al Pacino well . . . At the end of shooting it occurred to him that he wanted his name as big as mine on the billing. I had never made any trouble with such problems before but this time I refused. I should have crushed the jumped-up little prick like a common or garden fly' (Brando).

With the exceptions of Duvall, Caan and Brando these remarks were made for 'puff' articles appearing at the advent of the film or the sequel, but they also do add something to earlier remarks made by Brando's colleagues. In any case, Coppola is far from being a diplomatic filmmaker of the old school: worth noting is his further comment that Brando was a tower of strength to cast and crew, and also this: 'The things they were going to fire me over were, one: wanting to cast Brando. Two: wanting to cast [Al] Pacino. Wanting to shoot it in period. The very things that made it different from any other film.' He was, of course, proved right, and he should also be praised for his work on the script: though credited to both him and Puzo, it was much superior to the book – the junk had gone, the Harold Robbins stuff. What's left was a vivid picture of an incredible kind of private enterprise, etc.

The problem of handling a vast and teeming subject was solved by concentrating on the main handful of characters and letting the rest dangle (a method adopted in another current movie, from another best-seller, a very different one, *Nicholas and Alexandra*). Gone was the dreary business of the marital problems of the Hollywood star, Johnny Fontanne, though he was retained – presumably to stress the fact that the Godfather's power spread to Hollywood. With the exception of Kay Adams (Diane Keaton), the nice non-Italian girl who falls in love with Michael (Pacino), none of the women matter at all – and the reaction of her family to her marrying a Mafia man is barely touched on. She serves a plot function; as does the Corleone girl who marries the thuggish husband – because he'll be the decoy to lead to the death of Sonny (James Caan). Mother (Morgana King) is but glimpsed: her grief when the Godfather is wounded is of no account.

And so it goes. Other gang-leaders appear to be consulted or to be threatened, and in both instances to be gunned down. The corrupt police chief (Sterling Hayden) is murdered by Michael after that memorable meal in Brooklyn. The family cohorts, including Hagen (Robert Duvall), the consigliore or lawyer, do little more than dance attendance on the Godfather and the two sons who matter. The casting is perfect: the few familiar faces and the many unfamiliar ones. Pacino grows from callow kid to the new leader; Caan is cheery as the extrovert Sunny. Brando manages to look like an old man. His gestures are slow, his hands eloquent in a lordly, elderly-Italian manner. He looks at people the way old men of power look at people, inquisitively, graciously. He smiles mirthlessly, and talks in a hushed, authoritative voice, and the authority remains when he's off-screen. It's a construction job rather than a performance, but there's no strain and nothing jars – which is rare when actors play characters older than their years.

Brando's notices were the best he had had in a long while, but there were some dissenting voices. John Simon was one: 'The acting is predominantly good, with the exception of the highly touted and critically acclaimed performance of Marlon Brando in the title part. Brando has a weak, gray voice, a poor ear for accents, and an unrivaled capacity for hamming things up by sheer underacting – in particular by unconscionably drawn-out pauses. His make-up is good, to be sure, but only when the character is near death does Brando's halting, wheezing performance lumber into sense. The rest of the time he is outacted by Al Pacino, Richard Castellano, Robert Duvall and so lowly a talent as James Caan's.'

Whether it was worth his trouble (other than in restoring his prestige, in commercial terms) is something else again. Both he and Coppola said they saw the story as a metaphor for the US. Violence, and organized violence is, as we're often told, part of the American way of life. Everything in the movie is part of the American way of life. Coppola compared the Mafia in the US to American infiltration in Latin America, while Brando felt – he told *Life* magazine – 'the picture made a useful commentary on corporation thinking in this country'. Everything in the movie is true – Coppola, for instance, feels that no previous film had managed to paint an honest picture of Italian-American families, but this particular family is not typical and the film – like the book – is finally ambivalent about their trade. There's no message and no moral: the family will go on with a new leader, and society will continue to look away or, at best, compromise.

Coppola intended no more. This is a film of tremendous accomplishment. The Sicilian scenes escaped the patronizing tone of most American films about Italy, the period detail is remarkable – but despite the incidentals, despite the skill and the transparent honesty, the 1932 *Scarface*, at half the length, is more exciting. And it's far less likeable than either *Gone With the Wind* or *The Sound of Music*, both of which it surpassed as the most financially successful film of all time, as the saying goes.

Before it was premiered, however – in March 1972 – Brando had begun another film which would be as much – if not more – discussed: *Last Tango in Paris*, or, to give it its correct title(s) – for it was a French–Italian co-production with only minimal American backing, *Dernier Tango à Paris* or *Ultimo Tango in Parigi*, to be directed by Bernardo Bertolucci, then riding an art-house crest after *Il Conformista*. His players on that occasion, Dominique Sanda and Jean-Louis Trintignant, had originally been cast, but she became pregnant and he decided that he was too prudish. Alfredo Grimaldi, who had produced *Queimada!*, sent the screenplay to Brando, believing that Brando would enjoy a further flirtation with the European cinema – given that the director would prove to be more malleable. The female lead would be a virtually untried actress, Maria Schneider, who happened to be the illegitimate daughter of Daniel Gélin, a friend and admirer of Brando. The combination of star and director excited the press office of United Artists (handling the French end of the production and world distribution). Paramount were offered distribution because they had handled *Il Conformista* in the US but they forecast a repetition of the *Queimada!* quarrels and wouldn't go ahead with Brando. Grimaldi tried companies the world over and discovered that the man once thought of as the screen's first actor was to all intents and purposes unfinanceable. Grimaldi finally convinced United Artists that the film could be brought in for very little cost, and that turned out to be $1,430,000 – of which UA's contribution was a mere $800,000. 'Marlon took very little up front,' said Grimaldi, which would seem to contradict the salary announced as $200,000 plus the inevitable percentage.

It is true that the companies approached were as wary of the subject matter as of Brando, since Bertolucci intended to breach the frontiers of sex as portrayed on the screen – even though the end of the Breen Office had ushered in a flood of naked bodies humping and thumping. The U A press office tried to pretend that it was delighted by the combination of star and director without much success: but this combination with sex did interest the world's press, which began to throb in anticipation.

The film was invited, and sent, to the 1972 New York film festival, in the hope that favourable American reviews would avert the expected censorship problems in Italy; and an apparently eminent American critic, Pauline Kael, wrote a notice (in *The New Yorker*, which, parenthetically, once had a reputation for the concinnity of its writers) in which she claimed that the film was as important an event in the history of the arts as the first night of 'The Rite of Spring' in 1913. *Time* magazine did a cover story entitled 'Love and Death in Paris', and there were whispers about sodomy as well as speculation on the film's involvement with art and censorship (invoking memories of *A Streetcar Named Desire*). It opened in Paris, it opened in New York; it opened in London, shorn of the scene where Brando sodomizes the girl with his trousers on – by which time, the presses of the world had ensured that there wasn't a literate person in the world who hadn't heard of it. As it opened, United Artists were predicting that it would overtake *The Godfather* as the most successful film ever made.

You might consider what it was the public would find more enticing than Vivien Leigh loving Clark Gable, Julie Andrews carolling in the hills above Salzburg or the carnage of the Mafia: a melancholy anecdote about an American widower in Paris and the girl he picks up in an empty apartment. They are both looking for a flat; he (Brando) is mourning his wife, she (Maria Schneider) is about to marry a young movie director (Jean-Pierre Léaud). He is sulky and rude; she is bright, casual, unruffable. After the publicity, it is no surprise to find that he has pinned her against the wall within seconds and is unbuttoning his fly – uncomfortable and unlikely, but not, in the circumstances, entirely incredible. He proposes that they continue to meet for that purpose – no ties, no surnames, just sex for the hell or the fun of it. Given the hangdog expression adopted by Brando since the first frame, it is hardly surprising that this is his scene or wherever the action now is in Paris. More seriously, he is a man going downhill, expended, a man beaten-up by life and betrayed; he wants no commitment beyond the sexual one, but he finds, only too soon, that it isn't enough. He talks about his past and encourages her to talk about her life. In the end, when she tells him that her marriage is imminent, he follows her, pleading, 'You know you're a jerk. The best fucking you'll ever get is right here in this apartment.' He follows her home, and she takes out a gun and kills him – always a good way to end a movie which has run out of steam (this sort of 'stop' to a movie, a common let-out in several rotten films of the sixties and seventies, was considered indecent by earlier film-makers – see Frank Capra's memoir). Dilys Powell wrote in *The Sunday Times*: 'Bertolucci has been reported as making the usual glib pronouncements about the impossibility people "in our society" find in communicating with another. His idea, then, was to show two figures in isolation who communicate solely through sex.' Death, of course, is the final isolation, with death there is no further communication; but for a film-maker of any aspiration it's a cop-out.

This movie certainly raised doubts about Bertolucci's talent; it is altogether quieter and less glittering than *Il Conformista* and the other films which preceded it, but when it does liven up it is only too reminiscent of their virtuoso passages. We are relieved of the room in Passy quite early, via some glossy flashbacks; later, when Brando returns to his home, it turns out to be a flophouse (there's no reason why it shouldn't be, but no reason why it should be, either). We learn that his wife had a lover (Massimo Girotti), there are clients knocking to be let in. When one client deserts his whore, Brando tears after him for a spot of beating-up against modernist billboards (close-ups of billboards being de rigueur in all sub-Godard movies). The last tango itself takes place on a dance-floor eerily like that in *Il Conformista*, with Brando and the girl drunk on champagne, shocking the patrons as the lesbian dance shocked us in the earlier film.

At this point, Brando unlooses his trousers and exposes his behind to a patron – a practice called 'mooning', and indulged in as a joke, so went the publicity, on the set of *The Godfather* by Brando and other cast members. The practice suggests an infantilism hitherto unsuspected in a profession not noted for maturity, but the fact that it turns up here confirms a suspicion that Brando is the real *auteur* of *Last Tango*. Bertolucci said that they discussed each scene before shooting, in perfect accord, but the extent of Brando's participation can be gauged by another remark of Bertolucci's, that the film is 'a melange of Hollywood and European cinema', which it isn't at all: there's nothing of Hollywood in it. He also said that he 'decided that to suggest and allude instead of saying it outright would create an unhealthy climate for the spectator' – but the sex isn't explicit (the girl is seen nude, but Brando only in part and discreetly). These are the expected, bourgeois remarks from this *Italian* director: what he shows may be shocking to him – since his earlier films reveal no exhibitionist tendencies in the manner of Vadim or Ken Russell. His later films do, but this business has often shown that if you discover a way to attract world-wide attention you will plough the same old furrow again and again. The film is autobiographical, according to Léaud, saying that it was pulled two ways, with Bertolucci making him the adolescent movie-maker and Brando dealing with his 'sexual obsessions' – and he goes on to remark that Bertolucci 'was too embarrassed to cast a character close to himself in age', but this would not have been so had Trintignant played the Brando role.

Léaud was completely swamped and didn't like the result: 'Maybe the sympathetic thing is to say that there was a clash of styles – Italian, French and American', but then this nouvelle vague mascot was required to work horribly hard on Saturdays, because Brando refused to, and the crew were not to waste time. Bertolucci described Brando as 'an angel as a man but a monster as an actor' and admitted that he improvised (no cue cards!) much of the dialogue of *Last Tango*, including the reminiscences of his youth – dialogue which has all the scintillation and wit of the monologues in lesser Godard. As David Leitch wrote in *The New Statesman* (under a review headed '*Merde de Taureau*'): 'Brando's ad-libbing, dredged from that area of Hemingway the novelist was too rigorous to publish, speaks for itself. An amazingly deft amalgam of the worst of "To Have and Have Not" and "Across the River and Into the Trees".'

The dialogue of the 'love' scenes is, at least, of a new cinema level. 'What strong arms you have,' she says. 'The better to squeeze a fart out of you,' he replies, going on with the Red Riding Hood analogies to talk of crabs and putting his tongue in her rear. Later, she: 'What are we doing in this apartment?' He: 'Let's just say we're taking a flying fuck at a doughnut' – and that's the nearest this film gets to a glimmer of humour. As for the sodomy, him with his trousers on, using butter as a lubricant, you wonder that grown people can offer it as entertainment, or a comment on human behaviour or whatever. It is supposed to represent the degradation to which the girl has sunk, after which she must reassert sanity and return to her film director – but *Screw* magazine and *Playboy* would have us believe that it's common practice among 'liberated' couples; and, anyway, Brando degrades her even more heinously in his tirade – wanting to see her fucked by a pig, etc. He then goes home to look at his wife's corpse, abusing her in the same manner for about five minutes. The two scenes together make up the most repellently misogynist sequence of any movie yet made. They would be equalled in 1986 by Bertrand Blier's *Tenue de Soirée*, the tale of a gay man who wins another man away from his wife. One source says that Bertolucci originally envisaged *Last Tango* as a story about two men, but did not feel that the world was ready for that. The final scene of *Il Conformista* reveals that the hero's troubles are entirely due to his having suppressed his homosexuality – but that is one sexual perversion missing from those paraded in Bertolucci's films, suggesting that it is not a subject he finds of much appeal.

There was much speculation as to what extent Brando improvised the 'love'-making as he did the dialogue – as to how much it was his 'scene'. It is not hard to imagine the otherwise private Brando, a masochist in several previous movies, deciding on a Christ-like atonement for being a film star, purveyor of sexual excitement to the masses. He does succeed in holding his dignity, because of the sad lion's head and the uncanny way he has imagined himself into this gruesome, middle-aged failure – the most direct playing of a derelict by any Hollywood actor that the screen has known. (It is curious: Miss Schneider says, 'As he thinks himself old, only one thing interests him – his make-up. He is lazy, indolent . . . and he drinks too much. Only one thing interests him – love.') It is Bertolucci who becomes suspect. We do not know which of them made the new-to-them discovery that people play games during sex, but after a self-conscious display by Brando and Schneider it is Bertolucci, obviously, who cuts to a shot of two ducks – an unnecessary introduction to scenes of Léaud filming, and a very clumsy device.

The film abounds in such devices – like the razor Brando fondles – he may have a death wish, but it is a hack-movie way of creating tension. Bertolucci's central idea, that sexual congress with a stranger is a release from loneliness, was not new, but it was new for films – or almost: in *Mademoiselle*, directed by Tony Richardson and written by Jean Genet, an unbalanced schoolmistress and an Italian immigrant woodcutter come together from loneliness, and they too bay like dogs as a prelude to love-making; Brando had toyed with this script some seven years earlier before relinquishing it, but he had also claimed then that it was the only film he wanted to do. The situation could still make a good movie – there is strength in this room, and these two characters (and as played by these two); but it would have to be in either French or in English and not in this uneasy mixture. Anyone who has lived in Paris knows how easily bilingual French and Americans slip from one language to the other, but in this movie it's show-off, quite unnatural, as if United Artists wanted both an art movie and a commercial one – hedging their bets, the best of all possible worlds. What *is* here is inescapably dreary: two hours nine minutes of what might have been a footnote in Kraft-Ebbing.

The public sensed this; within a few months of the film's opening, United Artists revised their estimates of its eventual earnings. Its reputation as the most 'candid' major film yet made – outside the more consciously cheery soft- and hard-core pornographic movies – was offset by the fact that no one who saw it considered it erotic; but that was offset again by the fact that it was mentioned in all the arguments and battles waged over censorship in 1973 – and in fact it was banned in a handful of backward towns, as well as in Italy itself. Wherever possible, UA booked it into classy cinemas, many of which raised their price from three dollars to five – taking it to a domestic take of $16 million, but nowhere close to the $86,275,000 of *The God-father*. In Hollywood it was premiered at a hundred dollar black tie affair, attracting such notables as Cary Grant, who didn't know precisely what he thought of it, 'except that it did seem crude to me. I really don't know why Marlon made it'. The lady of the *New Yorker* did, but that put her in the position of having to defend the even more rubbishy movies Bertolucci subsequently made. In 1985 he explained that he was in analysis because he made 'such beautiful movies and no one goes to see them'. In 1987 he made *The Last Emperor*, which had much less of his customary sexual foolishness; it went on to win nine Oscars, including one for Best Director. It is one of the worst directed movies ever made. Let Brando have the last word (speaking to Adriano Botta for *L'Europeo*): 'This was a true film. I'll add that it is humane and poetic. Things which are too real always give us a sense of irritation, of nausea, and this film is real. It is difficult to create a work of art at any time and expect everyone to understand.' As to how much of him was in the role, he went on, 'Only a certain desperate melancholy. A gloomy regret. Self-hatred. All men, when they reach my age unless they are complete idiots must feel an emptiness inside, a sense of anguish, of uselessness.' Yet I would say this: the film was expected to be widely influential, and it did inspire a number of other third-rate film-makers to expect that their fantasies, usually sexual, would have infinite box-office pickings. From Franco Brusati's 1974 *Pane e Cioccolata* to 'Nic' Roeg's 1980 *Bad Timing* they failed to achieve that purpose, and most of them make *Last Tango* look like a blazing masterpiece.

There was another reason to discuss Brando in the spring of 1973. *The Godfather* brought him a slew of awards, despite the fact that his antics in *Last Tango* had alienated the industry more completely than his lack of drawing-power a year earlier. It was announced that Brando's Don

Corleone had won both the New York critics' award and the Golden Globe proffered by the Hollywood foreign correspondents, but he politely declined to accept either. He was nominated for an Oscar, but didn't acknowledge the missive from the Academy informing him of the fact. As he became odds-on favourite to win it was necessary to hold some seats at the Dorothy Chandler Pavilion in Los Angeles in case he decided to turn up – though there was every indication (see above) that he would emulate George C. Scott, who two years earlier had asked for his name to be eliminated from the nominations and who had ignored the ceremony, the statuette, etc. when it wasn't. After the festivities had started Brando's secretary arrived with an Indian girl, Sasheen Littlefeather, with a four-page speech and a mandate from Brando authorizing her to refuse the award – if given – on his behalf.

Her speech was on the injustices meted out to native tribes of America by the white settlers – a matter connected to the Academy Awards because 'the motion picture community has been as responsible as any for degrading the Indian and making a mockery of his character and describing him as savage, hostile and evil . . . I, as a member of this profession, do not feel that I can as a citizen of the United States accept an award here tonight.' There was more in the same vein, but the booers were trying to drown her out and she herself realized that the President of the Academy had meant it when he had threatened to have her hauled off if she exceeded the allotted two minutes. Miss Littlefeather remained composed as she bowed off, but then she was not without experience as a performer. Elsewhere in Hollywood she was known as Maria Cruz, a starlet, or Miss American Vampire, a title won in a publicity contest in 1971.

Brando later sent a copy of the speech to *The New York Times* and other papers, and it was admirably argued, if a bit naive in the belief that he was punishing the Academy or the industry for the treatment meted out to the American Indian by movies since their inception. But even before the revelation that Miss Littlefeather was not Miss Littlefeather, the whole thing had backfired: he had used Hollywood's gala night for politicizing; he had been too cowardly to come in person, and, worse, hid behind a woman's skirts; and Gregory Peck's comment was not entirely uncalled-for, that if Brando wanted to make a gesture he might have offered the Indians some of his enormous earnings from *The Godfather* and *Last Tango*. Few could disagree with John Wayne, the antithesis politically of all that Brando believed in: 'I think it was sad that Brando did what he did. If he had something to say, he should have appeared that night and stated his views instead of taking some little unknown girl and dressing her up in an Indian outfit. What he was doing was trying to avoid the issue that was *really* on his mind, which was the provocative story of *Last Tango in Paris*.' Since Wayne is Wayne, let us return temporarily to that topic and let *him* have the final word. He hadn't made a point of seeing the film, he confessed, but Brando 'is one of the finest actors we've had in this business, and I'm only sorry he didn't have the benefit of older, more established friends – as I did – to help him choose the proper material in which to use his talent'.

As far as the Oscar ceremony was concerned, what was uncomfortably clear was that Brando's rejection of the award was entirely consistent with the worst of his public behaviour since he first achieved fame: he was showing off in the worst sort of megalomaniac film star manner. Peter Ustinov put it this way: 'I admire George C. Scott enormously but for him to refuse awards, and for Marlon Brando to refuse awards, is another way of accepting them with more noise than is normal.' Brando acted in the way most convenient to him, typically misunderstanding the actual importance of the Oscar ceremonies: if the cause was really dear to him, he could have gone on every talk-show in the US to air his views. This was pointed out to him, and he accepted an invitation to appear in Dick Cavett's show in July, when he talked about the Indian cause with, said *Variety*, 'conviction and indignation'.

He said that his next film would be about the cause, and he turned down the sequel to *The Godfather*, or, rather, he said he would only do it for a ridiculously high price – $500,000 plus 10 per cent of the profits, said *Variety*, for what was merely a cameo role. Paramount declined to meet his price, which gave him the last laugh, since it took only $30,673,000 at the box-office, or just over one-third of that earned by *The Godfather*, despite the fact that both films had been praised by the press and both won a Best Picture Oscar. It seemed that the public didn't want a Brandoless *Godfather* too much. It is true that Paramount kept coming after Brando: they may not have wanted him for *Last Tango*, but they were going to get him for *Child's Play*, based on a Broadway thriller about warring schoolteachers; James Mason was to play the other one and it was the first movie of the Broadway producer David Merrick, directed by Sidney Lumet, who assured everyone concerned that he could handle Brando. It was Merrick who couldn't, so that after many differences he left the cast and was replaced by Robert Preston – and the film's box-office failure may have convinced Brando of his re-acquired infallibility, since most of the brouhaha surrounding *The Godfather* and *Last Tango* had concerned him.

'Marlon wanted the moon and stars,' said Robert Evans, explaining why Brando did not play the title-role in the 1974 remake of *The Great Gatsby*, planned to star Evans's then wife, Ali McGraw – which was why so many other star actors had turned it down. 'The fact that Paramount approached Marlon really makes you wonder. Didn't anyone [there] bother to read the novel?' asked Robert

Redford, noting that Gatsby was almost twenty years younger than Brando – but who, despite that, would surely have been more appropriate in the role than Redford himself. Evans considered Brando's demand was such 'because he was angry at not having a bigger percentage of *The Godfather*. I told him we did not have that kind of budget and he said, "Well, take a slice of *Godfather*."'

Last Tango and the Oscar business had undone much of the good done by *The Godfather*, and the industry continued to evolve, moving away from the prima donnas and the legends. He was no longer the industry's rebel, but a pariah, an outsider; no longer the golden boy, but a chubby middle-aged man with a gaunt face and grey locks falling to his shoulders. He spoke of retiring, and terminated his contract with his agent, saying that he doubted whether he'd need him again. His indifference to his career had probably been increased by his last two films, which had restored him to glory and a seemingly limitless earning capacity (on 4 September 1973 *Variety* reported that Brando had pocketed $1,600,000 of his 'cut-off' profits from *The Godfather*, and that his agent was estimating that he would earn $3 million from *Last Tango*). Besides, after stuffing your cheeks with cotton-wool for the highest-earning film ever made, and baring your soul for the most-discussed movie in a decade, what is there left to do? Maybe it has something to do with the way he looked in *Last Tango*, or the effect of the whole depressing enterprise, but one was tempted to see him as a spent force.

14
Taking the Money and Running

As far as the industry was concerned, Brando was back at the top – though it was a fact not universally pleasing. He received another Oscar nomination – his seventh – for *Last Tango*; he was 6th in the exhibitors' box-office top ten in 1972 and 10th in 1973. The Oscar went to Jack Lemmon for *Save the Tiger* and Brando continued to find himself attacked. The television presenter Rona Barrett in her capacity of Hollywood gossip columnist wrote a syndicated article demanding to know why Brando was using his vast earnings from *The Godfather* and *Last Tango* on developing Tetiaroa instead of giving them to the Indians.

Some months later he announced that he was giving a site of forty acres in California back to the Indians. It was the traditional home of the Chumash tribe which he had recently purchased, and he hoped that others would follow his example; but AAISA – the Survival of the American Indian Association – chose to sell it to real estate developers, with Brando's approval, since insurance and taxes did not, in the end, make it too welcome a gift.

Burt Reynolds, himself part-Indian, criticized this transaction when interviewed by Roderick Mann: the gift, he said, turned out to be hypothetical since Brando had only wished to re-establish his prestige. Let us remain for a moment with Reynolds, who said that he could write a book on Brando, since for the last seventeen years he had been hearing strange stories about him: 'He's an extraordinary man. He's the best actor of his profession . . . a genius, and even when he's bored he's better than most others at the top of their form.' But, Reynolds said, he had preserved an adolescent mentality: 'When he isn't acting and you speak to him it's like talking to a blind wall: indeed, it's even worse since you can always suppose that there's someone behind the wall.'

For his part Brando is even less complimentary: 'As for Burt Reynolds, you reassess him the more when he is dark and hairy, then the more he is virile. I think he drinks hormone-based potions and has had a transplant of black hairs.'

In the same interview he had harsh words for Robert Redford and Ryan O'Neal, and implied that with the exception of Jack Nicholson – with whom he was then working – the only young actor whom he admired was Dustin Hoffman: 'He has talent. He should get out from under that nervous personality which he got under his skin in *Midnight Cowboy* and then one could see whether he's really a complete actor.'

Also in the interview he explained what he was doing at this time: 'I did a lot of things. I participated in a little war between the Indians and the pale skins, I made love, I got fat, I got thin, I read several completely idiotic books and I cried a lot. When things aren't going well I cry. And then also, I accumulated a lot of money and dispensed it "scientifically".'

He did not say that he had been trying to wrest a script from Dee Brown's eloquent study of a tragic episode in Indian history – the Battle of Wounded Knee in 1876 – 'Bury My Heart at Wounded Knee'. Employed to work on it was Abby Mann, whose television plays and films – *Judgement at Nuremberg, Ship of Fools* – showed him to be of the required liberal persuasion but uninspired as a dramatist. After three attempts at a screenplay Mann left without acrimony: 'Marlon makes wonderful contributions,' he said. 'He can sit down and improvise better than I can write it.' As in the case of *One-Eyed Jacks* Brando turned to a young and newly-acclaimed director, Martin Scorsese, whose *Mean Streets* had not long opened. Speaking of their work together Scorsese doesn't mention Dee Brown's book, but he does specify a film on the American Indian and does say that they finally spent all night trying 'to map out' a script before giving up. As reported, Pontecorvo was prevailed upon to take over, with the bitterness of filming *Queimada!* now in the past: this time he enjoyed the experience of working with Brando – and of talking to his Indian friends; his connection with the project ended when Brando failed to get financing. It is not known whether this was before or after December 1974, when this item appeared in the magazine *Take One*: 'Marlon Brando, star and co-producer of what he says will be his last film, *Wounded Knee*, has so far talked Steve McQueen, Barbra Streisand, Jane Fonda, Paul Newman and Lee Marvin into working on the film for union minimum.' A year later the film was on the schedule of the producer John Foreman, who had partnered Paul Newman on some very successful films, including *Butch Cassidy and the Sundance Kid*. 'I am a firm believer in the maxim that you can't have a tiger without its stripes,' he said, adding significantly, 'There *are* certain things about Brando: he doesn't return telephone calls, he does break appointments. But what he brings to a part far outweighs the problems.' That was the last the outside world heard of the project.

Brando turned his attention instead to *The Missouri Breaks*, hoping that that might be 'a serious study of the American Indian'. 'Gee, Marlon, not at these prices,' replied the director, Arthur Penn, referring to the salaries being paid to Brando and his co-star, Jack Nicholson. Nicholson had moved house and now lived near Brando, whom he referred to as 'the guy on the hill. He's the one to beat.' He mentioned that he wanted to work with him, and the item in an interview caught the attention of Elliott Kastner, who had produced *The Night of the Following Day* and *The Nightcomers*. He had an outline for two male stars, rather in the manner of *Butch Cassidy and the Sundance Kid* – though as yet only tentative, as penned by Thomas McGuane; with the assurance of his stars' interest he soon had a group of tax shelter investors and a director, Penn, who later observed wryly, 'The picture took only a few months to shoot but the deal lasted nearly a year.' He also said: 'I think we were victims of our own version of the cavalier attitude of the seventies. We took the money and ran. Remember, that was the movie that broke the million-dollar barrier for two actors – Brando and Nicholson got one and a quarter million each for that film.' That was, for five and ten weeks' work respectively; had the film gone into profit Brando stood to get 11.3 per cent of all gross receipts over $8,850,000 and Nicholson 10 per cent of those over $12.500.000.

While negotiations proceeded Penn and Kastner were commuting between Los Angeles – to confer with Nicholson, the South-Pacific – to see Brando, and London – where McGuane was making on *92 in the Shade*. Of the three, the South Pacific was the most dispensable because it was the least accessible; London was the most important, since the screenplay wasn't working. Penn says that McGuane was working on the script of *92 in the Shade*, but it is more probable that he was supervising the editing, for the film opened a good nine months before *The Missouri Breaks*: he was making his directorial debut on this Florida-based tale, and it was clearly important to him. At all events, he did not supply the completed screenplay Penn thought necessary – which may well be why Brando thought the Indian problem might be included in a subject basically concerning rustlers and ranchers. Once again for him filming began without the words to work from – and precipitously, for not only had United Artists scheduled the film to open for the Memorial Day weekend, in 1976, but Nicholson had numerous future commitments (partly as a result of being newly-Oscared for his role in *One Flew Over the Cuckoo's Nest*).

Said the actor Dennis Quaid, who wasn't in the film but who experienced the location shooting because his brother Randy was: 'It was real chaotic. Making up the script as they went along. They had about nine different versions of each scene. Fascinating! I don't know if I was Brando's tutor, exactly. I play guitar, of course, and they stipulated I should show him a few chords for the mandolin he used in one scene. That's all. Least I got to meet my idol – a very nice man. After that, I quit being impressed by people. Including him. Everybody has snot coming out of their noses once in a while, right?' Kathleen Lloyd, a newcomer cast in the female lead, was less complimentary: 'Marlon changed his lines all the time. He changed his costume and character interpretation. He even changed his accent from scene to scene which absolutely amazed me.'

Penn, however, defended Brando: 'Marlon's a thorough professional. He knew his lines perfectly.' He admits that Kastner was not of the same opinion: without his knowledge, Brando had agreed to remain after his cut-off date, to get 'whatever was necessary to finish the film' – but Kastner, fearful that that was his last day, was rushing about the set holding up Brando's cue-cards, which, when the actor saw them, made him look in any other direction. Kastner was less amused by this than the rest of the cast and crew.

The story is as old as Western movies: the enmity between the ranchers and the cattle rustlers, with Nicholson

leading the latter and Brando as the 'regulator' hired by
the former. But like some other 'debunking' films of the
70s, traditions are upended and it's part of the thesis that
the lawman should be the villain and the rustler the hero –
but Brando's performance prevents this idea from being
effective. He is first seen hanging along the side of a horse
in the manner of the drunken Lee Marvin in *Cat Ballou*,
except that he isn't drunk. He wears his hair like a hippie,
keeping it in place with a bandana; he has an Irish accent,
which he loses when – for obscure reasons – he imperson-
ates a priest (equally oddly, he gets into drag at one stage);
because of his binoculars (apparently common in the old
West) he seems to be a voyeur. He even has a bathroom
scene with lots of foam, but not enough to hide a body at
his age better covered up. His horse and he chew on the
same carrot and might be even more intimate: he likes to
sing to him. There is no reason why a lawman shouldn't
be eccentric, but this one gives the impression of being
stark, staring mad.

Said Andrew Sarris in the *Village Voice*: 'You really
have to see Brando and Nicholson to experience the extraordinary lack of electricity between them' – and that is
mainly because Brando destroys every scene in which he
appears. 'He's making a complete ass of himself' was
Stanley Kauffmann's verdict in the *New Republic*, which concluded, 'If Brando doesn't like acting, why doesn't he quit?'
John Simon found Brando's performance 'utterly lament-
able . . . even more slatternly and self-indulgent than his
bloated physique. Starting with a correspondence-school
brogue and bits of mannerisms left over from *The Nightcomers*, an effeteness and smarminess . . . He comes across
as a mixture of Rod Steiger doing Hennessy and Tallulah
Bankhead doing Tallulah.'

Simon considered that only Nicholson 'comes out of
this mess well-nigh unscathed' and few would disagree.
Penn looked back on the experience and observed that he

would never again be tempted to do anything for the money. The film took a mere $6,752,000 at the American box-office, thus ensuring that Brando would get none of his unmerited profit participation.

When I asked Elia Kazan whether he had seen *The Missouri Breaks* he replied, 'The man must really despise his profession to give a performance like that.' He also said, 'I think the whole picture was unfortunate, that from the beginning he wished he hadn't done it. The worst kind of betrayal in life is self-betrayal. I think he began to something which he must regret, which is, well, like George Scott, he is embarrassed by being an actor. He didn't like the profession, or said he didn't. He hated it, he said. Finally he began to do something for the money like *Superman*. Three weeks, three million bucks. There was a time he could have done absolutely anything, any picture that he wanted – he could have had them written for him, he could have chosen his material. He didn't do it.'

Apocalypse Now was made before, but released after *Superman*. The idea of re-setting Conrad's novel 'The Heart of Darkness' in the present day was that of John Milius, and in 1967 George Lucas was to have directed it for Francis Coppola's company and Warner Bros – till Warners' then management went cold on Coppola's company. When Coppola was 'hot' again, after the two *Godfather* films, there was a more favourable response, even with the hefty budget of $13 million. United Artists was not prepared to foot the entire bill, so Coppola sold the rights in several foreign territories – including the ambitious EMI in Britain – though none with an advance of more than a million dollars. These distributors wanted the guarantee of star power – and there were two roles of star dimensions, Willard and Kurtz. Willard was offered to Steve McQueen who turned it down twice – first because he didn't feel right for the role and then, after some rewriting, because he didn't want to take his children on a location shoot of seventeen weeks. Kurtz was offered to Brando, who indicated through his lawyer, Norman Garey, that he wasn't too interested. When Al Pacino discovered that he couldn't fit Willard into his schedule Coppola turned back to McQueen, but this time for the part of Kurtz. Since that required only three weeks' work McQueen agreed to do it, but only at the $3 million offered for the more arduous role. Coppola thought this might be feasible if he could get James Caan for Willard at a reasonable price, i.e., $1,250,000 – but Caan's agent held out for $2 million. Willard was then offered to Jack Nicholson, who was otherwise engaged; so was Robert Redford – though he was prepared to consider playing Kurtz, since it required so much less work on location. Coppola then dispensed with the idea of McQueen as Kurtz and offered it to Nicholson, who was still too busy. It was then rewritten to suit Pacino, who refused to commit himself – at which point Brando's lawyer suggested that Brando would take it if the price was right: $3,500,000 plus a percentage. That precluded having another major star as Willard, and that role went to Harvey Keitel, who was however fired after the first few days' shooting. He was replaced by Martin Sheen, whom Coppola had bumped into in an airport lounge.

Production began in April 1976 (with Brando not starting work till the end of the summer, which he wanted to spend with his children) and it was in an unfinished state when it was premiered at the Cannes Film Festival three years later – since Coppola wanted to test audience reaction. By the time it opened in the US in August we knew more about its cost than was good for it. It had become the most expensive film since *Cleopatra* – though some even more expensive films were in the works – and would have to take $40 million to break even. The negative cost had escalated to $31,100,000, much of that due to weather conditions and Sheen's heart attack: UA involvement had risen to $20 million, though that included a loan to Coppola, who had sold or hocked most of his properties – and had, including that loan, an investment of $18 million in it.

The gist of his promotion was that the film was beyond criticism, because it was an honest attempt to comment on the Vietnam War; it was also 'rich and multi-levelled' with an ending 'like a Jungian exercise'. Thus he was scathing about critics who were less than enthusiastic: 'It's outrageous to make the effort I did and be greeted by slapdash attitudes and big egos.' Vincent Canby responded to that in *The New York Times*: 'It's a serious attempt to deal with the manifold meanings of the American involvement in Vietnam but . . . is it to be a Philistine to suggest that though there is nothing wrong with personal movie-making, there is something slightly askew with personal movie-making on the grandiose scale of *Apocalypse Now?*' In Britain John Coleman in the *New Statesman* and Peter Ackroyd echoed this opinion, though their main complaint concerned the pretension of the finale.

That is when Brando appears. Willard has a series of adventures when sent up river to assassinate Kurtz, a brilliant, distinguished Green Beret officer who has gone native and started his own kingdom of deserters – a theme, in fact, calling to mind Graham Greene rather than Conrad and descending to any number of daft jungle movies in which the hero stumbles on a mad ruler. Kurtz himself wanders about in a kaftan, his face in part-shadow, clearly as mad as a hatter, reading T. S. Eliot's 'The Hollow Men', Fraser's 'The Golden Bough', Weston's 'From Ritual to Romance'. These cultural references are supposed to justify Coppola's claim of 'multi-levelled', flattering spectators recognizing them. He would seem to be ambivalent towards Kurtz; a photograph of Charles Manson the mass-murderer propels us back to 1968, a time of American madness, flower power and gutter-level philosophy. The ending is less a Jungian exercise than a way of stopping a story which has no further way to go.

Brando's performance – for the first time in his career – is dwarfed by his material, which is not to say that the material is good. Most accounts suggest that he was responsible for most of his own dialogue – and therefore with the film's deterioration in the final sequence. Although till them it has the confidence of its own considerable ambitions it must be reconsidered in the light of Coppola's later work, i.e., *One From the Heart* and *The Outsiders*, other examples of 'personal' film-making which rank among the most misconceived and pretentious ever to see the light of day. The first, in particular, lost a small mint of money. *Apocalypse Now* took $38 million domestic, a noble achievement, but not, in view of the cost, one likely to have United Artists' executives dancing in the streets. Coppola would be the last person to recoup, but he predicted a series of reissues starting in 1986 when the rights reverted to him. He was also confident that it would never be sold to television. He was wrong on both counts.

Superman – The Movie was also initially plagued by casting problems. The heyday of the comic strip hero was probably soon after he first appeared, in 1938. He featured in a television series of the 50s, but that was eclipsed by the camp success of his rival, Batman, in the 60s. The resulting movie, *Batman*, caused no box-office rush, and the big screen Superman was originally envisaged as a medium-budget imitation of the James Bond films. The idea came from Pierre Spengler in association with the Salkinds, father Alexander and son Ilya. Alexander Salkind was one of the ambitious fly-by-nighters who had plagued the French film industry almost since its inception; in 1963 Alexander with his father Michel produced Orson Welles's *The Trial* which left a lot of bills unpaid – and which was perhaps only finished because Welles paid the cast with his own money. In 1971 Alexander and Ilya produced the

Spanish-French-Lichtenstein *The Light at the End of the World*, a Jules Verne tale with Kirk Douglas and Yul Brynner, after which they were joined by Spengler and good luck for *The Three Musketeers*, directed by Richard Lester. Mario Puzo was assigned to write the screenplay, which was thought too heavy, so the producers turned to a team which had written a Broadway musical based on the comic strip – Robert Benton and David Newman, in fact more famous for the screenplay of *Bonnie and Clyde* (the final screenplay was credited to all three writers, plus Newman's wife Leslie).

The project looked permanently stalled at one time, as so many writs were flying about London: no case came to court, probably due to the intervention of Warner Bros, who were investing in the production. Another more certifiable cause of delay was the casting of the title-role. Robert Redford was always the first choice, but he didn't like the screenplay; Warren Beatty and even Charles Bronson were mentioned. According to Ilya Salkind, he was 'going bananas' over the casting when the phone rang: 'It was an agent friend and he asked, almost casually, whether I would be interested in having Marlon Brando in the cast. He said he thought Marlon would do it if the terms were right.' The agent we may assume to be Brando's lawyer, who from the days of helping him battle Anna Kashfi was now representing such other show business figures as Frances Coppola and Gene Hackman – who was signed for *Superman* immediately after Brando. The rest of the casting was then easy, with an unknown, Christopher Reeve, signed to play the title-role – which was seriously sought by Sylvester Stallone, who had just scored his big success in *Rocky*. Brando had veto right on casting, Stallone consoled himself with that success, wondering whether Brando would think he was doing a cheap imitation of him in the love scene in *Rocky*.

Brando was also getting $3.7 million for what amounted

to twelve days' work. Production was also switched from Italy to Britain, since Brando was unable to set foot in Italy without the risk of an arrest on an obscenity conviction for *Last Tango*. Guy Hamilton was replaced as director by Richard Donner, fresh from *The Omen*. Said Donner: 'Two days into the role he came to me late in the afternoon and said he had a cold and was still a bit jet-lagged. Would I mind if he finished early that day? That floored me. Knowing how little time we had with him, I'd even been figuring out what it would cost us every time he went to the lavatory. Now this. But I said the only thing I could say: "You're Marlon Brando. How can I stop you?" Then he said, "Tell you what, I'll give you an extra day. How about that?" Well, at his salary that extra day was worth a fortune. And it meant that we could get everything we needed. So, I sent him home happily.'

The film, in my opinion, is a triumph, an entertainment for children that will endure as long as *The Wizard of Oz*, but all that concerns us here is the prologue. It takes place on the planet of Krypton, where a panel of elders is condemning to death some malefactors. The adjudicator in white is Brando in a curly silver wig; in his argument with some other elders (Trevor Howard, Maria Schell, Harry Andrews) we learn that the planet is about to be destroyed; after consultation with his wife (Susannah York) he decides to send their son to the planet Earth. Krypton falls apart and thus, after twenty minutes, there depart from the film half the stars who got their names on the posters, sometimes with only a couple of lines each. The whole sequence is, as subsequent events prove, unnecessary, and not a patch on what follows.

The public flocked to it, and although it had ended up by costing an astronomical $55 million it took in over $82 million in the US/Canadian market, the highest such sum in the history of Warner Bros. A sequel was not so much on the cards as almost in the can. Even as *Superman* premiered it was said that from forty to sixty per cent of *Superman II* had already been shot. Something similar had happened with *The Three Musketeers*, when the Salkinds negotiated with the cast additional fees for work which they had already done. The situation this time was more complicated, since they sacked Donner and replaced him with Richard Lester, who had directed both the Dumas films. Spengler and Lester claimed that only ten per cent of what he had shot was used in *Superman II*. The chicanery went back a while, according to the *Los Angeles Times* which reported (3 April 1980) that Alexander Salkind had demanded $15 million from Warner Bros in order to release the sole negative of the first *Superman* for its projected première in December 1978, at which time he was arrested in Switzerland, accused of stealing $20 million from a German company owned by William Forman, a Los Angeles tycoon – but escaped a remand in jail by claiming immunity as a Costa Rican diplomat: the case was settled out of court.

It is much less clear what happened when the participants of *Superman* discovered that much of what they had worked on was already earmarked as *Superman II* – and there might have been more of it, had the producers had the funding. The four main complainants seem to have been Donner, Puzo, Brando and Margot Kidder, who so delightfully played Superman's girlfriend, Lois Lane. 'I've been told not to talk about it but I don't care. They are truly despicable people and it's time it came out,' she told a reporter, adding, 'They tried to screw me out of $40,000 which was a huge amount of money to me . . . They were behaving totally illegally and it ended up costing them over a million.' As far as Brando was concerned, he had sued for $50 million within a month of the film's opening, alleging that he wasn't being paid his share of the gross receipts; as far as *Superman II* was concerned, he forbade the use of his image unless a further large fee was paid –

causing most of his footage to be reshot with Susannah York, though he could not prevent a brief cut-in from the earlier film being used in flashback. Nothing is known of a settlement, but since *Superman II* was almost as big a hit as its predecessor it was probably amicable on all sides.

Brando's contribution to the saga was summed up by the critic Jack Kroll in *Newsweek* and by Billy Wilder. The former observed: 'Brando has become a beguilingly monstrous grotesque of fatherhood and authority in *The Godfather* and now as Jor-El . . . a bit like an intergalactic Liberace in his vanilla wig and fluorescent caftan.' Said Wilder: 'Mr Marlon Brando got, for an aggregate of twenty minutes on the screen in *Superman* and *Apocalypse Now*, more money than Clark Gable got for twenty years at MGM.' But I cannot move on without noting that Robert Redford was critical: the stars of today, he observed, were less interested in their fans than their bank accounts . . . 'Some among them can retire to an island, transforming it bit by bit with millions of dollars into a paradise reserved exclusively for millionaires.' He considered Brando correct, he went on, in taking what he could get for *The Godfather*, since the film rested on his shoulders, 'but despite my admiration for his talent – one of the finest actors of his generation – I can't help thinking his demands, for the secondary role in the first *Superman*, excessive'. The reason he himself had accepted a huge sum for *A Bridge Too Far* – $2 million, though he didn't say so – was to cut short the arguments of the director, Richard Attenborough, and because he had 'enormous obligations'. The industry was in a crisis, he concluded, but unlike certain 'superstars', he didn't want to make it worse. Brando had his revenge: asked about the stars who had followed him he described them as 'All monkeys who have learnt their lesson by heart. Where would they be if I hadn't showed them the way?' Redford he found especially objectionable: 'He's only a dumbbell who moves his arms about like the sails of a windmill. If that's the new style of acting, I know nothing about it.'

Another who admired him was Barbra Streisand. Brando had appeared in three of the biggest hits of the decade; he might have been in a fourth – the 1976 remake of *A Star is Born*, thus getting a second crack at the role he had turned down in the 1954 version. According to Frank Pierson, who directed, there was a crisis when Streisand and her producer-lover, Jon Peters, insisted on having Brando at any price. (Kris Kristofferson played the role.) Streisand herself said that it was her dream to act with him; that every time she received a script she thought, 'Can Brando do this?' – which may be why in 1979 he was asking $3 million plus 25 per cent of the receipts to co-star with her. No further details were made available and the film was never made.

'The finest actor who ever lived,' she called him. 'To me, he's a phenomenon . . . He has done enough good work to last for two lifetimes. What people don't understand is the pain of it all, the pain of performing, the pain of getting up in front of the cast and the crew and delving into your guts and exposing yourself. And he knows that pain and he doesn't choose to act, except, perhaps, for money now. Which is a very valid reason. I mean, in his position and point in life, where he would like to relax and live on his island in Tahiti and be left alone.'

15
Stalled

In 1979 Brando did his first acting for television for almost thirty years. Two years earlier an ABC mini-series, *Roots*, had been watched by more people – 66 per cent of the audience, or 130 million – than any other programme in the history of American television. It was a dramatization of Alex Haley's novel chronicling his family history from the time they were rounded up as slaves in Africa to the emancipation at the time of the Civil War. *Roots: the Next Generations* took up the story in 1882 and continued to the present day, with James Earl Jones playing Haley. Brando reputedly telephoned Haley to ask whether there was a role for him, knowing from the first series that most of the whites in the saga were not portrayed sympathetically. He played one of the nastiest of all, George Lincoln Rockwell, the American Nazi who in the 60s had been interviewed by Haley for *Playboy*. He was on screen for less than ten minutes, chanting racist jingles and spraying his office with disinfectant – and later winning an Emmy award as Outstanding Supporting Actor. The producer, David Wolper, told the press that he was paid much less than he deserved; and that he gave the fee to charity.

A year later Wolper and Brando were in conflict over *Hanta Yo*, which was to explain an Indian family to television audiences in the manner of Haley's work; but the author of the original novel, Ruth Beebe Hill, was not an

Indian and it contained numerous inaccuracies. Brando, in conjunction with an Indian group, the Black Hills Treaty Council, managed to persuade Wolper to make changes to the text and to the title – which became *The Mystic Warrior*. As such it limped into view four years later, to little or no interest.

One who commented on Brando's performance in *Roots II* is the actor Roy Scheider: 'Within five minutes you totally understand why that man's brain is so twisted. You find yourself thinking, Why don't they leave him alone? I mean, if he played Hitler, you'd love him.' Let us stay with the interview, since Scheider is so revealing: 'Now, *there* is a strange animal . . . Marlon is a pure piece of animal flesh. He's pansexual, beyond normalcy of any kind. He's so delicate. He can outfeminize any woman in any scene. He became more vulnerable than Blanche du Bois.' Referring to the interview Brando gave to *Playboy*, Scheider went on, 'Without meaning to – in fact, while trying to say just the opposite – Brando revealed that he still loves acting. That drive that made him a great actor is still there. As sour and twisted and jaded as he's become, as much as he now wants to be remembered as a philosopher, a philanthropist, as savior of the Indians, the joy of the performance is still in him . . . He's still an artist.' Scheider concluded: 'Marlon has screwed up a lot of roles in recent years, just deliberately shit all over the director and the script and everything else. Still, the talent is there, and once in a while he'll give you a few minutes of his special genius, and then it's magic time.'

George C. Scott was of similar opinion. He started by agreeing that Brando may have wasted his talent, but only because it was 'so colossal'. He had no doubt that Brando had or has 'authentic genius in his field' and he explained why: 'The thing about his genius is the originality, the freshness that he brought to acting. Just overwhelming. Nobody had seen anything like that before. I never had. And certainly nobody else had. Brando is in a class by himself. Been there for years. I can't conceive of a man who has suffered through more disappointing experiences than he has professionally. I'm not the least surprised that he doesn't want to work or that he wants eighty zillion dollars to work. I mean, if I were him, I would have told them to go fuck themselves a long time ago.'

When Scott gave this interview he had just finished work on *The Formula* with Brando, written by Steve Shagan from his novel and directed by John D. Avildsen – a team which some years earlier had made an excellent film on contemporary California, *Save the Tiger* with Jack Lemmon. The title of the new film referred to a synthetic fuel secretly developed by the Germans during the War and which, rediscovered because of a series of murders, threatens to destroy the profits made by today's oil barons. Scott, top-billed, was to play the detective investigating the killings. Brando was then approached to play an oil tycoon, for three sequences only – two of them quite long, but with approximately twenty minutes screen time, for which he would get $1 million. Scott believed it would be a timely and important film. Brando is quoted as saying, 'Of course, it won't be a hit. But nothing serious is.'

Shagan gave *The New York Times* a detailed description of working with Brando, starting with the first script conference – when he and Avildsen were told by Norman Garey to wait (for hours as it turned out) for a summons to the Brando mansion. There, Brando went minutely through the script, urging more emphasis on its anti-capitalist aspects and driving Shagan spare because he wasn't allowed to smoke during the hours that he was there. Throughout the house there were large signs saying 'No Smoking'. Of the two actors together Shagan said 'I sensed a loss of purpose, a sense of betrayal, a feeling that they don't want to work anymore, a sense that they have come to think of acting as playing with choo-choo trains. And, of course, they both refused to accept Academy Awards.'

He went on, 'George is always the first one on the set. He's prepared and he has great respect for the script, but he's tough on the director. Marlon improvises constantly. You never get the same reading twice, and he leans toward the director and is rough on the writer. George once asked Marlon, with very good humor, I must say, "What are you going to say this time?" Marlon said, "What difference does it make? You know a cue when you hear one." I was surprised how well they got on.' Scott himself said about this: 'With Marlon, I wouldn't want to do an entire film with the little darling, because he would drive you crazy, but I find him a wonderful man with a magnificent sense of humor . . . He is dreadfully slow. He thinks about everything and does it over and over. Marlon would improve *all* the time. I'm not sure about the rest of us, but he's always working at it, discovering the part. It's amazing.'

His efforts were not rewarded. Portly, bald – with strands of white hair combed across his scalp – and sporting granny glasses, he adopts a mischievous air which suggests that he was enjoying himself for the first time in a movie since *Guys and Dolls*, but his is less a performance than caricature, with no more depth than a sheet of cellophane. There was no 'magic time'. The film itself turned out to be yet another in the genre of *Marathon Man* and *The Boys from Brazil*, in which the evil doings of the Nazis are found to be the cause of murder and mayhem these many years later: now and then – for instance, in a scene in a seedy hotel lobby, in the character of the enigmatic beauty (Marthe Keller) who helps Scott – it looks back to the first and best of all such movies, *The Third Man*: but the twists in the plot are absurd, the hoped-for seriousness all but swamped by them. It led to a rift between writer and director, since Shagan as producer denied the final cut to Avildsen, who sought unsuccessfully to have his name taken off the credits. Neither critics nor public was impressed, and it took only a paltry $3.7 million (domestic) on a heavy $15 million investment. MGM in desperation changed the slogan to 'The Movie the Oil Companies Don't want You to See', but the public still didn't want to see it. History repeated itself: as after *Mutiny on the Bounty*, the studio reported that it was only interested in medium-budget films. The new chairman, Frank Rosenfelt, told stockholders that $15 million was the absolute 'ceiling' for any movie.

The public had been flocking to such films as *Star Wars*, *Jaws*, *Close Encounters of the Third Kind* and *Star Trek*; in 1981 it would show enthusiastic support for *Raiders of the Lost Ark*, which also boasted no stars to speak of. Despite Paul Newman – demonstrably with more box-office clout than Brando – and a dozen other names, the $20 million *When Time Ran Out* collected less than $2 million in the domestic market. It was inconceivable that Brando's contributions to *Apocalypse Now* or *Superman* had been responsible for their popularity, as the failure of *The Formula* seemed to prove: and he had been paid a sum in excess of $50,000 for each moment of his brief appearances. Once again, he was 'dead' as far as the industry was concerned.

None of the projects announced for him looked viable, starting with *Saud*, a biography of Ibn Saud Abd al'Aziz, the first king of Saudi Arabia, with a $12 million budget financed by Arab oil tycoons with John Huston directing. There were discussions with George Englund on something to be called *The Smiling Buddha*, and producer Edward Montoro was offering an incredible $5 million plus 50% of the profits if Brando would play Picasso in a film biography. In 1981 there was a rumour that he would appear in John Boorman's *Excalibur*, with Faye Dunaway as Guinevere, Robert Redford as Lancelot and either Lee Marvin or Sean Connery as Merlin (none of whom appeared in the final film, which Boorman said he discussed only with Donald Sutherland). Equally name-strong was

The Godfather II in 1983, which would find him supported by Jane Fonda, Jack Nicholson and Dustin Hoffman, and also *Firebrand*, a life of Benvenuto Cellini directed by Terence Young, with Laurence Olivier, Marcello Mastroianni, Ornella Muti and Nastassia Kinski. In January of that year he was reported as on the verge of starring in *Fan Tan*, also directing, with Englund producing, and he was said to be discussing the role of Al Capone in *The Assassin*. In June 1986 the trade press announced that he might be coaxed out of retirement to play a Mafia chieftain in Michael Cimino's *The Sicilian*, from the novel by Mario Puzo – at $5 million for a three-week stint; in October he was scheduled, with the role still to be decided, for an ABC series produced by Harry Belafonte on the life of the jailed South African black activist Nelson Mandela – to be played by Sydney Poitier, with Jane Fonda as Molly Blackburn; and his was one of the first names to be mentioned for the title-role in Jean-Luc Godard's *King Lear* when that curiosity was first discussed. In August 1987 he was said to be shedding a hundred pounds to star in a television movie, *Legend*, about a star very like himself. A month later Paramount offered *The Presidio*, a cop thriller, but with only a few days to make up his mind: Sean Connery played the role.

In May 1988 he did begin filming again, on location in Zimbabwe for MGM, with Donald Sutherland co-starring: *A Dry White Season*, based on the novel by André Brink. The director is Euzhan Palcy, whose film about growing up in Martinique – where she also was born – *Rue Cases Nègres*, augured well for this story set in South Africa: but as of this writing the filmed material has been taken out of the director's hands by the studio. Within weeks of finishing the film Brando was scheduled to begin *Jericho*, a suspense thriller, written by himself, to be directed by Donald Cammell, best-known as co-director (with Nicolas Roeg) of *Performance*. The cult success of that film had led in the interim to only two completed films by Cammell, both of them box-office failures. The second of them, *White of the Eye*, made in 1986, was produced by Brando's old collaborator, Elliott Kastner, announced as the producer of *Jericho*. Because of his pretensions Cammell is not the sort of director the industry feels itself at home with, but Kastner obtained backing from two new companies, Emerald Films and the Cinema Corporation of America. Brando has also been announced to play Matthew Broderick's surrogate father in *The Freshman*, written by Andrew Bergman.

Brando's return to the screen may well have been occasioned by the need for money. In 1988 it was announced that he had put Tetiaroa up for sale. In April 1983 it had been struck by a hurricane so violent that it had virtually destroyed the hotel he had had constructed, wiping out most of his investment. In July of that year *Ciné-Revue* quoted 'friends' as saying 'He lives deep in solitude and practically hasn't been out for months. Marlon seems worn out. But you must understand that the financial catastrophe he has just undergone is very serious. He dreamed of creating something grandiose on "his" island. All that is gone today.' That solitude should not be taken literally, since according to the same source Brando was living with a Japanese lady, Yachio Tsubaki. It did not mention another blow to Brando at this time – August 1982, in fact – when his lawyer-agent Norman Garey committed suicide by shooting himself in the head, the victim of the sort of life from which Brando himself had been fleeing.

The article in *Ciné-Revue* also quoted an 'official' of Papeete who had recently met Brando: 'He always wears a kaftan to hide his obesity, but his face is horribly puffed-out. He never takes off his thick dark glasses, but I noticed that he was incapable now of wearing normal shoes because of his swollen feet.' Brando once observed that his tendency to be overweight surprised him as much as it annoyed him. A man of his temperament is unlikely to take patiently to slimming sessions, but bulk must limit him as an actor. Paul Newman, one year his junior, can still play ageing heroes; a fat actor perforce must play character roles.

We have an image of this secret Brando, as another generation once did of Garbo, glimpsed in grimy photographs boarding or leaving a plane, unrecognizable under hat and behind shades. Today's moviegoing generation know him like this – unless they take the trouble to seek out his films in revival houses or on television. As far as I can tell he holds no place with those stars of the 30s and 40s who still exert a powerful hold on movie buffs. And that is one reason why I have so often quoted other members of his own profession, for few actors have been so much admired. Here are three more, among the more talented of a younger generation. Anthony Hopkins: 'I hate polite actors. I like people like Marlon Brando who would dare to do that terrible film with David Niven called *Bedtime Story* and who did *Godfather* when people were complaining "he mumbles" and "I can't hear him". I heard every word. I thought the performance was brilliant. Whether the film is good or bad Brando is always compulsive viewing, like Sydney Greenstreet, the vulgarian of all time, or Peter Lorre, or even Bette Davis daring to do *Whatever Happened to Baby Jane*.' Brian Dennehy: 'I said to myself, "I'm the only person whose life has been changed by seeing this picture!" Then I talked to Al Pacino, Jimmy Coburn and the rest of the guys, and they all said "Yeah! *On the Waterfront* did it for me too". . . all these frustrated, runty, pimple-faced actors in Hollywood were thrust upon the Hollywood scene by that picture.' James Woods: 'It'd be pretty amazing to think of *me* shooting Darth Vader with a space-gun, like Marlon Brando in *Superman*. The greatest actor in the history of cinema – perhaps – and he's running around with white hair and a Krypton suit. Just something wrong about that.'

Let us move on to William Redfield's oft-quoted remark in 'Letters From an Actor': 'Laurence Olivier is less gifted than Marlon Brando. He is even less gifted than Richard Burton, Paul Scofield, Ralph Richardson and John Gielgud. But he is still the definitive actor of the 20th century. Why? Because he wanted to be.' I have no quarrel with this conclusion, but the rest of it is nonsense. It does, of course, place Brando in exalted company, but is Redfield judging these British actors on their stage or screen work? I saw Olivier on the stage more than a score of times, on most of which we were palpably in the presence of greatness. In terms of imagination, invention, skill and personality only Scofield came close to him. On both stage and screen Richardson could be as totally bad as he was wonderfully good on other occasions. Burton's early stage performances were hardly more than promising; few of his film performances show any gift whatsoever. Gielgud had not the range of Olivier; I did not see his celebrated Hamlet, but his Benedick was perfect and his Prospero very fine. Olivier's Richard III, Mark Antony, Shylock, Othello, Coriolanus and Macbeth are literally incomparable; but if we speak of only his screen performances we can summon *Pride and Prejudice*, *That Hamilton Woman*, *49th Parallel*, *Carrie*, *The Entertainer*, *The Prince and the Showgirl* and his three Shakespeare films as at least showing Olivier to be as 'gifted' as Brando at his best.

Even the cameo roles Olivier did in late middle age contain some rich performances; even when acting – as he admitted – for money in his old age, even in material as feeble as *The Betsy*, he was never as embarrassing as Brando in *The Missouri Breaks*. He has been thought of as the world's best actor not only because he played the classics so superbly but because he went on doing so, accepting the challenges open to a leading actor, till well past middle-age. As England's greatest actor, he was loved within the industry and without; and he climaxed his career by heading Britain's National Theatre.

But America's greatest actor, having achieved some sort of notoriety for sodomizing a girl with his trousers on, withdrew except for some rare and highly lucrative performances in cameo or smallish roles, ranging in quality from the competent to the contemptible. More sadly, given his stand on Civil Rights, but not because of that, he remains a matter of doubt and distrust to his fellow-countrymen. Whatever it is that spurs an actor on – money, the need for affection, the need for display, ambition, power, creativity – it could hardly be for this.

'I have never been conscious of any need other than to show off,' Olivier once confessed. Brando was a great actor when he shared the feeling. Those of us who found his early work so impressive hope that he can still be stirred; we hope that *A Dry White Season* will show him again at the peak of his powers. Although he has had his share of disappointments he has also made some foolish choices. One thing is abundantly clear: it has not been the career it should and could have been. As Joseph L. Mankiewicz said: 'Marlon is or was one of the great acting talents of our time. What happened, I really don't know. No one really knows. He could have gone on from *Caesar* to do almost anything he wanted.' He himself said – as long ago as 1972 – that he no longer despised acting, but the effort seemed too great: 'You have to upset yourself. Unless you do, you cannot act. And there comes a time when you don't want to anymore. You know a scene is coming where you'll have to cry and scream and all those things, and you can't just walk through it; it would be really disrespectful not to try to do your best.'

One last quotation, from the actor Edward Albert, who lived near Brando in Tahiti and talked to him one day: 'Brando talked about the problem of being a public personality, about how important it is to keep your own life –

your own center – within yourself. I don't think anyone *knows* Brando, but I have the feeling that he believes somewhere along the line he missed something he could have done, something he could have *been*. This sounds strange, but it's as if somebody had put an angel inside of him, and he's aware of it, and it's more than he can *contain*. I walked away from Brando's house that day feeling very sad, very lonely.'

Bibliography

Alpert, Hollis: *The Dreams and the Dreamers*, New York, The Macmillan Company, 1962

Atkinson, Brooks: *Broadway*, London, Cassell, 1970

Bacon, James: *Made in Hollywood*, New York, Contemporary Books, 1977

Capote, Truman: *The Dogs Bark*, London, Weidenfeld & Nicolson, 1974

Carey, Gary: *Marlon Brando The Only Contender*, London, Robson Books, 1985

Coward, Noel: *Diaries*, London, Weidenfeld & Nicolson, 1983

Crist, Judith: *Take 22, Moviemakers on Moviemaking*, New York, Viking, 1984

Davis, Bette: *The Lonely Life*, New York, G. P. Puttnam's Sons, 1962

Downing, David: *Marlon Brando*, London, W. H. Allen, 1984

Fiore, Carlo: *Bud, the Brando I Knew*, New York, Delacorte Press, 1974

Funke, Lewis and Booth, John E.: *Actors Talk About Acting*, New York, Random House, 1961

Geist, Kenneth L.: *Pictures Will Talk, The Life and Films of Joseph L. Mankiewicz*, New York, Scribners, 1973

Gielgud, John: *An Actor and his Time*, London, Sidgwick & Jackson, 1979

Golson, G. Barry (Ed.): *The Playboy Interview*, New York, Playboy Press, 1981

Graham, Sheilah: *Scratch an Actor*, London, W. H. Allen, 1969

Hamblett, Charles: *Who Killed Marilyn Monroe?*, London, Leslie Frewin, 1966

Hardwicke, Sir Cedric: *A Victorian in Orbit*, London, Methuen, 1961

Higham, Charles: *Brando The Unauthorised Biography*, London, Sidgwick & Jackson, 1987

Higham, Charles and Greenberg, Joel: *The Celluloid Muse*, London, Angus & Robertson, 1969

Hirschhorn, Clive: *Gene Kelly*, London, W. H. Allen, 1984 (revised edition)

Hotchner, A. E.: *Sophia Living and Loving, Her Own Story*, New York, William Morrow, 1979

Houseman, John: *Front and Center*, New York, Simon & Schuster, 1979

Houseman, John: *Run Through*, New York, Simon & Schuster, 1972

Houseman, John: *Unfinished Business*, London, Chatto & Windus, 1986

Huston, John: *An Open Book*, New York, Alfred A. Knopf, 1980

Kashfi, Anna and Stein, E. P.: *Brando for Breakfast*, New York, Crown, 1979

Kazan, Elia: *A Life*, New York, Alfred A. Knopf, 1988

Knight, Vivienne: *Trevor Howard, a Gentleman and a Player*, London, Muller, Blond & White, 1986

Logan, Joshua: *Josh*, New York, Delacorte Press, 1976

Mankiewicz, Joseph L.: *More About All About Eve*, New York, Random House, 1972

Marx, Arthur, *Goldwyn*, New York, W. W. Norton, 1976

Mason, James: *Before I Forget*, London, Hamish Hamilton, 1981

Morella, Joe and Epstein, Edward: *Brando, The Unauthorised Biography*, New York, Nelson, 1973

Redfield, William: *Letters From an Actor*, London, Cassell, 1967

Ross, Lillian and Ross, Helen: *The Players*, New York, Simon & Schuster, 1962

Selznick, Irene Mayer: *A Private View*, London, Weidenfeld & Nicolson, 1983

Simon, John: *Reverse Angle*, New York, Clarkson Potter, 1982

Thomas, Bob: *Brando*, London, W. H. Allen, 1973

Thomas, Tony: *The Films of Marlon Brando*, Secausus, Citadel Press, 1973

Thomas, Tony: *Ustinov in Focus*, New York, A. S. Barnes, 1971

Vickers, Hugo: *Cecil Beaton*, London, Weidenfeld & Nicolson, 1985

Williams, Tennessee: *Memoirs*, New York, Doubleday, 1975

Winters, Shelley: *Shelley*, London, Granada, 1981

Zec, Donald: *Some Enchanted Egos*, New York, St Martin's Press, 1973

My special thanks to Elia Kazan, Joseph L. Mankiewicz, Fred Zinnemann, Sheilah Graham and Neil Sinyard. My thanks to the various books listed above, and the following publications, all used in my research: *Ciné-Review*, *The New York Times*, *New York Post*, *New York Herald Tribune*, *New York World Telegram*, *New York Journal American*, *Time Magazine*, *Esquire*, *Variety*, *The Nation*, *Saturday Review*, *Playbill*, *Playboy*, *Show Magazine*, *Theatre Arts Monthly*, *Films Illustrated*, *Photoplay*, *Films and Filming*, *The Observer*, *The Guardian*, *The Sunday Times*, *the New Statesman* and *Time Out*.

Also to the *British Film Institute* for the supply of photographs number 1, 2, 4, 5, 6, 7, 9, 10, 11, 12, 16, 19 and 21 which are reproduced courtesy of the BFI.

Filmography

1950   The Men
Stanley Kramer Productions–United Artists. Director: Fred Zinnemann. Producer: Stanley Kramer. Story and screenplay by Carl Foreman. Music: Dimitri Tiomkin. Photographed by Robert de Grasse. 85 minutes. New York premiere: July. With Marlon Brando (Ken), Teresa Wright (Ellen), Everett Sloan (Dr Brock), Jack Webb (Norm), Richard Erdman (Leo), Arthur Jurado (Angel), Virginia Farmer (Nurse Robbins), Dorothy Tree (Ellen's mother), Howard St John (Ellen's father), Nita Hunter (Dolores).

1951   A Streetcar Named Desire
Charles K. Feldman Group Productions–Warner Bros. (When Feldman's agreement with Warners expired, distribution was taken over by 20th Century-Fox.) Director: Elia Kazan. Producer: Charles K. Feldman. Screenplay by Tennessee Williams, from his own play, adapted by Oscar Saul. Music: Alex North. Photographed by Harry Stradling. 122 minutes. New York premiere: September. With Vivien Leigh (Blanche du Bois), Marlon Brando (Stanley Kowalski), Kim Hunter (Stella), Karl Malden (Mitch), Rudy Bond (Steve Hubbell), Nick Dennis (Pablo Gonzales), Peg Hillias (Eunice Hubbell), Wright King (the young collector).

1952   Viva Zapata!
20th Century-Fox. Director: Elia Kazan. Producer: Darryl F. Zanuck. Screenplay by John Steinbeck, from *Zapata the Unconquered* by Edgcumb Pichon. Music: Alex North. Photographed by Joe MacDonald. 113 minutes. New York premiere: February. With Marlon Brando (Emiliano Zapata), Jean Peters (Josefa Espejo), Anthony Quinn (Eufemio Zapata), Joseph Wiseman (Fernando

Aguirre), Arnold Moss (Don Nacio), Lou Gilbert (Pablo), Alan Reed (Pancho Villa), Margo (Posadera), Harold Gordon (Don Francisco Madero), Mildred Dunnock (Senora Espejo), Frank Silvera (General Huerta), Nina Varela (Aunt), Florenz Ames (Senor Espejo).

1953 Julius Caesar

Metro-Goldwyn-Mayer. Director: Joseph L. Mankiewicz. Producer: John Houseman. From the play by William Shakespeare. Music: Miklos Rozsa. Photographed by Joseph Rutternberg. 121 minutes. New York premiere: June. With Marlon Brando (Mark Antony), James Mason (Brutus), John Gielgud (Cassius), Louis Calhern (Julius Caesar), Edmond O'Brien (Casca), Greer Garson (Calpurnia), Deborah Kerr (Portia), George Macready (Marullus), Michael Pate (Flavius), Alan Napier (Cicero), John Hoyt (Decius Brutus), Tom Powers (Metellus Cimber), Rhys Williams (Lucilius).

1953 The Wild One

Columbia. Director: Laslo Benedek. Producer: Stanley Kramer. Screenplay by John Paxton, based on a story by Frank Rooney. Music: Leith Stevens. Photographed by Hal Mohr. 79 minutes. New York premiere: December. With Marlon Brando (Johnnie), Mary Murphy (Kathie), Robert Keith (Harry Bleeker), Lee Marvin (Chino), Jay C. Flippen (Sheriff Singer), Peggy Maley (Mildred), Hugh Sanders (Charlie Thomas), Ray Teal (Frank Bleeker).

1954 On the Waterfront

Horizon–Columbia. Director: Elia Kazan. Producer: Sam Spiegel. Screenplay by Budd Schulberg, suggested by articles by Malcolm Johnson. Music: Leonard Bernstein. Photographed by Boris Kaufman. 107 minutes. New York premiere: July. With Marlon Brando (Terry Malloy), Eva Marie Saint (Edie Doyle), Karl Malden (Father Barry), Lee J. Cobb (Johnny Friendly), Rod Steiger (Charley Malloy), Pat Henning ('Kayo' Dugan), Leif Erickson (Glover), James Westerfield (Big Mac), John Heldabrand (Mutt), Rudy Bond (Moose), John Hamilton ('Pop' Doyle), Martin Balsam (Crime Commissioner), Pat Hingle (bartender).

1954 Désirée

20th Century-Fox. Director: Henry Koster. Producer: Julius Blaustein. Screenplay by Daniel Taradash, from the novel by Annemarie Selinko. Music: Alex North. Photographed by Milton Krasner. CinemaScope. De Luxe Colour. 110 minutes. New York premiere:

November. With Marlon Brando (Napoleon), Jean Simmons (Désirée), Merle Oberon (Josephine), Michael Rennie (Bernadotte), Cameron Mitchell (Joseph Bonaparte), Elizabeth Sellars (Julie), Charlotte Austin (Paulette), Cathleen Nesbitt (Mme Bonaparte), Evelyn Varden (Marie), Isobel Elsom (Mme Clary), John Hoyt (Talleyrand), Alan Napier (Despreaux).

1955   Guys and Dolls

Samuel Goldwyn Productions–Metro-Goldwyn-Mayer. Director: Joseph L. Mankiewicz. Producer: Samuel Goldwyn. Screenplay by Mankiewicz, based on the play with book by Jo Swerling and Abe Burrows, adapted from a story by Damon Runyon. Music and lyrics: Frank Loesser. Photographed by Harry Stradling. Cinemascope. Eastman Colour. 149 minutes. New York premiere: November. With Marlon Brando (Sky Masterson), Jean Simmons (Sarah Brown), Frank Sinatra (Nathan Detroit), Vivian Blaine (Adelaide), Robert Keith (Lt Brannigan), Stubby Kaye (Nicely-Nicely Johnson), B. S. Silver (Big Jule), Johnny Silver (Benny Southstreet), Sheldon Leonard (Harry the Horse), Dan Dayton (Rusty Charlie), Regis Toomey (Arvid Abernathy).

1956   The Teahouse of the August Moon

Metro-Goldwyn-Mayer. Director: Daniel Mann. Producer: Jack Cummings. Screenplay by John Patrick, based on his play, adapted from the novel by Vern Sneider. Music: Saul Chaplin. Photographed by John Alton. CinemaScope. Metrocolor. 123 minutes. New York premiere: November. With Marlon Brando (Sakini), Glenn Ford (Captain Fisby), Machiko Kyo (Lotus Blossom), Eddie Albert (Captain McLean), Paul Ford (Colonel Purdy), Jun Negami (Mr Seiko), Nijiko Kiyokawa (Miss Higa Jiga).

1957   Sayonara

Goetz Pictures Inc.–Pennebaker Productions–Warner Bros. Director: Joshua Logan. Producer: William Goetz. Screenplay by Paul Osborn, from the novel by James A. Michener. Music: Franz Waxman. Photographed by Ellsworth Fredericks. Technirama. Technicolor. 147 minutes. New York premiere: December. With Marlon Brando (Major Lloyd Gruver), Miiko Taka (Hana-ogi), Red Buttons (Airman Joe Kelly), Patricia Owens (Eileen Webster), Ricardo Montalban (Nakamura), Myoshi Umeki (Katsumi), Kent Smith (General Webster), Martha Scott (Mrs Webster), James Garner (Captain Bailey), Doug Watson (Colonel Calhoun).

1958   **The Young Lions**
20th Century-Fox. Director: Edward Dmytryk. Producer: Al Lichtman. Screenplay by Edward Anhalt, from the novel by Irwin Shaw. Music: Hugo Friedhofer. Photographed by Joe MacDonald. Cinema-Scope. 167 minutes. New York premiere: April. With Marlon Brando (Christian Diestl), Montgomery Clift (Noah Ackerman), Dean Martin (Michael Whiteacre), Hope Lang (Hope Plowman), Barbara Rush (Margaret Freemantle), May Britt (Gretchen Hardenberg), Maximilian Schell (Hardenberg), Dora Doll (Simone), Lee Van Cleef (Sgt Rickett), Liliane Montevecchi (Françoise), Arthur Franz (Lt Green).

1960   **The Fugitive Kind**
Jurow–Shepherd–Pennebaker–United Artists. Director: Sidney Lumet. Producers: Martin Jurow, Richard A. Shepherd. Screenplay by Tennessee Williams and Meade Roberts, from the play by Williams, *Orpheus Descending*. Music: Kenyon Hopkins. Photographed by Boris Kaufman. 121 minutes. New York premiere: April. With Marlon Brando (Val Xavier), Anna Magnani (Lady Torrance), Joanne Woodward (Carol Cutrere), Maureen Stapleton (Vee Talbot), Victor Jory (Jabe Torrance), R. G. Armstrong (Sheriff Talbot), Emory Richardson (Uncle Pleasant), Spivy (Ruby Lightfoot).

1961   **One-Eyed Jacks**
Pennebaker–Paramount. Director: Marlon Brando. Producer: Frank P. Rosenberg. Screenplay by Guy Trosper and Calder Willingham, based on the novel *The Authentic Death of Hendry Jones* by Charles Neider. Music: Hugo Friedhofer. Photographed by Charles Lang Jr. Vistavision. Technicolor. 141 minutes. New York premiere: March. With Marlon Brando (Rio), Karl Malden (Dad Longworth), Pina Pellicer (Louisa), Katy Jurado (Maria), Ben Johnson (Bob Amory), Slim Pickens (Lon), Larry Duran (Modesto), Sam Gilman (Harvey), Timothy Carey (Howard Tetley), Miriam Colon (Redhead), Elisha Cook (Bank Teller).

1962   **Mutiny on the Bounty**
Arcola–Metro-Goldwyn-Mayer. Director: Lewis Milestone. Producer: Aaron Rosenberg. Screenplay by Charles Lederer, based on the novel by Charles Nordhoff and James Normal Hall. Music: Bronislau Kaper. Photographed by Robert L. Surtees. Ultra Panavision 70. Technicolor. 185 minutes. New York premiere: November. With

Marlon Brando (Fletcher Christian), Trevor Howard (William Bligh), Richard Harris (John Mills), Hugh Griffith (Alexander Smith), Richard Haydn (William Brown), Tim Seely (Edward Young), Percy Herbert (Matthew Quintal), Gordon Jackson (Edward Birkett), Noel Purcell (William McCoy), Duncan Lamont (John Williams), Chips Rafferty (Michael Byrne), Ashley Cowan (Samuel Mack), Eddie Byrne (John Fryer), Frank Silvera (Minarii), Tarita (Maimiti).

1963 The Ugly American

Universal–International. Director and producer: George Englund. Screenplay by Stewart Stern, based on the novel by William J. Lederer and Eugene Burdick. Music: Frank Skinner. Photographed by Clifford Stine. Eastmancolor. 120 minutes. New York premiere: April. With Marlon Brando (Harrison Carter MacWhite), Eija Okada (Deong), Sandra Church (Marion MacWhite), Pat Hingle (Homer Atkins), Arthur Hill (Grainger), Jocelyn Brando (Emma Atkins).

1964 Bedtime Story

Lankershim–Pennebaker–Universal International. Director: Ralph Levy. Producer: Stanley Shapiro. Screenplay by Shapiro and Paul Henning. Music: Hans J. Salter. Photographed by Clifford Stine. Eastman Colour. 99 minutes. New York premiere: June. With Marlon Brando (Fred Benson), David Niven (Lawrence Jamison), Shirley Jones (Janet Walker), Dody Goodman (Fanny Eubank), Aram Stephan (Monsieur André), Parley Baer (Col Williams), Marie Windsor (Mrs Sutton), Rebecca Sand (Mrs Trumble).

1965 Morituri retitled The Saboteur, Code Name 'Morituri'

Arcola–Colony–20th Century-Fox. Director: Bernhard Wicki. Producer: Aaron Rosenberg. Screenplay by Daniel Taradash, based on the novel by Werner Jörg Lüdecke. Music: Jerry Goldsmith. Photographed by Conrad Hall. 122 minutes. New York premiere: August. With Marlon Brando (Robert Crain), Yul Brynner (Captain Müller), Trevor Howard (Colonel Statter), Janet Margolin (Esther), Martin Benrath (Kruse), Hans Christian Blech (Donkeyman), Wally Cox (Dr Ambach).

1966 The Chase

Horizon–Lone Star–Columbia. Director: Arthur Penn. Producer: Sam Spiegel. Screenplay by Lillian Hellman, based on the novel and play by Horton Foote. Music: John Barry. Photographed by Joseph LaShelle. Panavision. Technicolor. 133 minutes. New York premiere: February. With Marlon Brando (Calder), Jane Fonda (Anna Reeves), Robert Redford (Bubber Reeves), E. G. Marshall (Val Rogers), Angie Dickinson (Ruby Calder), Janice Rule (Emily Stewart), Miriam Hopkins (Mrs Reeves), Martha Hyer (Mary Fuller), Richard Bradford (Damon Fuller), Robert Duvall (Edwin Stewart), James Fox (Jake Rogers), Diana Hyland (Elizabeth Rogers), Henry Hull (Briggs), Jocelyn Brando (Mrs Briggs), Katherine Walsh (Verna Dee), Lori Martin (Cutie), Marc Seton (Paul), Joel Fluellen (Lester Johnson), Nydia Westman (Mrs Henderson), Bruce Cabot (Sol), Eduardo Ciannelli, Grady Sutton (Guests at party).

1966   **The Appaloosa** (in Great Britain: **Southwest to Sonora**)
Universal. Director: Sidney J. Furie. Producer: Alan Miller. Screenplay by James Bridges and Roland Kibbee, based on the novel by Robert MacLeod. Music: Frank Skinner. Photographed by Russell Metty. Techniscope. Technicolor. 98 minutes. New York premiere: September. With Marlon Brando (Matt), Anjanette Comer (Trini), John Saxon (Chuy), Rafael Campos (Paco), Miriam Colon (Ana), Emilio Fernandez (Lazaro), Alex Montoya (Squint-Eye), Frank Silvera (Ramos).

1967   **A Countess from Hong Kong**
British: Universal. Director: Charles Chaplin. Producer: Jerome Epstein. Screenplay by Chaplin. Music: Chaplin. Photographed by Arthur Ibbetson. Technicolor. 120 minutes. London premiere: January. With Marlon Brando (Ogden), Sophia Loren (Natascha), Sydney Chaplin (Harvey), Tippi Hedren (Martha), Patrick Cargill (Hudson), Michael Medwin (John Felix), Oliver Johnston (Clark), John Paul (Captain), Margaret Rutherford (Miss Gaulswallow), Angela Scoular (Society Girl), Charles Chaplin (an Old Steward).

1967   **Reflections in a Golden Eye**
Warner Bros: Seven Arts. Director: John Huston. Producer: Ray Stark. Screenplay by Chapman Mortimer and Gladys Hill, based on the novel by Carson McCullers. Music: Toshiro Mayuzumi. Photographed by Aldo Tonti. Panavision. Technicolor. 109 minutes. New York premiere: October. With Elizabeth Taylor (Leonora Penderton), Marlon Brando (Major Weldon Penderton), Brian Keith (Lt-Col Morris Langdon), Julie Harris (Alison Langdon), Robert Forster (Private Williams), Zorro David (Anacleto), Gordon Mitchell (Stables Sergeant), Irvin Dugan (Captain Weincheck).

1968 **Candy**
American–French–Italian: Selmur Pictures (Hollywood)–Dear Film
(Rome)–Corona (Paris). Distributed by Cinerama. Director: Christ-
ian Marquand. Producer: Robert Haggiag. Screenplay by Buck
Henry, based on the novel by Terry Southern and Mason Hof-
fenberg. Music: Dave Grusin. Songs sung by The Byrds and Step-
penwolf. Photographed by Giuseppe Rotunno. Technicolor. 124 min-
utes. New York premiere: December. With Ewar Aulin (Candy),
Marlon Brando (Grindl), Richard Burton (McPhisto), James
Coburn (Dr Krankheit), Walter Matthau (General Smight), Charles
Aznavour (The Hunchback), John Huston (Dr Dunlap), John Astin
(Daddy/Uncle Jack), Elsa Martinelli (Livia), Ringo Starr (Em-
manuel), Enrico Maria Salerno (Jonathan J. John), Sugar Ray Rob-
inson (Zero), Anita Pallenberg (Nurse Bullock), Lea Padovani
(Silvia), Florinda Bolkan (Lolita), Marilù Tolo (Conchita), Nicoletta
Machiavelli (Marquita), Umberto Orsini (1st Hood).

1969 **The Night of the Following Day**
Gina–Universal. Director and producer: Hubert Cornfield. Screen-
play by Cornfield and Robert Phippeny, based on the novel *The
Snatchers* by Lionel White. Music: Stanley Myers. Photographed by
Willy Kurant. Technicolor. 93 minutes. New York premiere:
January. With Marlon Brando (Bud), Richard Boone (Leer), Rita
Moreno (Vi), Pamela Franklin (The Girl), Jess Hahn (Wally),
Gérard Buhr (Gendarme).

1970 **Queimada!**
Iralian–French: P.E.A. (Rome)–Les Productions Artistes Associés
(Paris). Distributed by United Artists. Director: Gillo Pontecorvo.
Producer: Alberto Grimaldi. Screenplay by Franco Solinas and Gior-
gio Arlorio, from a story by Pontecorvo, Solinas and Arlorio. Music:
Ennio Morricone. Photographed by Marcello Gatti and Giuseppe
Bruzzolini. De Luxe Color. 132 minutes (112 minutes in the U.S.A.
and Britain). Italian premiere: January. New York premiere: Oc-
tober. With Marlon Brando (Sir William Walker), Evaristo Marquez
(José Dolores), Renato Salvatore (Teddy Sanchez), Norman Hill
(Shelton), Tom Lyons (General Prada).

1971 **The Nightcomers**
Scimitar–Avco Embassy. An Elliott Kastner–Jay Kanter–Alan Ladd
Jr Production. Director and producer: Michael Winner. Screenplay
by Michael Hastings, based on characters created by Henry James.
Music: Jerry Fielding. Photographed by Robert Paynter. Techni-

color. 96 minutes. New York premiere: December. London premiere: May 1972. With Marlon Brando (Peter Quint), Stephanie Beacham (Miss Jessel), Thora Hird (Mrs Grose), Harry Andrews (Master of the House), Verna Harvey (Flora), Christopher Ellis (Miles), Anna Palk (New Governess).

1972   The Godfather
Alfran Productions–Paramount. Director: Francis Ford Coppola. Producer: Albert S. Ruddy. Screenplay by Maria Puzo and Coppola, based on the novel by Puzo. Music: Nino Rota. Photographed by Gordon Willis. Technicolor. 175 minutes. New York premiere: March. With Marlon Brando (Don Vito Corleone), Al Pacino (Michael Corleone), James Caan (Sonny Corleone), Richard Castellano (Clemenza), Robert Duvall (Tom Hagan), Sterling Hayden (McCluskey), John Marley (Jack Woltz), Richard Conte (Barzini), Diane Keaton (Kay Adams), Al Lettieri (Sollozzo), Abe Vigoda (Tessio), Talia Shire (Connie Rizzi), Gianni Russo (Carlo Rizzi), John Cazale (Fredo Corleone), Rudy Bond (Cuneo), Al Martino (Johnny Fontane), Morgana King (Mama Corleone).

1972   L'Ultimo Tango in Parigi/Dernier Tango à Paris/Last Tango in Paris
Italian–French: P.E.A. Cinematografica (Rome)–Les Artistes Associés (Paris). Distributed by United Artists. Director: Bernardo Bertolucci. Producer: Alberto Grimaldi. Screenplay by Bertolucci and Franco Arcalli. Music: Gato Barbieri. Photographed by Vittorio Storaro. Technicolor. 129 minutes. New York premiere: October. Italian and French premieres: January 1973. With Marlon Brando (Paul), Maria Schneider (Jeanne), Jean-Pierre Léaud (Tom), Massimo Girotti (Marcel), Catherine Allégret (Catherine), Maria Michi (Rosa's mother).

1976   The Missouri Breaks
EK–United Artists. Director: Arthur Penn. Producer: Robert M. Sherman. Screenplay by Thomas McGuane. Music: John Williams. Photographed by Michael Butler. De Luxe color. 126 minutes. New York premiere: May. With Marlon Brando (Robert Lee Clayton), Jack Nicholson (Tom Logan), Randy Quaid (Little Tod), Kathleen Lloyd (Jane Braxton), Frederic Forrest (Cary), Harry Dean Stanton (Calvin), John McLiam (David Braxton), John Ryan (Si), Sam Gilman (Hank Rate).

1978   Superman
British. Dovemead–Warner Bros. For International Film Produc-

tions. Director: Richard Donner. Producer: Pierre Spengler. Screenplay by Mario Puzo, David Newman, Leslie Newman, Robert Benton, based on the characters created by Jerry Siegel, Joe Shuster. Music: John Williams. Photographed by Geoffrey Unsworh. Technicolor, Panavision. 143 minutes. New York premiere: December. With Christopher Reeve (Clark Kent, Superman), Margot Kidder (Lois Lane), Gene Hackman (Lex Luthor), Valerie Perrine (Eve Teschmacher), Ned Beatty (Otis), Jackie Cooper (Perry White), Marc McClure (Jimmy Olsen). Krypton: Marlon Brando (Jor-El), Susannah York (Lara), Trevor Howard (1st Elder), Harry Andrews (2nd Elder), Jack O'Halloran (Non), Maria Schell (Vond-Ah), Terence Stamp (General Zod). Smallville: Glenn Ford (Pa Kent), Phyllis Thaxter (Ma Kent), Jeff East (Young Clark Kent).

1979   **Apocalypse Now**
Omni Zoetrope–United Artists. Director and Producer: Francis Coppola. Screenplay by John Milius, Coppola, based on 'The Heart of Darkness' by Joseph Conrad. Music: Carmine Coppola, Francis Coppola. Photographed by Vittorio Storaro. Technicolor. Technovision. 141 minutes (70 mm) or 153 minutes (35 mm, with end title sequence). New York premiere: August. With Marlon Brando (Colonel Walter E. Kurtz), Robert Duvall (Lt Colonel Bill Kilgore), Martin Sheen (Captain Benjamin L. Willard), Frederic Forrest (Hicks), Albert Hall (Chief Phillips), Sam Bottoms (Lance B. Johnson), Larry Fishburne ('Clean'), Dennis Hopper (Photo-journalist), G. D. Spadlin (General Corman), Harrison Ford (Colonel Lucas), Jerry Ziesmer (Civilian), Scott Glen (Captain Richard Colby).

1980   **The Formula**
Metro-Goldwyn-Mayer. A CIP feature. Director: John G. Avildsen. Produced and written by Steve Shagan, from his own novel. Music: Bill Conti. Photographed by James Crabe. Metrocolor. 117 minutes. New York premiere: December. With George C. Scott (Lieutenant Barney Caine), Marlon Brando (Adam Steiffel), Marthe Keller (Lisa), John Gielgud (Dr Abraham Esau), G. D. Spradlin (Clements), Beatrice Straight (Kay Neeley), Richard Lynch (General Kladen/Frank Tedesco), John van Dreelen (Hans Lehman), Robin Clarke (Major Tom Neeley).

1988   **A Dry White Season** (in preparation)
Metro-Goldwyn-Mayer. Director: Euzhan Palcy. Based on the novel by Andre Brink. With Marlon Brando, Donald Sutherland.

Index

244

RICHARD BURTON

My Brother

GRAHAM JENKINS

Richard Burton was one of the greatest actors of our age –
and one of the wildest. He is as famed for his reckless life
off-stage as for his brilliant and sensitive roles in
productions as varied as Antony and Cleopatra, Where
Eagles Dare, Under Milk Wood and Camelot.

Now Graham Jenkins gives the family-eye view of his
brother's turbulent and contradictory career: the brilliant
classic roles and the ham Hollywood moneyspinners; the
chequered relationship with Elizabeth Taylor and his three
other marriages; the public image of the jetsetting playboy;
the private passion for his family and for Wales – and the
battles with alcohol which finally killed him. Above all, this
intimate and controversial biography shines with the magic
of Richard Burton, flawed genius and enduring friend.

'The stories of wine, women and lusty song acquire a new
credibility from this close and apparently unembittered
source'
DAILY TELEGRAPH

0 7474 0351 1   BIOGRAPHY   £3.50

CARY GRANT
A TOUCH OF ELEGANCE
WARREN G HARRIS

Cary Grant, adored throughout the world as the witty, debonair star of over seventy films, cultivated a screen image of ageless style which masked a private life of insecurity and tragedy.

Born in Bristol as Archie Leach, the man who would rise to play leading roles alongside such screen goddesses as Marlene Dietrich and Marilyn Monroe, was the son of an alcoholic clothes-presser and of a mother who disappeared suddenly when he was ten. Grant thought she'd abandoned him only to discover twenty years later that she'd been committed to a mental asylum. The trauma cast a shadow over the rest of his life.

In this fascinating and compelling biography Warren G Harris reveals all about Grant's five marriages, his affairs, his rapid ascent to stardom in Hollywood, his nervous breakdowns, his alleged bisexuality and his mid-life liberation through LSD therapy. It is a story of a life of magnificent achievement, of success mixed with despair, of stardom – of a man of incomparable charm, known as the 'epitome of elegance'.

0 7474 0202 7   BIOGRAPHY   £3.50

TREVOR HOWARD

A GENTLEMAN AND A PLAYER

VIVIENNE KNIGHT

Trevor Howard, perhaps the greatest British film actor of his generation, famed for his compelling roles in films ranging from the classic BRIEF ENCOUNTER to the contemporary WHITE MISCHIEF, is a man of intriguing enigma and contradiction. A hell-raiser and drinker, but always the perfect gentleman, he considers acting a game and plays it for the highest stakes.

In this definitive and entertaining biography, Vivienne Knight reveals the truth behind one of the most popular and well-loved actors Britain has ever produced.

0 7474 0055 5   BIOGRAPHY   £3.50

As Time Goes By
The Life of Ingrid Bergman

LAURENCE LEAMER

In a career that spanned forty years, Ingrid Bergman brought her astonishing screen presence to star in a string of classics – *Casablanca*, *Joan of Arc*, *For Whom the Bell Tolls*, *Notorious*. She was adored for her transcendent beauty, her devotion to her family, her vulnerability.

Yet, of all Ingrid Bergman's stunning roles, none was as dramatic as her own life. Behind her idealised Hollywood image was a passionate and daring woman who craved excitement and adventure, a woman who had many affairs, a woman who followed her heart into the biggest celebrity scandal in post-war film history.

AS TIME GOES BY is the riveting and sometimes shocking story of a woman of fierce ambition and strong desires, a story of love and lust, of public image and private truth.

'At once chilling and fascinating. No film of Ingrid's will look quite the same again' Sheridan Morley

0 7221 5493 3   BIOGRAPHY   £3.95

The *true* story of the Cannon Film Empire

HOLLYWOOD A GO-GO

ANDREW YULE

Hollywood film moguls Yoram Globus and Menahem Golan of the Cannon Film Group are a phenomenon of 80s enterprise. With next to no capital and by wheeling and dealing their way up the film industry hierarchy, they have established the Cannon Group as a massive, international film empire.

But the downside of this glittering success story is only now being told. The list of films produced by Cannon includes some of the shoddiest fare ever foisted on the public and most have been box-office disasters. Their accounting methods are under investigation and their sources of finance uncertain. How then have they inspired such confidence in the business world?

In this fascinating and hard-hitting account, Andrew Yule blows the lid off the Cannon go-go boys and provides a unique insight into the more buccaneering aspects of modern entrepreneurial practice.

0 7221 9389 0   NON-FICTION   £3.50

A CANDID PORTRAIT OF BETTE DAVIS BY HER DAUGHTER

My Mother's Keeper

B. D. HYMAN

Bette Davis was never a typical Hollywood star. She was tough, smart, aggressive, gifted and bitterly determined. It was those qualities that made her one of the most legendary and charismatic actresses of her generation.

But the stormy personality that drove her to the top knew no rest behind the scenes, and those same qualities damned her personal life right from the start.

The broken marriages, the domestic violence and unhappiness, the vicious battles with The System – all of it is here, told by the only person who knows Bette Davis well enough to tell it, her daughter, B. D. Hyman.

Written with compassion, humour, understanding and searing honesty, this is the story of the real Bette Davis – more controversial , more shocking and more moving than any character she ever played
on film.

BIOGRAPHY   0 7221 4837 2   £3.50

A selection of bestsellers from SPHERE

FICTION

THE PALACE	Paul Erdman	£3.50 □
KALEIDOSCOPE	Danielle Steel	£3.50 □
AMTRAK WARS VOL. 4	Patrick Tilley	£3.50 □
TO SAIL BEYOND THE SUNSET	Robert A. Heinlein	£3.50 □
JUBILEE: THE POPPY CHRONICLES 1	Claire Rayner	£3.50 □

FILM AND TV TIE-IN

WILLOW	Wayland Drew	£2.99 □
BUSTER	Colin Shindler	£2.99 □
COMING TOGETHER	Alexandra Hine	£2.99 □
RUN FOR YOUR LIFE	Stuart Collins	£2.99 □
BLACK FOREST CLINIC	Peter Heim	£2.99 □

NON-FICTION

MARLON BRANDO	David Shipman	£3.50 □
MONTY: THE MAN BEHIND THE LEGEND	Nigel Hamilton	£3.99 □
BURTON: MY BROTHER	Graham Jenkins	£3.50 □
BARE-FACED MESSIAH	Russell Miller	£3.99 □
THE COCHIN CONNECTION	Alison and Brian Milgate	£3.50 □

All Sphere books are available at your local bookshop or newsagent, or can be ordered direct from the publisher. Just tick the titles you want and fill in the form below.

Name _____

Address _____

_____

Write to Sphere Books, Cash Sales Department, P.O. Box 11, Falmouth, Cornwall TR10 9EN

Please enclose a cheque or postal order to the value of the cover price plus:

UK: 60p for the first book, 25p for the second book and 15p for each additional book ordered to a maximum charge of £1.90.

OVERSEAS & EIRE: £1.25 for the first book, 75p for the second book and 28p for each subsequent title ordered.

BFPO: 60p for the first book, 25p for the second book plus 15p per copy for the next 7 books, thereafter 9p per book.

Sphere Books reserve the right to show new retail prices on covers which may differ from those previously advertised in the text elsewhere, and to increase postal rates in accordance with the P.O.